NO BAG
FOR THE
JOURNEY

One Man

One Bicycle

One Outrageous Journey of Faith

Even our best efforts and purest motives are clouded by our frail and corrupted human nature. But the love and grace of a sovereign God gets us where He wants us to go.

By Joseph R. Martin

Forward by Ashley Null

Book Production Services provided by
David G. Young, Newsmaker Publishing Services
website: www.newsmakerpublishing.com

ISBN: 978-1-4507-3953-5

Library of Congress Control Number: 2010916396

Printed in the United States of America
Comfort Press
Glenshaw, PA
www.nobagforthejourney.com

Dedication

I want to dedicate this book, first of all, to all those well meaning souls who strive to attain the love and approval of God and others and find themselves totally exhausted.

And secondly, to the Bill Mahers and Richard Dawkins of the world who, for whatever reason, rail against the very God who gives them breath even though He has revealed Himself so clearly.

May we all learn to recognize God's hand at work in the world and in our lives.

Acknowledgements

First of all I need to thank all the people in the book that assisted me across the country. They were like God's hands passing me from town to town as in a fire bucket brigade. Without any one of them my ride would have stalled.

Next, I need to thank the many friends and writing experts that helped complete this work: First, my good friend Dorothy Saladiak for helping revive this project and encourage me to finish after it sat dormant for years; Greg Wilson for giving me an eye for clichés; Jen Kissel for her professional editing and advice that made me feel and look like a real writer; Kathy Walzer for her proof reading; and my dear friend Dave Young who redefined generous by offering his professional layout skills and publishing expertise near gratis and turned this idea into a finished product way beyond my expectations.

Lastly, I want to thank my parishioners at the Church of Our Saviour who gave me a place of rest and allowed me to continue my journey and grow in my understanding of God's sovereign grace as I completed this work. May we all continue to trust God more completely.

Preface

This book did not turn out anything like I imagined. First, the bike ride itself completely obliterated any concept of adventure I might have had before I began. Second, and most importantly, the impact the ride would have on my understanding of God and my future vocation was totally underestimated. What began as a somewhat naïve personal journey of faith, filled with all kinds of intangible motives, turned out to be an accelerated entry into the ordination process for the priesthood along with a radical reorientation about God that would not even begin to be understood for years to come. This most crucial reordering of my concept of God is best described as going from the "all-assisting, always available co-pilot, ready to accommodate my every need," to the "completely Sovereign, all Loving, Ruler of my destiny, intentionally guiding my steps despite my tendency to run in the wrong direction."

Along with those major developments has come the humbling and comforting realization that this same Sovereign God is completely able and willing to act on behalf of His people without us having to earn or contribute to His generosity in any way. Granted, in the case of my bike trip, I had to get on the bicycle and push on the pedals, but in the overall outcome of the ride, and the multiple circumstances completely beyond my control that turned out in my favor, I learned very quickly that I had nothing to bring to the table that ultimately could influence the outcome of the ride in any way.

Such a passive understanding of God's goodness seems to contradict the very nature of a physically demanding endeavor such as a bike ride across the country, but in the end, as I believe the story bears out, the physical contribution on my part vanishes in comparison to the extravagant and miraculous provision consistently supplied by God Himself. Any other interpretation, for me, would either be the pinnacle of human pride and arrogance or the unscrupulous trust in chance and coincidence. My intellect and experience will not let me go in either of those directions.

Of course that's just my take on it. Everyone is free to draw their own conclusions. But any way you look at it, the ride is a fascinating experience and one that I'm grateful to be able to share. I hope everyone will enjoy the journey, and, if possible, even be encouraged and strengthened in his or her own faith.

Thanks for taking the time to read about my journey.

Gratefully,

Joseph Martin

Contents

Foreword

The Greater Grandeur of God's Grace

Whate should you do? You thought becoming a Christian would enable you to fulfil your dream of becoming a professional tennis player with a computer ranking. That didn't work out. So you decided to try your hand at banking, but that didn't feel like the right way to serve Christ. So you decided to devote all that discipline and dedication you learned in sports to serve God as a youth minister. Endless nights of hanging out with teenagers at high school football games and fast food restaurants. Countless conversations as their friend trying to help them cope with the ever-present challenge of being a teen. You deeply cared about the town's youth because you wanted them to know that Jesus did too. But you also always made an effort to be real so that they would think Jesus was too. Nothing, however, you ever did seemed good enough and in your mind that includes your current youth ministry. So there you are single, 33 years old and so incredibly far away from being that guy voted "most popular" by his senior class. So what should you do now? Run away from it all by doing something extraordinary like taking a six-week bike trip across America!

And just to make things really interesting, a proper challenge, a real test not only of your physical manhood but also of your spiritual strength as a hard-core follower of Jesus, why not refuse the usual support system of an accompanying van or fellow riders or a clear idea where you are going to stay each night or even a credit card as a last-ditch back-up when all other things fail. Why not go all out? Practice Extreme Christianity. Ride alone and trust God to provide. If you preach living by faith is the true Christian way, why not for once just do it! At last, be a spiritual athlete for Jesus.

And that's exactly what Joseph Martin did for forty-three event-filled days from San Diego, California, to Ambridge, Pennsylvania, during July and August 1990. He set off to encounter the greatness of God and to try to reconnect with some sense of greatness in himself. What he discovered along the way was not so much the importance of greatness but the incredible power of graciousness, both God's and other people's. For God used Joseph's journey across America to begin the long process of breaking him free from all those years conditioned by sports to base his identity on his own current performance. God wanted Joseph to learn deep in his heart to look only to Christ's loving performance for him on the cross for his self-worth. Over and over again, God providentially met Joseph's every need, not because he deserved it as a reward for the extreme effort of the bike ride or even because of the radical faith by which he rode. No, God provided Joseph daily manna just because that is the kind of God he is. As the waves of unmerited grace kept washing over Joseph, an overflowing gratitude slowly welled up in his heart, altering his attitude about life and his sense of direction for his future. Much to his surprise, despite all of the incredible sights of natural beauty he saw and the impressive acts of physical prowess he was able to perform, Joseph's abiding, life-changing memory of that incredible time was the greater grandeur of God's grace.

One of my favorite sayings is:

> God's love takes us on journeys we do not wish to go,
> makes us travel by roads we do not wish to use,
> always to take us to places we never wish to leave.

The compelling story of Joseph Martin's journey across America only confirms the truth of that saying. For time after time, each day's uncertainty, hardships and forced reliance on God's intervention end in Joseph's eventually arriving for the night at a new place so special, so filled with love and acceptance for him, that he finds it difficult to leave the next morning and start the process all over again.

I was so deeply touched to see God's grace so consistently at work in Joseph's circumstances and his heart that I could not put the book down. Of course, he is not the only Christian to struggle with a performance-based misunderstanding of the Gospel. All too often we evangelicals preach that we are saved by God's grace but live like we are sustained by our own sweat. I found that I was comforted and encouraged in my walk with Christ by reading of the utterly grace-given comfort and encouragement that Joseph constantly received during his biking safari. Even when his obliviousness to its true source at times bordered on presumption, God's loving provision for his needs still faithfully flowed. Joseph's winsomely honest and well-written account left me refreshed for my own journey and deeply grateful to God for it.

So fasten your seatbelt, turn the page and begin the next, better chapter in your Christian life.

The Rev. Canon Dr. John Ashley Null, Former Rector (1988-90)
St. Andrew's Episcopal Church, Liberal, Kansas
Host Parish for Day 23

December, 1989

Introduction

Deciding to Ride

I t was a disappointing youth group meeting; low turnout, no new kids, and kind of flat. As we were leaving the sterile meeting room of the Home Health Care storefront office that we were using for the meetings, it felt as if everyone was thinking the same thing—this group would be so much better if we had more people—but no one said anything because we really did enjoy each other's company and nobody wanted to spoil the moment. But the disappointment still lingered, at least in the youth leader. We straightened up the molded plastic chairs, turned out the lights, and filed out the door onto the sidewalk of Merchant Street, the main drag in Ambridge.

Like many towns in Western Pennsylvania, Ambridge was once a mighty steel town on the outskirts of Pittsburgh but after the collapse of the steel industry had fallen on hard times and lost much of the industrialism and prestige that it once had. Now, relying on small businesses and the service industry, the prideful town was trying hard to keep a positive image along Merchant Street while figuring out how to turn things around. One sure sign of life was Police Station Pizza two buildings down. As usual, the takeout-only hot spot was hopping with kids hanging out on the sidewalk and sitting on parked cars talking and having a good time. I recognized most of them because for two years I had been the chaplain for the high school football team and attended all of the Friday night games, usually ending the night like half the student body with a white bakery box loaded with hot, square pizza slices before going to bed. My idea to hold the youth meeting in the Home Health Care building two doors down from the pizza shop was done in hopes of inviting more kids to the group. It wasn't working despite the convenient location and I knew why they weren't coming.

The same reason I didn't go to a youth group when I was in high school—my friends and I simply had better things to do. Our families didn't go to the same church, some didn't go at all, so there wasn't any reason for us to hang out and play silly games with kids we didn't know very well when we could be doing something more fun. On top of that, most youth group kids seemed kind of out of touch and a little goofy.

Youth Group meeting on Merchant Street

But that wasn't the kind of group I was running. We did share a common interest in Jesus and spiritual matters but we also had a good time together and we certainly were not goofy or out of touch. My God, I had received the "Most Popular" senior notable in high school, for crying out loud; being considered goofy never crossed my mind. There had to be a way to get more everyday kids into our group.

After the meeting we piled into my big, brown, three-quarter ton Suburban and drove five miles down Highway 65 to Sewickley, the wealthy town next door that had a modern, brightly furnished Eat 'n Park restaurant where we often went to eat, talk, and basically enjoy each other's company. Afterwards, I dropped everyone off at their homes one by one, and headed home to my one-room apartment above the cigar store three blocks down from the pizza shop. "Apartment" might have been somewhat of an exaggeration since my 8 x 10-foot bedroom was actually an unused section of the church office that had been offered to me by the Church of the Savior when I decided to start the youth ministry in Ambridge. The space had been donated to the church by the owner of the store and local insurance businessman, Jim Simon, and we all had pitched in for the renovation. The décor was a little sparse, and I shared a common bathroom with the office, which sometimes presented a challenge, but with free rent it was one way to try to get a youth ministry up and running. That night, as I tried to fall asleep in my little white-walled cell block, my mind churned with thoughts about the evening and what was going on with my unsuccessful ministry and pitiful life.

A few weeks later while sitting in the doctor's office reading last month's *People* magazine, I came across an article about a lady who rode a horse across the country to raise money for cancer. I was captivated by the thought of a person putting so much effort into a cause she believed in. I sat back and let the story sink in. Then, very subtly, like a whisper in the back of my mind, surfaced the most radical thought of my life: "If a normal person can ride a horse across the country for her cause, why can't a youth leader do something just as radical for his?"

At that moment, as I raised my head and stared at the waterfall painting on the waiting room wall, something stirred inside me. It was as if the sleeping athlete in me that had been dormant for over six years had come alive. Once an impassioned tennis player, practicing five hours a day, running wind sprints, and grunting out "kangaroo" jumps, I had spent the last six years rehabilitating a herniated disk in my lower back, with no particular goal or ambition in mind except to get healthy. Suddenly a renewed passion had come alive inside me and the seed for the bike trip had been planted.

That afternoon I went to the Sewickley YMCA as usual, to do my standard workout of riding the stationary bike, going through the Nautilus machines, and lifting light weights, but this time my attitude was different: I was in training, I had a goal, and my mind was racing.

Weeks on the stationary bike went by without me sharing the idea with anybody. I knew some people could handle riding a bike across the country in an organized group with van support, meals, lodging, and experienced leaders. That was almost understandable, and for a good cause, maybe even commendable. But the idea growing in my mind was way different from that. The desire developing inside me was to ride alone, with no support team, no tent, and no sleeping bag, staying in churches and trusting God for all my needs.

And that wasn't even the whole of it. Somewhere deep within me was another motivation for making the ride that that was far beyond youth ministry. This strong, inner drive was impossible to describe but equally impossible to deny. It had something to do with the intangible side of life, spiritual matters such as faith and emotions that clearly exist but are much harder to put a finger on. The best I could describe it was as a need to know God better; somehow to know

Coach Kam and the Ambridge football team prayer time

more convincingly that the God I talked about to teenagers was more than a mythical old geezer in the dry pages of the Bible, but one who really did part the sea, raise the dead, and feed five thousand. Something along those lines was driving me and if I thought most people would not understand the ride in terms of youth ministry, I knew no one would understand the inner drive, especially since I really didn't understand it myself.

The idea became real one cold evening in January as I ate dinner at the Eat 'n Park with a friend visiting Ambridge from San Diego. Ned was an ordained minister who came to Ambridge occasionally to take courses at Trinity Episcopal School for Ministry. He knew about my youth ministry and had been a person I knew would at least listen with an open mind. As I shared the idea, Ned not only embraced the trip but offered to make his home in San Diego my starting point. And to add to the excitement, Ned knew a man who had made such a trip himself. He suggested I give him a call and get some advice. The ball was rolling.

Training continued at the YMCA during the cold winter months as I logged hour after hour on the stationary bike pumping away and dripping with sweat. Plans also began to take shape. I called Ned's friend, Al, in LA , who rode across the country with an organized group that left out of LA and took a northern route across the Rockies. He suggested I contact the "touring counselor" at the Southern California AAA and see if they could recommend a southern route leaving from San Diego. "Are you sure you want to take a southern route during July?" Al asked. "Yes, that's my plan," I said, thinking to myself, "Hey, I grew up in Florida. How much hotter could Arizona be?" Al also put me on to another man, Ray, in San Diego who had also made a cross-country trip. While he rode, his wife, Chris, drove the van each day to the chosen destination and waited for Ray to arrive. Then they would load up and drive to the hotel for a shower, food, and a nice bed; a workable strategy and a great way to see the country, but not the plan brewing in my mind. I called Ray and Chris anyway and they took great interest in my trip and volunteered to help any way they could.

After working on my proposed route, I sent it to "Norty" at the Southern California AAA and asked him to check it out and rework it for safe bike travel. He sent me back detailed maps and a ton of helpful information. Next, I had to work out lodging. Having never made an overnight bike ride I wasn't exactly sure how to split up the trip, but using the mileage markers on a typical road map, I picked out thirty-five towns along the route that I thought I could reach in one day's ride. Since I planned not to ride on Sundays I figured I could make the trip in forty days. It had a good ring to it anyway. I got out my National Episcopal Church Directory and sent a postcard to every Episcopal church, if there was one, in each of my thirty-five towns explaining that I was an Episcopal youth leader riding across the country and asking if they would put me up for the night when I passed through. I waited for the responses.

```
                    Joseph K. Martin
                    1200 Merchant St.
                    Ambridge, PA 15003
                    (412) 266-4412
      Dear Pastor,

      My name is Joseph Martin  and I'm a youth minister  at
      the  Episcopal Church of  the Savior in  Ambridge, PA.
      This summer, from July 8 to Aug 16, I will be making a
      cross-country bike trip starting in San Diego to raise
      awareness and  support for youth ministry  in Ambridge
      and the  wider Church. My route is taking me near your
      area and I  wanted to know, if I need to, could I call
      you  for some hospitality.  I may  not need to  but if
      that would  be ok, could you drop me a postcard before
      June 25  with a phone number to call? Thanks, I'd love
      to meet you this summer.
                          In Christ,
```

As spring arrived and the ground began to thaw I was eager to get out on the road. The only problem was I didn't own a road bike. I had never been a serious biker but only took up riding when I injured my back six years before while living in Tampa and decided it was the best way to exercise since I couldn't run. My method at the time was to ride a bike standing upright on the pedals without sitting on the seat. This allowed me to keep my back straight and rotate my legs as if I were running but without the pounding. After a year or so in that routine I moved to Ambridge to go to the seminary for a one-year lay ministry program, and began riding normally on a five-speed hybrid bike that became my recreational friend for the next three years. Now that winter was fading and it was time to get off the stationary bike and put in some serious road miles, I needed more than my hybrid.

The solution came one day while working with my friend David fixing up bicycles that had been donated to his ministry to send to Africa. In the collection of used bikes I noticed an old, yellow, Schwinn ten-speed that needed some work but looked promising. We agreed that a donation to the ministry in return for the bike would be ethical. Whether it was or not, I'm not sure, but I gave David ten dollars for the bike and took it home to fix up for the road.

The thing weighed a ton. It brought back memories of ninth grade when my friend Judd got a beautiful forest green one for his birthday. It was the smoothest and most sturdy bike I had ever ridden, and I felt so cool riding it; probably didn't hurt that Judd was the coolest guy in the school, but, anyway, that was a long time ago. This yellow version had seen better days, but after a little fix up it was ready for the road. I didn't feel quite as cool riding it as I would have in ninth grade but that really wasn't the goal.

By this time the word was out at my church about the trip. One couple invited me to move into their house for the three months prior to the trip as I did my final road work. Bruce and Helen Camlin lived in the suburbs outside of Ambridge, which would make life more peaceful than in my second floor Merchant Street apartment above the cigar store. Summer nights there could be a little annoying. One hot night I was trying to sleep, as I usually did, with my windows open when I heard the sound of running water outside my second floor window. It was two o'clock in the morning as I looked down from my window to see a drunk neighbor below, on his way home from the bar across the street, leaning against the telephone pole relieving himself. It sounded like a race horse standing in the stall before the big race. Another night I was awakened by a loud crashing sound on the main street. A bar patron parking his car along Merchant Street had opened his door just as a passing car sped by, ripping the door off the hinges and pinning it to the front fender. The guy in the car, as much traumatized as angry, jumped out of the wide open exit that used to be a door, shouting obscenities and chasing the hit-and-run driver down the road. All to say that sleeping and training at the Camlins' house would be helpful.

Just as training began I decided to fly to Louisiana to visit my good friend and Episcopal priest Lee Jaster and his wife, Roxanne, for Easter. Because I was in tunnel vision about the ride and felt the urgency to ramp up the training, I asked if they knew anyone with a bike I could borrow during my visit. Sure enough they did and had the bike in the garage when I arrived on the Thursday before Good Friday. The next day after the Good Friday service at Fr. Lee's church, I quickly changed into my shorts and T-shirt, anxious to hit the open road. I had looked on the map and picked out a long, two-lane highway that looked like a good training route, and after a quick farewell, off I went, full of energy and ecstatic about getting out on the road. After a couple of hours I found myself cranking away on a lonely highway with no cars in sight and the Louisiana sun beating down on my neck. Having not yet trained in such heat and humidity in Pittsburgh my energy level began to drop and I found myself cranking away methodically, looking down at the worn asphalt and not paying much attention to the road ahead. Even when a car would approach from either direction I could hear the sound in time to make sure I was far enough over in my lane, but that didn't happen very often.

After a long quiet stretch I heard the faint sound of a car approaching from the distance ahead of me and since it was in the oncoming lane and didn't pose any problem for my lane I paid even less attention. As the noise grew louder and the car drew closer I looked up as part of my normal routine to watch it pass by and nearly jumped out of my skin. Approaching me head-on at a frightening speed was the grill of a large sedan passing the oncoming car side-by-side and totally covering my entire lane. Instinctively I swerved off of the road just as the speeding monster whizzed by, nearly knocking me over with wind power. Trembling uncontrollably, I dropped the bike in the grass beside the road and sat down, trying desperately to console myself back to some form of sanity. It was undoubtedly the closest I had ever come to staring death in the face and the shock was crippling. Nothing could stop the shaking.

When I finally regained enough composure to get back on the bike I headed straight back to the Jasters' house and parked the bike in the garage. Lee and Roxanne were in the kitchen when I came in and by the look on my face they knew something serious had happened. I told them the story, much to their horror, as the three of us thanked God for my safety and agreed together that that was the end of the bike trip idea. It just wasn't worth the risk. I didn't get on the bike for the rest of the visit but spent the next two days mulling over the near-death experience while mourning the real death of the bike trip. Returning back to Ambridge and sharing the experience and the decision with my pastor, Joe Vitunic, we both agreed that wisdom had won out and it was time to move on.

Days passed in Ambridge as I halfheartedly went through the motions with my youth ministry and contemplated the depressed state that had settled into my soul. Exercise at the Y was a drag and biking held no interest at all. This condition continued for a good week until one afternoon I went to visit another good priest friend, the Rev. George Pierce, and told him my story. George had had a similar yearning as a missionary in Africa when he decided to leave the village where he was ministering and take a journey in his jeep into the wilds of the African countryside. It was a dangerous and unexplainable trip but he felt the need to do it anyway. Far away from camp, in the sweltering heat of a deserted African dirt road, the jeep broke down, leaving him stranded in the middle of nowhere. The situation seemed life threatening and hopeless until he noticed a vehicle approaching from the distance. It was a vendor on his way to a village who happened to have a part for the jeep and was able to replace it right there on the spot. George cranked up the jeep and completed the journey back to camp. He told me it was the experience of lifetime, a time with God that he would never forget.

Listening to George I could almost feel the life coming back into my body as his story validated all I had felt about my trip before the near-fatal incident. He didn't tell me what to do, but by the time I said good-bye and headed home, the excitement had returned and I was ready to resume training. As soon as I got home I pumped up the tires of the old yellow Schwinn and took off for a ride. A few days later I broke the news to Joe, much to his disappointment. As a pastor and father figure to me, his regard for my safety far outweighed whatever other reason I had for making the trip, and he wasn't the only one. But the training continued and during the next two months I logged hundreds of miles on the old Schwinn with even greater determination.

A good friend, Josie, had put out a milk carton at her hair salon for donations toward my trip and in the two months had collected over $500. I accused Josie of putting most of it in herself but she denied it. Either way, the time had come to get a real road bike, and thanks to Josie and friends, I had the money.

One good thing about Ambridge was its exceptional bike shop. It was the place I went to buy the five-speed hybrid years before when I showed up in Ambridge without a bike and an anonymous check showed up in my student mailbox at the seminary. I can remember standing in the hallway holding the check in my hand and sharing with one of the African students how I had been looking at a bike in the bike shop but didn't expect to spend so much money on a new bike. "I'm just not sure what to do," I said, holding a check for the cost of the bike in my hand. Without hesitation, with his big African smile, he replied, "Buy the bike!" I walked down Merchant Street, cashing the check at the bank on the way, and bought the bike.

Aside from that small miracle, the Ambridge Bike Shop was also the place where serious bikers came from all around to gear up with the highest quality biking equipment. The owner, Larry, knowing me as a customer and as the local youth guy, and being an avid biker himself, took interest in the trip and offered to help me out. The day I came to the shop to talk about a bike, he took me down to the basement where he kept his overflow inventory and picked out an 18-speed touring bike that a guy had ordered but never came to pick up. It was my size and even though not the top of the line, it was the sweetest bike I had ever considered owning. Larry assured me it would make the trip and after a quick test ride around the block and a reasonable charge of $300, and some expert fitting by Gary, the store manager, I was soaring down Merchant Street like a kid on Christmas morning. While riding home on my new machine the thought struck me, "We're actually going through with this!" I could hardly contain myself.

One concern remained, and that was housing. With less than a month away from my July 3 departure to San Diego, I had received only thirteen responses from the churches that had received post cards. The element of faith and trust was becoming a real issue. What about food and lodging on the other twenty-seven nights? The $200 left over from the collection box at Josie's salon wasn't going to cover it. I had already decided to make Josie's collection box my support, but should I take more just to be safe? How about a trusty credit card in case an emergency pops up?

After a considerable amount of prayer and internal debate I decided to go with the $200 from the collection but still wasn't sure about the credit card.

What else to bring was also an issue. Between the AAA information and magazine articles from the bike shop, the list of necessary items ranged from foul-weather gear and tents, to medical kits and spare spokes. I finally settled on what I considered the bare minimum. The following is my list of items for the trip: bike, a rear rack with two side panniers, one handlebar pouch, three water bottles, two pairs of biking shorts, four long- sleeve T-shirts, one pair of cotton shorts, one pair of running shorts, two pairs of boxers, two short-sleeve T-shirts, three pairs of short socks, one pair of all-purpose (non clip-in) biking shoes, flip-flops, gortex rain suit, thinsulate long-sleeve undershirt, toothbrush, toothpaste, soap, wash cloth, beach towel, maps, camera, bike lock and cable, tire repair kit, two extra tubes, three-inch mini flashlight, bandana, sunscreen, lip balm, baseball hat, sunglasses, Bible, journal, helmet, and biking gloves. No spare parts, no tent, no sleeping bag, and, finally, after much soul searching, no credit card, just $200. I didn't talk much about that decision with anybody.

The final piece fell into place when USAir responded surprisingly to my request for air travel by offering me a free one-way ticket to San Diego. The only fee I had to pay was $35 for shipping the bike. I remember opening the mail and holding the ticket in my hand with mixed emotions: the exuberance of receiving such generosity from the airlines, countered by the gut-wrenching certainty of a departure date. Now, with ticket in hand, there truly was no obstacle preventing the trip. All I had to do was show up at the airport with my bike in the provided box and away we would go.

On Tuesday, July 3 that's what I did. My friend Bob came by in his pickup truck and we loaded up the white box and black panniers in the back and headed for the airport. The night before I had carefully followed the packing instructions by removing the pedals and front wheel, loosening the neck and twisting the handlebars ninety degrees, and fitting everything securely inside. Now, with the box lying flat in the truck bed in view through the rear window, Bob and I tried to talk normally as we drove to the airport. Bob was a good Christian friend and had been an encouragement for the ride from the beginning but conversation was hard that morning. At the curbside I checked the box, and with panniers in hand and holding back some unexpected emotions, gave my friend a hug and choked out a positive, "See you in six weeks." "I'll be here," he said, with one last boost of confidence before climbing into the cab and driving off. And there I was, standing alone on the sidewalk with no real obligations to worry about and no one who really needed me for the next six weeks.

Making my way to the boarding gate, I handed the attendant my boarding pass as the feeling of commitment rushed through my body. I had boarded a lot of planes in my life but walking down the long corridor toward the plane door felt like walking into the Twilight Zone. I found my seat, put my gear in the overhead compartment, and sat down, waiting for takeoff. Early on in the decision to make the trip I had a strong urge to journal the trip so I pulled out my 5 x 8-inch spiral notebook and made my first entry. Here's what I wrote as I waited for takeoff:

No Turning Back, Tuesday, July 3

Right now I'm on a USAir 737 bound for San Diego with my bike in a box and everything I'll ride with in the overhead compartment. Without a tent or a sleeping bag, or much extra clothes besides riding gear, I look like I'm ready for an afternoon at the beach rather than a cross-country bike trip.

One reason I'm glad you're reading this book is because I've busted my tail training and I'd hate to think it was only for myself. I'm thinking mainly of the hundreds of miles I've ridden in the past couple of months. It seems like a dream as I remember those days fighting the biting wind and cold in early April, sloshing through torrential rains and thunder storms, inhaling road dirt from passing trucks, enduring long hot rides in June to the point where I strained just to make it home, oozing off the bike and wobbling down the driveway like a wet noodle; it has to benefit someone other than me.

Please, though, no pity, I actually loved every minute of it. Gritting my teeth and taking my body to the limit has always been a favorite pastime of mine and I'm thankful for the opportunity to do it once again. The only problem is that in the past I've had a tendency to work hard and gut it out only to quit before I accomplish what I set out to do. I pray this time will be different.

My hope is that by making this trip I might do something to benefit the teenagers in the town of Ambridge and, if possible, lots of people across the country and the world.

I don't know what else to tell you about the book because at this point my journal pages are empty and only time will tell what lies ahead. I do feel like we are in for the experience of a lifetime and I hope you will stay with me for the entire ride.

Landing

Touching down in San Diego gave me goose bumps as I stared out of the airplane window. I had grown up in the Florida beach scene, but something about California felt electric, even the sky seemed to be plugged in with its cool neon blue. Couple that with the excitement and anticipation of the trip and my metabolism was racing like a bull rider waiting for the gate to open. Grabbing my panniers out of the overhead compartment, I walked off the plane and down the Jetway buzzing from head to toe; I was in San Diego and there really was only one way back.

Ned was waiting for me at the baggage claim where we located my white box and headed for his mini pickup truck. As we placed the box in the back of the bed, I noticed another biker on the sidewalk at the curbside unpacking his bike right there and getting ready to ride from the airport. A brief thought shot through my mind of how much more daring and adventurous that was than the way I was doing it, but I didn't have time to think much about that. Soon Ned and I were pulling away and heading down the road, talking and enjoying the drive.

Bluffs over San Diego

And what a drive. It felt like riding through a movie set. Everywhere I looked were more beautiful people with great tans and cool clothes, skateboards, surfboards, rollerblades, mountain bikes, and everything else fun and cool. The energy seemed to be everywhere and everyone seemed to be into it one way or another. I felt as if I had landed on a different planet, the contrast between old and industrial Ambridge, and new and recreational San Diego could not have been more captivating. I just couldn't wait to put my two-wheeled machine together and join the scene.

The wires on my Avocet electric trip meter had been damaged during shipping but Ned's electrical engineering son happened to drop by and after a little solder and a few minor adjustments we were ready to ride. Naturally, I headed for the beach. Having grown up on the Gulf Coast my seagull senses headed me straight to the coast, with a little help from the map. As I rode I began to notice that even though a standard of coolness permeated everything, there was also an individualism that allowed everyone to customize their coolness in their own way. If someone liked fluorescent orange swimming trunks, that was cool. If others liked gray baggies, that was cool too. The refreshing thing was that people seemed free to express themselves and be individuals and nobody seemed overly concerned with one another as everyone went about their own business.

This kind of coolness, I decided, was called funk. It was a kind of subtle, do-your-own- thing individualism that seemed to define the beach life. The bumper sticker on an old VW van summed it up, "In Funk We Trust." As I rode my bike along the cliff overlooking the immense Pacific Ocean and the variety of beach activities down below, I couldn't get that phrase out of my mind. I liked funk. Being free to express myself and do as I pleased sounded refreshing. Sure beat the heck out of control and unrealistic expectations, but

What a cool place.

it felt a little flimsy. As I thought about making my trip I needed something more solid to rely on. As corny as it sounded, something in me was clinging to the old line, "In God We Trust." I just wasn't comfortable doing this thing my own funky way.

Day 1

Saturday, July 7, 1990

San Diego, CA to Boulder Oaks, CA

56 miles

9:30 a.m. to 5:30 p.m.

A Wimpy Start

If ever I had any feelings of being some kind of biking he-man, my first day on the road put an end to that. In fact, the way I started the trip was so contrary to my original strategy it haunted me like a bad image.

My original plan was to leave Ned's house on Friday and spend the weekend with Ray and Chris Crater, the couple I had contacted in January, on the Island of Coronado and leave for the trip from there on Monday, July 9. Chris, however, suggested over the phone that I get the first day's ride out of the way on Saturday the seventh since I didn't have a place to stay lined up for the first night. She would drive out to my destination (like she had done for Ray) at the end of the day and pick me up and bring me back to their house. Then, on Monday morning, Ray would drive me back to where I left off and I could take it from there on my own. It sounded like a typical "mom" idea but I begrudgingly agreed to do it anyway. After all, for someone who had never ridden on the highways of California, or taken an overnight bike trip anywhere, it did make sense. Plus, I always found it easier to agree with Mom.

I spent Friday night at Ned's house in Point Loma, and on Saturday morning, July 7, headed out for Boulder Oaks. With bike fully loaded, I rolled through the quiet streets of San Diego, feeling a little nervous but totally pumped about the day's ride. The sky was a perfect San Diego blue and I could think of nothing I'd rather be doing than pedaling along, free as a bird, toward a totally unknown destination. The only drawback was the nagging guilt for getting picked up at the end of the day.

I made my way over the San Diego River and headed east on Friars Road. That's me, I thought, for the next forty days, a bike-riding monk, traveling the desert and talking with God.

San Diego had the most biker friendly roads and accommodating drivers I had ever experienced. Not once did I find myself teetering on the edge of an uneven pavement, bouncing through potholes, or swerving through dirt and gravel because some angry Neanderthal wanted to squeeze me off the road. None of that in San Diego. In Funk We Trust, be cool to bikers and all that. Following the San Diego River and winding around Jack Murphy Stadium was ideal, your typical Saturday morning bike ride in Southern California.

I almost blew it, though, when I decided to break from my charted route and check out a road that looked more adventurous. Even though San Diego was a great place, I was ready to get away from the city scene and experience the great outdoors. Mission Gorge Road looked like the way to go, at least on the map. I got to the intersection and turned left, but before I knew it I was heading straight down, I mean half-pipe straight down. One problem with maps is they are only two dimensional. Everything looks flat. I guess I should have known by the name Mission Gorge but the road was anything but flat, and before I reached warp speed I squeezed hard on the brakes and pulled over to the curb to rethink

CA freeway entrance

this idea. I knew the universal law of biking: "What goes down must come up," and the coming up is usually not worth the thrill of going down. I decided to turn around and climb back to the flat road before I really had to pay.

A few miles later on my prescribed route, I realized what a wise decision I had made as the road I was riding on became the top rim of Mission Gorge, an immense canyon down below. Climbing up the other side of that canyon would have been murder. My mind began to wander, "Like some of the gorges I've been down in my life. Going down was a breeze, but hitting the bottom and trying to climb back out was a pain." I thought of the time in tenth grade when a cop brought me and a friend home for drinking. When I left my house that night with my friends, my relationship with my parents was "on the charted course," you might say. I was a good kid, got along with my brother and sister, played little league baseball, mowed the lawn, went to church, and basically enjoyed life in my family. And, if the truth be known, I really didn't enjoy drinking at that stage of my life, but liked hanging out with my friends. When I left my house that night I didn't realize how steep the grade was I was heading down. My friends had heard of a party at a kid's house whose parents were away and naturally we headed in that direction. Along the way one of the guys pulled out a bottle of liquor that he had taken from his parent's house and we started passing it around. I really didn't have a taste for hard liquor but took sips with the others because I was part of the group. Some of the guys, though, really put it down and one friend in particular was a mess by the time we got to the party. He ended up in the bushes in the front yard of the party house while other kids mingled in the yard and flowed in and out from the parked cars to the wide open front door.

When two police cars pulled up, everyone scattered like mice. Feeling relatively innocent and not thinking I had much to be afraid of, I didn't run and ended up talking to one of the cops in the front lawn. He asked me to wait there for a minute and after finding my plastered friend in the bushes returned and asked us to get into the car. We dropped my friend off at his house and then the cop let me sit in the front seat as we talked reservedly on the way to my house. One tidbit we discovered was that he knew my dad from patrolling around his business in another part of town. I felt like that might be a plus, but the cost in reputation was more than I imagined. When we pulled into my driveway, little did I know how the downhill slope on which I had been riding would bottom out. The change of expression on my mom's face said it all when I walked in the kitchen door, quickly followed by a uniformed police officer. Her joyful greeting abruptly changed to bewilderment as the ominous presence of a police officer stood in our kitchen for the first time ever. My dad quickly joined us and the four of us discussed the episode until the officer dismissed himself and left us to deal with the situation.

As I pedaled my bike along the rim of Mission Gorge, I realized how quickly and permanently my downhill ride had altered the relationship between me and my parents, even though, as a teenager, I didn't have a clue. The climb out would be a slow one, and reaching the original level of trust and innocence I had before the incident would be a tough ride if even possible at all. And it wouldn't be the last one. "Oh Jesus," I thought, "thank you for pulling me out of life's gorges. Please keep me on your road."

Gradually, my peaceful streets turned into bustling California suburbs with busy streets, malls, fast food joints, and weekend warriors gearing up for fun. That's when my contemplative joy ride got a wake up call. Something felt strange in my rear wheel and when I looked down I noticed for the first time in my biking career a squishy back tire. Feeling inconvenienced but not overly stressed, I pulled into the Shoney's restaurant parking lot and dismounted along the curb underneath a tree near the drive-in window.

During my training days I thought it might be a good idea to practice fixing a flat but I never had one and felt I could handle it when the situation came up. The truth be told, I really didn't want to loosen the rear wheel of my brand new bike if I didn't have to, and also figured, being a mechanical engineer and car buff who had rebuilt car engines since high school, I could take the rear wheel off an 18-speed bike when the time came. Now was the time.

I unhooked the small elastic cords that secured the two panniers to the black aluminum rack over my rear wheel and laid the packs in the grass. I released the nifty clip on my handlebar pack and laid the black canvas bag beside the other two. "Hi, welcome to Shoney's, can I take your order?" The drive-thru order board asked. I continued with my job. "Hi, welcome to Shoney's, can I take your order?" it asked again. I must have heard that question fifty times as the convertible Mustangs and beach-bound Jeeps cruised through the drive-in on their way to another carefree day in their familiar world. And there I was, a complete stranger, 2,700 miles from home, changing the tube on the rear wheel of a touring bike. Good thing Larry at the bike shop had equipped me with the little plastic tire tools I needed to get the tire off the rim. After fiddling for a while I stuffed in the new tube, pumped in a little air with my handy bike pump, worked the wheel back onto the chain and into the slot without getting totally greasy, tightened the quick release lever, and finished pumping her up. I remounted my packs, put on my white Nike baseball hat and red Oakley shades and took off. The first day out was already more than I expected.

As the miles clicked by, the noonday sun intensified while the hype of the suburbs gradually transformed into quiet back roads. I was headed for the

Pine Valley

mountains. Point Loma was about thirty-feet above sea level; Laguna Summit, where I was headed, was about 4,000. Not a bad climb for a flatlander. Gradually, the mountain scenery began to change and so did my miles per hour. At about 2,500 feet I had to leave the frontage road I had grown comfortable with and get onto Interstate 8 to continue the climb. Staying in the emergency lane and looking out over the mountainside was worth the effort, though. Near Descanso Junction, around 3,000 feet up, I came upon a scenic pull-off and decided to take a break. The view was fantastic.

I walked my bike to the railing not far from two long-haired guys standing in front of their old Chrysler, smoking dope and looking out over the mountains. My attempt to strike up a conversation never really got off the ground as we talked in short sentences mainly about San Diego and the mountain sunset. Based on outward appearances I guess we didn't have much in common but I wanted somehow to bring God into the picture so I pressed on. "Do you guys think much about God when you come up here?" I asked. "Not really," the one said. "They say you can tell something about the creator by looking at His creation," I continued. "Uh," the other said without turning his head. Long silence. "Well, you guys take it easy," I said. I walked back to the road and pushed off, thanking God for the beauty of His creation and for the euphoria I was feeling in being on this journey. I realized trying to share those feelings and expecting two perfect strangers to relate and interact with me was a little crazy; I was in a world of my own.

Chris met me in Pine Valley as we had planned but then suggested I try to make Boulder Oaks, another eight miles or so. "What for?" I thought. "I've been on the road for seven hours, covered fifty miles, and climbed 4,000 feet. Not a bad Saturday's ride." But she persuaded me to press on, so off I went. The ride turned out to be a breeze and I even met up with a nice married couple training for an upcoming race. We rode together in the peaceful scenery outside Boulder Oaks to a little wooden shack of a gas station where Chris was parked. There we hung out on the edge of the gravel parking lot in the shade of some beautiful oak trees, drinking Gatorade and talking about bike adventures. I didn't have many to talk about yet but they encouraged me in my adventure. We said good-bye and Chris and I loaded up and headed back to Coronado.

Feeling a bit drained, I talked with Chris about the day's highlights, then put my seat back and stared out the side window replaying the scenes of the day and thinking about what was ahead. If there ever was a definition of surreal, my mind was in it. I had no categories for what I was experiencing.

We arrived home in an hour and a half or so and after a nice cool shower, dinner, and a lazy, peaceful, sunset walk on the beach, I felt like a renewed person. I still had this nagging feeling that I had wimped out by riding in a car and messed up the spirit of the trip. That night Ray and I spent time together talking strategy and cutting my thick stack of maps from the AAA down to only the sections I needed and taping them together into a nice thin collection. Also, after my first day of mountain climbing, I was convinced that weight reduction was essential and I had to make some cuts in my belongings. The items to go were my bike lock and cable and my original Bible that was no longer necessary since Ned had given me a much smaller one. The weight savings was significant. I went to bed replaying the events of the day and thinking about the ride ahead. "Good thing tomorrow is Sunday," I thought. I wanted to go to church one last time to pray and ask for God's blessing before leaving for real.

Day 2

Sunday, July 8, 1990

Coronado, CA

Does It Get Any Better Than This?

On Sunday, July 8, I experienced a wave of emotion beyond any level I had ever felt in my life. It happened during a walk on the beach after church and a terrific brunch with Ray and Chris at the Officer's Club. Changing into my shorts and walking toward the beach under the perfectly blue sky and bright summer sun brought joy to my soul I could hardly contain. Approaching the beach and inhaling the clean, cool, ocean air as the waves crashed gently on the sand produced peace within me that only the ocean could.

Frisbees flew, families played, and sun-soakers hung out for that perfect tan. Some hung out more than others but that was just part of the scene. As I walked along the waterline, bare feet in the wet sand, sun and blue sky overhead, listening, seeing, smelling and feeling the perfection of my situation, an unexpected flood of wonder and goodness filled my senses. Could life get any better for me at this moment? Six months ago I didn't even know the island of Coronado existed, but there I was, walking on a beautiful beach, feeling as healthy as I had ever felt, being provided for perfectly by strangers I had met over the phone six months before who had become like family, and getting ready to depart on the most exciting adventure of my life. My senses were ecstatic with all the positive input and my emotions soared with excitement about being alive.

The only way to describe my feelings is that I felt as if I were walking side by side with the Creator, Jesus, Himself, the one "through whom all things were made," the Bible says. As if the whole creation, in all its perfection, was pointing to Him, and every fiber in my body was trying to take it all in, while at the same time trying to respond with an equal amount of gratitude, and feeling totally unable to do either. I felt like one of the grains of sand on the beach and at the same time like a friend of the Most High God. Peace enveloped me and I wanted time to stand still. Later that evening I wrote the following entry in my journal:

Tomorrow I leave Coronado; Me, an 18-speed bicycle, and 15 pounds of belongings, heading into the desert. I have to admit a large part of me wants to stay right here. I like Sunday brunch at the Officer's Club. I like afternoon walks on the beach. Will life still be so wonderful on those days of desert and mountain riding? Will I still be at peace when I find myself in the middle of nowhere without the stability and luxury of Coronado? God only knows. He knows my thoughts and feelings before I even think or feel them, I guess I'll have to wait and see. Lord, I trust you as the one who holds me in the palm of your hand.

Day 3

Monday, July 9, 1990

Boulder Oaks, CA to El Centro, CA

66 miles

7:15 a.m. - 1:30 p.m.

Words Unspoken

Waking up on Monday, July 9, was a quiet, almost somber affair, with every thought in my head focused on the ride ahead. Athletes call it "putting on the game face," tuning out every distraction in order to maximize your potential and face your opponent. Today I didn't need a coach to remind me of those things. The reality of the ride was upon me and the time to launch out had come. No more training, no more planning, no more regular daily routines, familiar faces, showers, or pillows; just 2,700 miles of unknown pavement.

I walked quietly to the bathroom and stared in the mirror above the sink. "I guess this is it, no turning back now." And with a short pause and slight raising of the eyebrows I commenced my normal routine of washing, praying, stretching, and packing.

During my prayer time, I hardly knew what to say. I felt more like listening. Kneeling by my bed, I read a passage from the Gospel of Matthew when Jesus told his disciples, "And surely I will be with you always, to the very end of the age." A quiet voice in my mind reminded me that indeed the Lord had been with me this far and was not going to leave now. I got up and went through my stretching, sit-ups, and push-ups with a deep inner peace and strong sense of assurance.

Ray had been in the kitchen fixing breakfast and was ready to get me started out right. After a sizeable spread of pancakes, juice, milk, and cereal, I felt ready to ride. We loaded up my bike and headed for Boulder Oaks.

It was a quiet ride as Ray and I both stared straight ahead through the windshield. I felt as though both of us had a lot on our minds but didn't really know how to express it with each other. It reminded me of similar rides I had taken with my dad during my high school and college days. We would be riding in the car in silence or maybe engaging in general conversation when I had some huge issue swirling around in my head just dying to be talked about. Who knows why I didn't let it out? Sometimes I felt as if we both had something more significant to say but neither one knew where to start. So we would get to our destination and go about our business and forget all about it. Maybe it was only me who had something to say and just couldn't get it out. For some reason though, I kept it inside, waiting for the invitation to speak but it didn't come. Then again why should it? Were people supposed to know what I was thinking and ask me to share it? I guess I thought they should.

On the way to Boulder Oaks, Ray and I seemed to be in the same situation. I had a lot of thoughts on my mind about the trip, our friendship, saying good-bye, and all that, and I felt as though Ray, having made a similar ride himself, knew the excitement and nervousness I was feeling and had plenty of thoughts of his own. Why wasn't he talking about them? Could it be the near fatal accident he had on one of his bike rides? Whatever the reason, the fact that Ray was about the same age as my dad and had treated me like a son during my stay in his home made the silence punishing.

Looking out the side window I thought of the day when Ray took it upon himself to go to the bike shop and buy me a little device called a flip-stand. It's a small wire clip that mounts underneath your frame behind the front wheel and holds the tire in place when you park the bike. Since most touring bikes don't have kickstands you usually have to lean the bike against a wall or pole and if the front wheel is free to steer, it can turn and the bike tumbles. Ray and I fit the flip-stand on my bike in his garage, tinkering together like a father and son. Of all the men in California, how did I get involved in a relationship like that? The emotion was beginning to swell.

Approaching Boulder Oaks and pulling into the little gas station underneath the huge oak tree, I realized nothing like I was thinking would be said. Once we began unloading my bike and attaching all the gear there would be no time for emotional discussion. That's just the way it works. After squeezing my lunch into the top of the bulging side pack, we hugged briefly and said good-bye for the last time. Swinging my leg over the bar and placing my left foot in the pedal strap, I pushed off and pedaled slowly out of the parking lot onto the quiet highway heading east. Once on the road, I lifted my right hand off the handlebar and turned my head slightly to give Ray one last wave good-bye. My heart seemed to be shouting, "I love you!" across the parking lot, but no words came out. I turned back to the road ahead of me, eyes watering, and pedaled on, thinking someday I'd get the chance to let the words come out, then thinking I probably wouldn't. "I love you Ray," I said under my breath.

Capt. Ray Crater

The heat intensified as the quiet, cool mountain morning turned into barren, sandy, hot, brightness. I pedaled all alone on the untraveled, two-lane access road along I-8 and felt fear for the first time. The aloneness of being in such a harsh and faraway place and the frightful realization of the thousands of miles ahead suddenly hit me without warning, creating a sick, nervous feeling in my stomach. In some places the desolate road was so cracked and bumpy, as if tree roots bulged underneath the pavement, that I thought my packs were going to bounce off the bike. Years of heat and pounding sunlight had turned the asphalt road into what looked like a dried-up, African mud bed.

Cracked Frontage roads

At 10:30 in the morning I came upon a dot on the map called Ocotillo and decided to take a break under a small tree next to a tiny building with a white-pebble parking lot. After finding a hose and filling my bottles with fresh, cool water and eating some fruit and a peanut butter sandwich, I loaded up and walked my bike back to the road. As I moved out from under the shady tree, the sun beat down on me like a heat lamp over a cafeteria food line. My long-sleeve white T-shirt, riding gloves, baseball hat with the handkerchief hanging down my neck, sunglasses, and sunscreen formed the only barrier between my skin and the sizzling rays. And as long as I kept moving I at least had a "breeze" to reduce the heat.

Along with the extreme conditions, though, I still felt a subtle comfort of the presence of God throughout the day. When my helmet, which I hung on my handlebar while traveling the lonely roads, bounced off on a big bump, it caught neatly on my rear wheel locking lever and hung there so I didn't even have to backtrack to pick it up; I just stopped briefly, reached down and picked it off the lever, and was on my way. Later on, when the heat was becoming unbearable in the noonday sun, I came upon the first tree I'd seen in fifteen miles and pulled under its shade. Sitting on the ground I rested and drank water, dousing my head and shirt before pulling out for El Centro.

Entering El Centro I found myself frustrated over the torn-up roads and baked by the intense heat. While stopped at a traffic light and not knowing where to go, I asked a local guy in a worn-out pickup truck where 5th Avenue was. Speaking through his passenger window, he semi-shouted, "Where ya going to?" "Pittsburgh," I said somewhat jokingly, hardly believing the word as it came out of my mouth. "What are you trying to do, set a record or something?" "No, just trying to finish," I said half seriously. He chuckled, somewhat taken aback, and told me how to find 5th Avenue before rumbling off.

Following the simple directions I started thinking about what I had said. "Just trying to finish?" What the heck was that? Sure, I wanted to finish, which seemed more challenging now than ever, but I wanted to do more than just finish. That's the attitude I used to have Monday through Friday working at the bank. Just finish, make it to five o'clock, make it to the weekend, then live life. No way, there's got to be more to living than just finishing. What about enjoying the present? What about the ride? A scripture verse came to mind: "This is the day that the Lord has made, we will rejoice and be glad in it." "O God," I mumbled, "help me be joyful about these days."

When I rolled into the Episcopal Church parking lot in El Centro, a stay I had arranged while in San Diego, I was physically exhausted. The heat had evaporated nine bottles of water through my body and left me depleted. If not for the packets of "Emergen-C" ™ electrolyte supplement that my friend, Hazel, at DeWalt's Health Food Store in Ambridge had given me at the last minute, I would have been flushed out. When I added a packet of the orange powder to a bottle of cold water I would practically chug the whole thing, my body wanted it so badly, and I would feel an instant pick-up. Even still, by the end of the day I was worn out. The scary part was that most of the ride was flat or downhill. But I had made the first leg of the trip on my own and I was feeling good about my accomplishment.

The Rev. Jim and Dorothy Titcomb greeted me kindly and welcomed me into their home located next to the church. After a nice cool shower and a change into my street clothes, the three of us talked as Dorothy made me a sandwich. Afterward, I retired to my nice, clean guest room for a nap. "God is so good," I thought, as I dozed off in the cool A/C.

Later that afternoon Jim walked me through his backyard and gave me the tour of the church he had pastored for five years. Next we hopped in his car and cruised through the El Centro markets, gathering supplies for the Mexican dinner he was serving up that evening. Arriving back at the house I gathered even more items to be shipped back to Ambridge. Items to cut this time: the pants to my Patagonia rain suit, two of my four long-sleeve T-shirts, my third pair of socks, my second spare inner tube, and my beach towel; all making the sacrifice for the cause. That evening a friend came over and we had a major feast, much to my delight. On a normal day my appetite was known to be impressive, but after seventy miles in the desert it was almost scary. After dinner we talked until my eyes started to droop and I politely excused myself for bed. What a day, I thought, as I poured myself under the sheet, pondering my first overnight on the road.

Day 4

Tuesday July 10, 1990

El Centro, CA to Yuma, AZ

62 miles

5:40 a.m. - 11:30 a.m.

Beyond Planning

Jim and Dorothy stood in their nightclothes on the back patio in the pre-dawn darkness as I rolled my bike through the quiet backyard and into the empty church parking lot behind their house. Standing over the horizontal bar of my bike and strapping the Velcro across the back of my biking gloves, I noticed the faint, pink sunlight barely creeping up on the fresh, new morning. I slipped my left foot into the pedal strap and pushed off softly, waving one last time as they watched me pedal slowly and quietly out of view and onto the sleeping main street of El Centro.

Without cars or noise but only the methodical sound of sprockets turning through a well- oiled chain, my mind was free to replay the past seventeen hours of overwhelming hospitality and friendship that had been shown me on my first official overnight. Two perfect strangers had just welcomed me into their home, given me a comfortable room, fed me, talked with me, and sent me on my way without any obligation or personal gain. It was actually what I had envisioned for the trip but the reality of experiencing it was more than I could comprehend.

Even though I had done a reasonable amount of planning, trying to arrange places to stay before I flew out to San Diego, I still only had thirteen stops covered. When I arrived in San Diego, my first established contact was in Coolidge, Arizona, six days away through the desert. While in San Diego the gaps began to fill as my friend Ned put me on to Fr. Jim in El Centro and Tom in Yuma.

When I first called Jim, two days before leaving San Diego, I tried to explain what I was doing and asked if he would put me up for the night. Much to my surprise he wasn't very receptive, cautiously keeping me at bay with defensive statements such as, "I'm not sure if we'll be around that day." Just when I was about to give up trying to convince him that I was legitimate and hang up, somehow the word Ambridge came up again and we discovered Jim was the godfather of a friend of mine back at the seminary. Jim had gone to college with my friend's father and had not seen the father or the son in years. That small miracle opened the door for my stay in El Centro and the wonderful hospitality I had enjoyed.

With all those thoughts occupying my mind I wasn't even thinking about the sixty-mile, desert-dash to my next unknown contact in Yuma. With one simple call from San Diego the same day I called Jim, Tom in Yuma had agreed without hesitation to let me stay in his home. His priest, Tom Phillips, was a friend of the seminary in Ambridge, which I figured helped secure the invitation. I just hoped the hospitality would work out as nice as it had in El Centro.

As the mid-morning sun began to intensify I became subtly aware that the power of the desert sun was somewhat of a serious matter. Having grown up in Florida, running and playing tennis in the heat of the summer I thought I knew what heat was, but the intensity I was beginning to experience in the desert verged on lethal. My decision to leave before sunrise and finish before noon was a wise one, but would it be sufficient? I thought. I began to wonder as I approached Yuma.

During most of the morning thick clouds had covered the sky and protected me from direct sunlight, but by 10 a.m., the full intensity of the cosmic heat lamp had been unleashed, beating down on my back unmercifully and even heating the water in my plastic bottles to faucet-like hot water. I began to recognize my vulnerability. How much worse could it get? How much more could I take?

As the desert conditions began to consume my thoughts, I noticed up ahead, parked on the side of the highway in the emergency lane, an orange pickup truck with a man standing near the back. Rolling to a stop behind the truck I spoke out in my miles-away- from-home, friendly roadside voice, "How's it going?" hoping he would return in kind. "Just fine," he replied, with the friendly tone I was hoping for. "Where ya headed?" "Yuma," I replied somewhat apologetically, admitting in my tone I understood the perilous conditions under which I was traveling. "You need any cold water?" he asked, pointing to the large water cooler in the bed of the truck. He was a highway maintenance inspector and had pulled over to check some work being done on the highway. "Oh, man, that would be great, if you don't mind." "No problem, take as much as you want," he said, as I grabbed

my top two water bottles, dumped out the warm leftovers and commenced to drink the ice cold water and splash the refreshing liquid all over my face and head. After topping off my bottles and giving my heartfelt thank you for saving my life, I pedaled off, turning around to see if he was still there or if maybe he was an angel that had flown back to

Joe the water angel

heaven. About ten miles up the road when I passed him again parked on an overpass above the highway, I still wondered.

The surprise refreshment served me well but by the time I reached the outskirts of Yuma I felt as if I was riding inside a pizza oven. The brightness of the sun and the penetration of the heat seemed to be baking me on the inside and the out. As I followed the scribbled directions taken over the phone at Ned's house I didn't care what my accommodations looked like as long as I could just get out of the sun. I turned off the busy business district and made my way through the residential streets; trees began to appear and the houses became nicer and nicer. By the time I came to the end of my directions the blistering desert had given way to peaceful, tree-covered lawns, and eventually into the shady, concrete driveway of a beautifully landscaped home.

I parked my bike in the open carport and was greeted by Natilia, an Hispanic housekeeper who invited me in and fixed me a small bucket of my favorite mix of apple juice, orange juice, water, and lots of ice, with a clump of cold grapes on the side for good measure. She then proceeded to escort me through the living room to the sliding glass doors opening onto the shaded patio and, unless I was hallucinating, a crystal clear swimming pool situated in the privacy of the tropical backyard. With my mouth hanging open and my brain in never-never land, I thought, "Dear God, if this is a dream, please don't wake me until after I fall into that water."

Pillar of cloud

Being a little road weary, and more thirsty than anything, I first stretched out on one of the rubber-strapped patio lounges with my ice-cold drink and grapes and just relaxed, trying to absorb all of the comforts of my newfound oasis. After a while I was awakened from my tropical daydream by the chatter of female voices. Tom's daughters, Toby and Sheryl, had come home for lunch after their morning classes at the local college and, after a short introduction, welcomed me into the kitchen to make a little lunch. Actually, my Dagwood sandwich, chips, fruit, and brownie were more than a little lunch, but I hoped they understood. We took our plates to the patio table and had a good time eating and talking together. They had obviously been informed about my coming and were not the least bit shy about my stay in their house. After lunch we hung out in the kitchen cleaning up and talking before they headed out for the rest of their day, Sheryl to her job and Toby to the mall with friends. None of that for me; my afternoon was booked up with swimming, lounging around the pool, and possibly gift shopping later if I felt like it.

As we were cleaning up, their dad and my contact, Tom, came home from his law office to check out the scene and meet this strange youth leader biking into town and staying at his house. He was a big but gentle man of genuine Christian faith and having similar athletic interests as me, we hit it off immediately. So much so, that when he asked me how long I was planning to stay, I found myself asking if I could take a day off from riding and stay one day to recoup from the heat. He agreed without hesitation, offering me free run of his tropical paradise and anything else I needed. On his way out to return to his office, he casually checked in on Natilia to see what she was preparing for dinner. That evening we gathered around the table like family, except for Tom's wife, who was out of town taking care of her parents, and once again, as I looked around the table at all the new faces, I marveled at how miraculously I had been taken in and treated like a family member.

Yuma the oasis

As the evening drew on and I learned more about the family, my respect for Tom also grew. He had lost a son to a fatal accident and had another son estranged from the family; Sheryl was actually not a sister but Toby's friend who had moved in so she could finish high school in a healthy family environment, and his in-laws were ill, requiring his wife to be away to take care of them. Then, a total stranger rides in on a bicycle to stay for the night. How much more could be going on under one roof? I felt grateful to be welcomed so openly and prayed that I could be of some help during my stay.

Day 5

Wednesday, July 11, 1990

Yuma, AZ

Day off

The Oasis

Sheryl & Toby

Even if I had only been on the road two consecutive days, I felt good about staying a day in Yuma. Maybe it was the pool. Maybe it was a subconscious fear of going back into the desert. Either way I was happy to be at the oasis.

During the morning I relaxed and wrote postcards on the round patio table by the pool. Only three days out and I had to tell my family in Tampa and my church friends back in Ambridge how everything was working out; they had to know about my fantastic time in Coronado, my stay in El Centro, and now my paradise in Yuma, and just how perfectly God was taking care of me.

Fr. Tom Phillips had invited me to his weekly men's lunch at a local restaurant to share my story. He had also offered the use of his church office to help me mail some gifts I had bought the day before, so around 10 a.m. I loaded up my post cards and gifts and rode over to the church to package and mail them back home. I had also arranged to meet Attorney Tom at the church for a ride to the restaurant. While I was packaging the gifts, he came by and offered to take everything to his law office to let his secretary mail them. I couldn't argue with a deal like that so I put everything in a bag and off we went to the restaurant. I felt as though everything was working out perfectly. Even the day before when I was looking for a gift shop, I didn't know which of the many touristy shops to choose from but felt led to a particular one. When I walked in the store, the lady working there complimented me on the Holy Spirit dove pin on my baseball hat and informed me that the owner was a Christian also. They had the perfect gifts

I wanted: a pennant for my godson, a thimble for Helen, who fed me for three months before the trip, a coloring book for my friends' little girls Susanna and Melissa, and an Arizona T-shirt for myself. Now, with the unexpected help from Tom, everything was on its way to its proper destination.

Tom and I rode in his comfortable, air conditioned Suburban to The Crossing, a nice, wood-table restaurant bustling with the lunchtime business crowd. We made our way through the tingling glass and mumbling conversation to the reserved section where Fr. Tom and ten other men were seated. Fr. Tom had saved me a seat next to him and greeted me kindly. The men sitting around the U-shaped table continued in individual conversation as Tom suggested various house specialties and informed me when I would speak. As the waitress made her rounds taking orders I could feel the typical butterflies fluttering around in my stomach that showed up whenever I spoke to a group, no matter how small or informal.

When the time came, Tom introduced me to the group and let me go. Looking around the table at the respectable group of businessmen, I began my talk with some introduction about myself to obtain a little credibility before sharing about the bike trip. I used the typical background information such as, born and raised in Tampa, mechanical engineering graduate of Georgia Tech, youth minister in Ambridge, student at Trinity Seminary, all the reputable attributes I could scrape up to convince them they were listening to a well-grounded, level-headed, graduate student instead of some hair-brained, cross-country bike rider. Having laid the foundation, I launched into the good part about my bike ride from San Diego to Ambridge, recounting the highlights and spotlighting the miraculous ways God had seen me through, remaining outwardly humble but expecting them to be totally impressed. Finishing with a few testimonies of God's goodness in getting me this far, I thanked them for having me and turned it back over to Fr. Tom. Thanking me for my story and opening the table up for discussion, he hardly got the words out of his mouth before the questions came flying: "Joseph, how familiar are you with this desert?" "Do you know it can get 130 degrees out there?" "Where is your next stop?" And on and on. Instead of being impressed by my gallant ride of faith, they seemed to be overly concerned about my crossing the desert in July. I was caught by surprise. Instead of being an inspiration, I was a concern. "Even if you make it to Globe," one man warned, "you're gonna have to walk most of the way up the mountain," and "Mule Creek Pass? No one can bike that."

All was said in a friendly manner but in the end I felt thoroughly deflated about my trip and somewhat reprimanded for riding in the desert this time of year. The meeting ended politely with everyone shaking hands and heading for the parking lot where Attorney Tom, Pastor Tom, and Chuck, another friend of theirs, hung around talking with me while the others left. Chuck knew a lot about the desert and expressed his deep concern and desire to help me out. My plan to try to ride 116 miles from Yuma to Gila Bend in one day was completely rejected and a new plan put forth. Chuck traveled the state selling sprinklers and knew a man who had a farm in Aztec, a speck on the map 76 miles from Yuma. Chuck would try to reach the owner, Pierre, and arrange for me to stay there for the night and would get in touch with me that evening. Tom knew a guy in Gila Bend and since I didn't have a contact there would try to line up something. I accepted all the help and concern even if I thought they were overreacting to the situation. In the back of my mind I figured I could take a break at Pierre's place for the afternoon and finish the ride to Gila Bend late in the afternoon. Basically, I had my mind set on the plan I had mapped out and wanted to stick to it even if everyone in Yuma thought it was crazy. It was the same attitude I had in Coronado -- thinking that Chris' sensible plan was somehow a wimpy capitulation of faith. I knew the Bible verse that said, "Without faith it is impossible to please God," but was risking my life in the desert more faithful than taking good advice and playing it safe? For some reason I thought it was.

Attorney Tom had to get back to work so Fr. Tom offered to take me home and invited me over to his house to hang out for a while if I didn't have anything else to do. Not really interested in riding my bike, I took him up on the offer and we headed to his house, arriving just in time to meet his wife and kids coming back from the grocery store. We helped unload the multitude of bags, which for a single guy seemed as if we were stocking a food pantry. My routine back home was a once-a-week grocery run, spending twenty dollars on eggs, bread, milk, tuna fish, spaghetti, and OJ. This grocery haul was the real deal, the kind real families with kids have. Afterwards, Tom and I sat down in his living room to talk a little more about my trip and address the concerns the men had at lunch. To aid the conversation, Tom brought out a plastic topographical map of Arizona that showed elevations and terrain very clearly as we began to trace my route through Arizona into New Mexico.

The desert terrain from Yuma, through Gila Bend, Coolidge, and Safford was just as expected; flat, dry, and sandy. The shocker, though, was the mountain region after I turned north and headed for New Mexico over the Continental Divide. There, the plastic map revealed the jagged, three-dimensional truth. Globe, where the men said I would have to walk, definitely took a steep rise. Mule Creek Pass, toward Silver City, New Mexico, looked like a cliff, the only way up by switch-backs that snaked their way back and forth up one side and down the other. My AAA maps hadn't shown anything like that, but what was I going to do, fly home? Tom was easy to talk with and agreed that the situation was difficult but not impossible. We gradually changed the subject away from the trip to more general talk about our lives, our families, and plans for the future, then Tom drove me back to the oasis in time for my scheduled tennis match with Sheryl.

What were we thinking? I'm sure we were the only people in Yuma playing tennis at three o'clock in the afternoon. With the sun straight up, the walk to the court was punishing enough. We spent most of the time sitting in the shade drinking water and talking rather than playing. As a youth leader I knew about looking for opportunities to talk with kids but this was beyond the call. When we came to our senses we returned to the oasis and plunged into the pool, the only sensible place to hang out.

After dinner, Chuck and his wife dropped by, along with two other men from the lunch, to visit and talk about my plans. Chuck had contacted Pierre, the farmer in Aztec, and everything was set for my stay the next day. All I had to do was call him from the I-8 truck stop six miles before Aztec. Tom had contacted his friends in Gila Bend and they said they would be waiting for me at their business on the main road into town. He also gave me the name of another friend in Globe, Arizona who would be waiting for my call when I got there in three days. In 24 hours, three contacts had been lined up and my itinerary altered with an additional stay in Aztec. Still lurking in the back of my mind was the pestering idea to keep my schedule and make Gila Bend by evening that same day.

To make the evening even more exciting, after everyone had gone home, a group of teenagers came by to see Sheryl and Toby. The hot item for the evening seemed to be the heated breakup of Toby and her boyfriend and everyone wanted to be involved. Pockets of conversation chattered around in various corners of the house and even I was asked for advice. Toby and I sat in the kitchen and talked as I had so often done with teenagers at youth group meetings and retreats. Like most young girls, it seemed all Toby wanted was a boyfriend who loved her and treated her kindly. Apparently this guy was nice most of the time but sometimes would become downright mean and aggressive.

All I could suggest was that she look for someone with a common faith in God who treats her with love and respect and go from there. "If that isn't what you're getting with this guy," I said, "keep him as a friend and keep your distance." We prayed about the situation and then went into the living room with the rest of the group. She continued to talk to her friends while I said goodnight to get ready for my departure in the morning. Lying awake and listening to the chatter in the other rooms I marveled at the way the stay had worked out and how accepted I felt by my new family. I hoped I had been helpful.

Day 6

Thursday July 12, 1990

Yuma, AZ to Aztec, AZ

76 miles

5:40 a.m. - 11:20 a.m.

Desert Dash

Sheryl surprised me by waking up at 5:00 a.m. to say good-bye. I felt honored by this un-teen-like act, even if her eyes never fully opened. Most teenagers I knew awake at five o'clock in the morning during the summer hadn't gone to bed yet. Sheryl broke the stereotype, even if she was sleepwalking.

After breakfast Tom and I loaded my gear into the Suburban and drove in the quiet dawn back to I-8 where I had rolled in on Wednesday. Standing on the side of the road with my bike packed and ready to roll, I said my good-bye to my new friend, thanking him for all his help over the last thirty-six hours. I felt that woozy feeling in my stomach and my eyes beginning to fill and knew it was time to push off. For the next couple of hours in the silence of the sunrise, I pedaled methodically on the empty highway and reflected on the events of the past two days. "How many more times could this happen?" I wondered.

With cloud cover accompanying me most of the morning I figured the ride to Aztec would be comfortable and not much of a challenge: seventy flat miles in the emergency lane of I-8 to Dateland, a call to Pierre, then a quick six to Aztec--piece of cake.

Sometime around 10:00 a.m., though, after four hours of cool, 90-degree pedaling, the clouds disappeared again and I was rudely reminded of how intense the sun could be at any unclouded moment.

By the time I pulled into the truck stop in Dateland I felt as wilted and limp as lettuce left in the cardboard box in the grocery store parking lot. Inside the little food mart I gulped down a quart of Gatorade in about two gulps while talking to Maria, the young Mexican girl behind the counter. Maria, like most people, was intrigued with my adventure and asked where I normally stayed at night. I told her there was no "normal" about this trip except that God had provided places so far and tonight I was staying somewhere in Aztec. She looked at me in surprise and said, "Where are you going to stay in Aztec, there 'eez' nothing in Aztec, do you know someone?" "I don't know him," I said, "but I'm supposed to stay with a man named Pierre." Immediately a slight grin came across her face indicating she knew something. "Do you know Pierre?" I asked. "Everyone knows Pierre," she said without offering any details. I didn't know what to expect and she wouldn't elaborate so after a pint of orange juice I made my phone call to Pierre. In our short conversation he sounded pretty normal to me, so I saddled up and pressed on for Aztec.

I soaked my handkerchief and shirt with cold water, put the wet handkerchief on my head followed by my white baseball hat and dashed the

Desert dash

final six miles in the intense heat with handkerchief flapping--feeling like Lawrence of Arabia galloping across the Sahara. After about five minutes my shirt and handkerchief were totally dry and I could hear the heat meter ticking as the intense sun extracted every ounce of energy and moisture my body could produce. Exiting the freeway, I pulled underneath the I-8 overpass and leaned my bike against one of the large concrete pillars supporting the huge super slab overhead. The only sign of civilization was the rundown, vacant gas station near by with boarded up windows and a rusty pole with no sign. Feeling a little light-headed and shaky, I climbed up on the three foot high concrete wall and lay down like a dead man. The temperature had climbed to over 100 degrees and relief from the direct sunlight was like heaven as I drifted off into a semi-conscious nap.

Some short time later I was startled out of my slumber by the sound of a vehicle pulling alongside my concrete resting place. The driver, on the far side of the well-worn, gold Bronco, I rightly suspected to be Pierre. Much to my surprise, on the near side, in the back seat, sat two little girls with their cute, inquisitive faces peering out of the window. I guess meeting a strange biker underneath the interstate would be a thrill for any young kids.

Pit stop under I-8

Pierre, a well-tanned, rough and handsome farmer, got out and greeted me with a firm, hard-working handshake and helped me load my bike into the back of the Bronco. The girls looked on silently from over the back seat. I climbed into the front seat as Pierre introduced me to his daughters, Velmay and Marnelle, and we headed down the long dusty road to his farm, talking freely and getting to know one another. Soon we were talking openly about our mutual faith in God and all doubts that Maria back at the gift shop had planted in my mind diminished.

Pierre was from South Africa where he had lost his wife to cancer while the girls were just babies. He came to America with the girls and $2,000 and now was managing a farm and doing quite well. He loved America and had a hard time tolerating the welfare system.

Continuing our lively conversation we pulled onto the long, dirt drive leading to the farmhouse, passing the large metal barns, equipment sheds, water tower, and separate bunkhouse. Inside the modern farmhouse, Pierre's girlfriend, Margaret, was preparing lunch. Pierre showed me my room and after a quick, cool shower I joined the group for sandwiches, watermelon, and friendly conversation. While we were eating, two young guys ventured through the kitchen door and Pierre casually made introductions. Johan and Peter were also from South Africa and had completed the equivalent of high school but had no idea what they wanted to do, so they came over to the U.S. with a six-month visa to check out the country. They didn't know Pierre when they arrived but after they ran out of money in California someone gave them Pierre's phone number and he agreed to let them live on the farm until they earned enough money to get back home. They had their own living quarters in the bunk house and when they weren't taking adventure trips in the little Chevet Pierre had loaned them, they were growing flowers and selling them to flower shops in Yuma. It was your basic, "I-don't-know-what-I-want-to-do-with-my-life" living at its finest and my bike trip fit right in, establishing instant friendships and giving us common ground to talk further. It was happening again.

After lunch I settled down in the peace of my own room for a quick nap, thanking God for his goodness and also pondering my next move. The day was still young and Gila Bend was only forty miles away.

When I roused out of my semi-sleep, not being much of a daytime napper, I realized how taxed my body was from the heat and how unattractive riding sounded at the moment. The thought was actually ridiculous. Not only did the temperature stay in the 100s well into the night making afternoon riding more deadly than the morning, my body was so depleted from the sun I needed serious replenishment before I could tackle any more desert riding at all, even in ideal morning conditions. A small voice in my head seemed to whisper, "Relax, taking a break is okay." The thought barely registered. To most people the idea probably made sense but to

Irrigation tank Jaque, Gideon

a compulsive, middle-child, people pleaser who spent most of his life striving to be the best and earn the approval of everyone on the planet, relaxation was never permissible. How could you achieve anything by relaxing?

That afternoon, with the temperature leveling off around 105, my new friends Jaque and Gideon came by to show me the secret to cooling off on the farm. With inner tubes in hand we climbed up the fifteen-foot metal ladder attached to the open-top irrigation tank and plunged into the cool water inside, floating, swimming, and talking in the steel swimming pool overlooking the blistering Arizona landscape.

As it turned out, Johan had grown up going to church as a child but had fallen away as he got older. Said it was too strict. Peter knew very little about God but found it interesting that God could have a plan for his life. Both guys were searching for their next move and agreed that coming to grips with the person of Jesus should be a priority. When our fingers began to wrinkle we climbed out of our metal swimming hole so they could go work on their flowers.

That evening, Pierre grilled steaks outside and we had a great meal together, followed by fireworks, complete with Marnelle and Velmay running around with sparklers. It was a real "Little House on the Prairie" moment. Before bedtime, I made my pre-dawn departure arrangements with Pierre, said goodnight to everyone and turned in—six friends happier than when I pulled in eleven hours earlier.

Day 7
Friday, July 13, 1990
Aztec, AZ to Gila Bend, AZ
40 miles
6:30 a.m. - 9:30 a.m.

Hit Man

Since Gila Bend was only forty miles away I decided to sleep in a little and not implement the pre-dawn departure routine, informing Pierre that leaving by 6:30 would give me plenty of cool, sub-100 degree riding. We had a nice breakfast of basically everything in the kitchen and then it was time to say good-bye to my new little sisters, Marnel and Velmay, and head back to I-8.

My bike was still in the truck from the day before, which seemed like two weeks ago, and as Pierre and I walked out of the door he handed me a $100 check for my ministry in Ambridge along with a five dollar bill with which to buy a lottery ticket at one of the convenience stores in my next town. I accepted the check with sincere gratitude and was touched again by his generosity, but I wasn't much into the lottery and politely explained my desire to trust God on a daily basis during the trip. "What if God wants to provide for your needs through the lottery?" Pierre asked. "Well," I answered, "I guess he could let you win and you could give me half." We laughed and took off for I-8.

After we unloaded and said good-bye under the I-8 overpass I pushed off and resumed my solo desert trek, pedaling methodically over the gray asphalt as my mind mused over the topic of the morning, this time focusing on the lottery ticket offer. It was a friendly gesture with good intentions to fund my every dream for kids in Ambridge, but I had never been a fan of the lottery and, frankly, had little regard for a system that preyed on the insecurities and fantasies of discontented people in order to fund more government programs and schools. To me it was simply a backdoor way of collecting tax money to help seniors and schools so the real tax money could be spent on even more programs. My emotions began to rise as I pedaled along and preached out loud to the air, "Great idea, let's tap into the insecurities and addictions of masses of people and encourage them to throw away their money in hopes of winning the 'big one' so we can support more government bureaucracy. Maybe we can offer free debt counseling to everyone who can't pay the light bill because they have two hundred dollars in worthless lottery tickets on their dresser every month!"

My cynical attitude picked up speed as I honed in on my real issue, "Why are people so willing to throw money at a game of chance rather than trusting God and living contented with his provisions?" In just seven days my concept of God's provision in everyday life had been so radically changed I could hardly contain myself. "Why are we so afraid to trust God?" I shouted "The scriptures are clear, 'No eye has seen, no ear has heard, no mind has conceived what God has prepared for those who love him.' Oh God, help us to love and trust you!" I cried.

Chuck & Suzie

On a break underneath an interstate overpass I pulled out my Bible and read from Isaiah about God pouring out His Spirit on the people and making streams flow in the desert. I began praising God with an indescribable joy and excitement, trusting he would see me through my desert journey the same way.

I reached Gila Bend at 9:30, looking for the contact Tom Phillips had lined up for me there. I pulled up to the converted former gas station right along the main road leading into town where Chuck and Suzie Meccia ran their fuel oil business. I leaned my bike against the glass front section of the building, locked my flip-stand on the front tire, and walked inside. A nice lady greeted me politely but with the usual reservation anyone would have meeting a total stranger biking into town in the middle of their normal work day. She was Suzie and told me about the motel right down the street where Chuck had arranged for me to stay and that she would meet me there to check me in. Sounded like a nice idea even though my first thought was, "Why not your house?" I kept that thought to myself as I mounted up for the ride to the Yucca Motel. Suzie followed shortly behind and met me in the lobby where she paid the Indian woman and said she would be back around noon to take me to lunch.

On my way to the room I marveled at my crazy trip; what was a Floridian from Pennsylvania doing in the Yucca Motel in Gila Bend, Arizona? After parking my bike in my room I quickly changed into my quick-dry bathing suit and headed straight for the pool I noticed on the way in. Refreshing is about as complete an understatement I can come up with to describe how good that pool felt. Nirvana might be a better word, whatever that's like. I floated on my back, sank to the bottom, and slithered around the cool water like a school kid. Afterward, it was back to my room to shower and get ready for lunch. The shower never happened because even the cold water was so hot I couldn't touch it. After letting it run and trying every combination of knob turning, I dried off and rested in the cool AC. Suzie came by and we met Chuck for a nice lunch and friendly conversation.

After lunch I rode down to the tourist information building and shot the breeze with the attendant and a local guy just hanging out in the AC. They showed me a better route from Silver City, New Mexico, to Las Cruces and Sonny, the local guy, told me of a cousin that had a farm at the border near Mule Creek. "You might need to stop there," he warned. "It's a real climb." On the way back to the motel I stopped by the Meccia's business and met Chuck and some of the workers. His daughter dropped by and somehow we got talking about desert "washes:" massive walls of water from heavy rains miles away in the desert rushing through dried-up creek beds and catching campers by surprise. These unexpected washes were known to take away campsites and even vehicles from unsuspecting campers. The moral of the story was: Don't take a rest in a dried-up creek bed. I pedaled back to my motel room and rested again in the cool AC.

For dinner I was on my own and meandered across the parking lot to the family diner next door. Sitting alone in the quiet and nearly empty dining room, feeling like an alien from a strange planet, I was delighted to overhear a family two tables over talking about St. Petersburg, Florida. My ears perked up like a jack rabbit's as I discretely leaned toward their table and tuned into the conversation. Waiting for the right opportunity, I politely broke in and we began talking across the tables as if we were American tourists meeting unexpectedly in a small French café—the bond was instant. They were on vacation with their teenage daughter and her friend and had another daughter, Julie, at Geneva College in Beaver Falls, Pennsylvania, right down the river from the seminary in Ambridge. She was interested in youth ministry and they suggested I give her a call when I got home. They were members of an independent church in "St. Pete" and delightful Christians. The conversation was just what I needed to

Waiting out the heat in Yucca Motel

ease the loneliness and get me ready for another day's ride.

Satan Has a Master

I woke up at 4:00 a.m. prepared for the toughest ride of the trip, and, actually, of my whole biking career: 80 miles of wide-open desert. For all practical purposes I had spent the whole day Friday waiting out the 104-degree heat getting ready for this ride, like a hit man hanging out in a cheap motel waiting to pull off a job. Now it was time.

The dark and quiet morning greeted me as I opened the door and rolled my tires across the threshold into the warm, still air, giving one last look around the room before turning off the light. Everything was just like I found it except for the unmade bed and empty water glass sitting on the night table, so I flipped the switch, shut the door, and walked my two-wheeled life support system into the parking lot. Because the sun wasn't even close to coming up and the pitch-black night made the road hard to see, I pedaled slowly toward I-8, holding my mini flashlight with three fingers against my handlebar to try to spot potholes, glass, muffler pipes, or any other foreign object that might wipe me out. Curving along the access road and approaching the entrance to the freeway, I passed the Gila Bend truck stop packed full of eighteen wheelers with their large diesels idling in the parking lot while their drivers sat inside chowing down before hitting the road. I wondered how many of those monsters I'd be seeing real soon bearing down in my rearview mirror.

As I pulled onto the lonely highway and headed east into the darkened desert, I noticed an unfamiliar sight that sent chills up my spine. Straight ahead, in the black horizon, flashed long, thin, jagged bolts of lightning, wickedly lighting up the dark sky and exposing the thick blanket of rain clouds that dominated the horizon. In the background rumbled the ominously delayed accompaniment of thunder. Continuing to pedal eastward, with the sky becoming dimly lit from the unseen sun rising secretly below the clouds, I could see huge rectangular blankets of rain hanging like black cloth beneath the clouds.

The day before I had heard reports about the monsoon storms that hit nearby Casa Grande causing serious damage, and was thankful at the time I was not one day further along on my schedule. But now, even the headlights on the oncoming traffic reminded me of the danger the locals had spoken of, of people literally swept off their feet by the driving rain, and livestock pummeled by baseball-size hail; all, I feared could be waiting ahead. I just knew everyone driving toward me thought I was insane riding a bike into a black death like that. I envisioned a Highway Patrol car speeding up and telling me to turn back, and thought about what I would say. Turning back was just not an option I was willing to consider.

Storm out of Gila Bend

As I rode, with fearful thoughts shooting through my mind at the crack of every lightening bolt, a monster eighteen wheeler surprised me from behind, blasting his horn as he blew by, hugging the white stripe right next to me. Every nerve in my body lit up like a row of red overload lights on a recording machine while my input meters pegged flat in the maxed out position. For the first time I really understood what was meant by "a bundle of nerves."

What happened next I cannot even begin to explain. From somewhere deep inside me rose something powerful that I can only attribute to the Holy Spirit, something that came alive in my body and seemed to rush to my defense. With an intense hatred for evil and Satanic forces that afflict God's people, I began to shout out loud, rebuking fear in the name of Jesus and commanding Satan to get away from me. I prayed out loud for Jesus to make a path for his servant and to calm the storm as he had done for the disciples long ago.

Continuing to pedal hard and praising God loudly like a Pentecostal preacher, I shouted declarations of his power and Lordship: "Praise your name, Jesus!" "Bless your holy name!" "You are Lord, You are the mighty One!" And on and on I went, pedaling east and making my declarations as, amazingly, the storm moved slowly south, taking its black clouds, lightning, and wide, gray sheets of rain with it. A few miles later, with the blackness far over the desert to my right, I found myself riding on a wet, rain-washed road with a wild rushing stream flowing in the desert beside me but not a drop

Storm clearing

Streams in the desert

falling from the sky. Coincidence? Natural weather pattern? Maybe. But suddenly the Bible verse from the day before popped into my mind and I could hardly control myself: "streams in the desert," "pour out His Spirit on the people." My spirit soared with thankfulness for such a loving and faithful God who continued to be involved in the affairs of his people, maintaining his uncontested authority over all of his creation. Coupled with the feeling of relief, safety, and joy like I never experienced before, I pedaled along the cool desert highway as carefree and happy as I had ever been in my life.

The temperature stayed in the mid 70s the entire forty-four miles to Stanfield, where I pulled into June Jones' Café to take a break and have a little lunch, or second breakfast since it was only 8:30 in the morning. Sitting alone with my ice water, staring out of the large, plate glass window, reflecting over the mind-boggling morning, I resolved to never be lukewarm in my witness for God again.

I arrived in Coolidge around one o'clock in the afternoon after an absolutely beautiful afternoon ride. A flat tire in Casa Grande and a missed turn cost me some time, but with the total trip ending up at eighty miles, the longest distance I had ever ridden in one day, and considering the crazy start, I felt good about the day's ride. Drained and exhausted, I wondered if the sun had been out the whole way and the temperature in the 100s as usual, if I would have made it at all.

Riding through Coolidge I mixed up my directions and was heading down the wrong road when a van pulled along side of me and the lady driver spoke through the passenger window, "Are you Joseph?" "Yes," I replied, a little surprised since I didn't know too many people in Coolidge, Arizona. It was the Rev. John Smith's wife, Kathleen, the family I was to stay with. She led me to their house, where I got cleaned up for lunch with the family, and then off to my room for a much-needed nap. Later in the afternoon we all went over to a church member's house for a fabulous swim, then back home for a little whiffle ball with the three boys, John, Chris, and Ryan, followed by a delicious chicken casserole, some friendly chatting, and, finally, to bed.

Feeling totally exhausted and slightly light-headed, I turned out the lights and shut down all emotional and physical synapses and flopped lifelessly into my single bed. Grateful that the next day was Sunday, I laid on my back, motionless, replaying the events of the day. It seemed like a dream. I hardly had categories for the intense experiences I had encountered: the massive intimidation of the storm, the nerve-wracking brush-by of the eighteen wheeler, and the extreme isolation and vulnerability of being alone and unprotected in the face of such unharnessed natural power—all met head-on by the surprising inner strength

that rose up out of nowhere to see me through, coupled with the timely movement of the storm. It was all way more than I had bargained for when I started the journey. "Oh, Lord, thank you for keeping me safe," I prayed. "Please forgive me if I have put you to the test. Amen."

Coolidge

Day 9
Sunday, July 15, 1990
Coolidge, AZ

Starting to Get It

Sundays are generally good days for reflecting and after the first week of the trip I had a lot to reflect on. The way each stop had worked out so far was overwhelming. I mean, Coolidge, Arizona? Six months before I couldn't find the place on the map but now I was staying with a minister and his family for the weekend, attending his Sunday church service, and being treated like a family member. One day behind in the schedule and I'd be spending Sunday in Gila Bend in the Yucca Motel – yikes!

Such goodness overwhelmed my capacity to comprehend it. A part of me wanted to take some credit, or at least feel a little satisfied, but I couldn't. My contribution had been fear and vulnerability, while God's part was complete love, power, and goodness. What was there to take credit for? My hope was that His goodness would continue throughout the trip.

Such were my thoughts during church that morning, along with mulling over the sermon about the "Sower and the Seed." The thought of sowing the seed of God's Word had captured me even as a new Christian and even more so since studying the preaching ministry of John Wesley in church history; a challenging undertaking, I thought--like climbing the mountain to Globe--but neither one impossible with God's help. I'd just have to deal with both as they came up. Also, that Sunday, I found myself identifying with Father John in his role as a minister. Not that I was ready to do it or anything but the role didn't intimidate me; at least not as I observed from the pew.

That night I packed a third box of unnecessary items to send back to Ambridge. The next day I would start climbing some serious mountains and I needed to shed some more weight. My wardrobe wasn't going to impress anyone but finishing the trip was the only thing on my mind and anything that wasn't absolutely necessary was going back.

Items to go this time: a Thinsulate, long-sleeve undershirt, two bungee cords, my new Arizona T-shirt, the reflector off the front wheel, and a compass. After a week on the road it seemed my faith to believe the Matthew 10 scripture that had inspired the trip had grown a little since I started, and trusting that God would continue supplying my needs was becoming slightly more believable. The proof was evident so far but we had a long way to go. Preparing for bed I felt as though tomorrow was a stepping-up day. The stretch to Globe had twenty-five miles of steep mountain road that the men in Yuma said I would have to walk up. I had butterflies but had already reviewed my options with Tom in Yuma, and making the climb was the only way. "Dear God," I prayed, "Thank you for getting me this far. Please keep me going." Every fiber in me raised a silent "Amen" as I determined more than ever to finish.

Swimming buddies in Coolidge

Day 10
Monday, July 16, 1990
Coolidge, AZ to Globe, AZ
66 miles
5:45 a.m. - 1:00 p.m.

Real Life or Rocky

Looking on the map at the road from Coolidge to Superior, all I could see was a thin, gray line on white paper for about thirty of the forty-mile stretch. In map language that says, "Don't count on a double cheeseburger and Biggie fries along the way. In fact, if you find running water you're doing good." That looked especially true between Florence and Florence Junction where the road was as straight as an arrow for sixteen miles then split off towards Globe in one direction and Apache Junction in the other. What that spelled to me was "nothing" with a capital "N;" cactus, tumbleweeds, and buzzards; thirty miles of perfect isolation to think about the mountain climb from Superior to Globe, which, by now, had been built up in my mind to Mount Everest proportions. I pictured myself pushing my bike straight up a narrow mountain pass like a rock climber.

Actually, thinking about the mountain climb wouldn't have bothered me so much if I hadn't picked up some kind of allergy in Coolidge that had my sinuses plugged up and my body feeling weak. On flat roads I could dog it and just plod along without much effort but climbing was a different story. Dog it up a mountain and you go backwards. I found myself repeating the scripture, "In my weakness He is strong. In my weakness He is strong. In my weakness…." I sounded like Dorothy chanting, "There's no place like home, there's no place like home." If only I had the red slippers.

After climbing about a thousand feet without much problem I still had the hardest part ahead—23 miles and about 3,000 feet up to Globe, not to mention getting through the Queen Creek Tunnel through Iron Mountain. Even the name was intimidating.

Simply put, Queen Creek Tunnel was not made for bikers. The opening was narrow and dark, barely wide enough for the thin, two-lane road to fit through, with the only escape from the road surface being a two-foot-high "sidewalk" (more like a thick curb) running alongside the road against the tunnel wall. The dark entrance reminded me of the Road Runner cartoon where Coyote flies into the black opening of a tunnel on his ACME rocket skates only to come back out on the front grill of a semi truck. Coyote always bounced back pretty quickly but somehow the thought wasn't quite as funny staring into the black tunnel.

A hit-and-run here might not be discovered for two days. Rather than make a mad dash on the road through the dark tunnel with no lights, hoping not to encounter traffic in either direction, I made the cautious decision to walk my bike through on the curb.

The problem was that the raised sidewalk was not wide enough for both me and my bike. I decided I would walk on the raised sidewalk against the tunnel wall and roll my bike with my left hand on the road below. Another Roadrunner scene came to mind as I pictured a big truck going in one side of the tunnel and then me walking out the other side holding nothing but the handlebars. Still not funny.

Walking quickly through the darkness of the tunnel I began thinking of how often my life had been influenced by Hollywood. Flashbacks of the Lone Ranger, Kung Fu, and Rocky filled my mind as I recalled how readily I latched onto certain characters, trying to emulate their life in one way or another, Rocky being the most profound example. I remembered the warm summer night walking alone on the beach after returning from my first Rocky movie, looking up to the sky and crying out to God to help me become a great tennis champion; and for the next four years, pouring myself into the dream like an Olympic athlete, training and practicing with the hope of making it to the top, the sound track alone lifting me to new levels of dedication. And I got the feeling I wasn't alone as many others, filled with inspiration, put on sweats and hit the gyms, tracks, and weight rooms in pursuit of the dream they never reached for until Rocky showed us how. The problem for me was the dream never materialized; the muscles got bigger and the intensity of competing and improving was exhilarating, but the new Rocky person never showed up; in the end it was the same me struggling with all my insecurities, fears, and weaknesses, never ending up yelling, "Adrian" above the roar of the crowd, and what's worse, years later still blaming my failure on the fact that I quit too soon and took the easy path of getting a normal job. But now was not the time to dwell on those haunting memories. Right now, I needed to concentrate on getting out of this tunnel and facing the real life challenge ahead of me.

On the way to Globe

Emerging from the black opening into the sunlit mountainous landscape, I braced myself for the infamous climb. Approaching the ascent I knew it would be a challenge but determined in my mind I would not be walking. Call it pride, stubbornness, or just the unspoken biker's rule, but with a low gear that moved at the pace of a slow walk, I was not getting off the bike. At times I felt like it would never end. With the sun beating down and not a breath of wind since I was riding at a walker's pace, it felt like I was riding a Stairmaster in a tanning booth. The big, positive difference, though, was the scenery: huge rock mountains towering majestically in front, beautiful deep canyons down below, all in panoramic view as I made my way through the pass. In the end it wasn't as bad as people had made it out to be, but along the way something else had begun to surface. By the time I cleared the summit and covered the remaining miles to Globe my body began to feel tingly and feverish as if I were coming down with something.

When I rolled into Globe and found a pay phone, I called Joe Albo, the attorney that "Attorney Tom" in Yuma had lined up for me. Joe was in a meeting but his secretary gave me directions to the office and told me to ride over. Pulling into the parking lot of the professional building I found myself feeling a tad out of place among all the nice cars. Then, leaning my bike against the rear of the building and walking through the glass doors brought new meaning to "out of place." Talk about clothes conscious; walking into the marble-and-glass professional building in biker pants felt like that familiar nightmare where you find yourself at the mall in your underwear—horrified, and always glad when you wake up—only this was no nightmare. On top of that I felt like death warmed over; my body feeling chilly and weak and tingling all over. If there had been a hole nearby I would have gladly crawled in and disappeared.

Two people sat in the waiting room as I walked up to the receptionist and introduced myself. The well-dressed and very attractive receptionist politely gave me the message that Mr. Albo would be in meetings all afternoon and had arranged for me to stay in a nearby hotel. She gave me directions and said Mr. Albo would call me when he was free. I thanked her and headed out. I was completely drained and all I wanted to do was get cleaned up and lie down. I made it to the hotel and all I could think of was what a gift from God hotels were: clean, quiet, private, with fresh towels, and TV. "Good-bye world," I thought, as I collapsed on the bed and shut down.

What someone had told me was a desert allergy that would probably clear up when I got into the mountains, had developed into a flu-type, sinus cold that had me laid out like the guy in the Nyquil commercials. While I was sitting on the john in the motel the phone rang and Joe offered to take me to dinner. I told him about my symptoms and he said he would call a local doctor friend who was a member of his church and see if he could see me. He said he'd be by to pick me up in about twenty minutes.

When I got off the phone and returned to the bathroom I discovered the toilet water was bright red with blood. Fear flooded my body and my mind ran wild with possibilities as I stared at the red bowl. Had I pushed my body past the limit? Was this the end of the trip? Would I have to quit and ride a bus home? What humiliation! I collapsed to my knees on the bathroom floor and prayed, "Dear God, what is going on? Please show me what to do." Slowly I picked myself off the floor and wobbled to the edge of the bed to put on my shoes.

Joe came by and picked me up and we went straight to his doctor friend's office. What a great guy Joe was. He showed genuine interest in me and youth ministry as our conversation flowed effortlessly all the way to the office. We were instant friends. His doctor friend was waiting for us before closing up his office for the day and let us in a side door since the receptionist had already gone home. After a quick greeting Dr. Durham and I stepped into the nearby patient room and began the checkup while Joe stayed back in the small waiting area. Both the checkup and the conversation flowed along normally, the checkup with the standard routine of squeezing my neck, looking down my throat, and checking my breathing, and the conversation about the obvious topic of the bike trip and youth ministry, until Dr. Durham asked an innocent and otherwise natural question: "Are you married?" At thirty-three years old I wasn't unfamiliar with the question and gave my usual reply, "Not yet. I'm waiting, but I don't really make enough money to support a family right now." "Why not?" "Well, I raise my own support and our budget is pretty small." "Are there other ways of earning money, did you go to college?" "Yeah, I guess so. I have an engineering degree but that's not really what I want to do with my life." "It might be a way to provide for yourself. It's not un-Christian to make a living and have a family, do you think?" "No, not at all. I hope to do that some day, but it just wouldn't work right now." "Well, don't wait too long."

His words followed the same reasonable logic I had mulled around in my mind a number of times but this time they seemed to reach down a little deeper. But the checkup was over and we didn't have time to dwell on the topic for long. The important thing was that he checked me out and determined I had a sinus infection and even gave me what I needed to clear me up. And the best news of all, the blood I saw was from some small hemorrhoids and was nothing serious. I just needed to be diligent with the Preparation H for the rest of the ride. Thank goodness, I thought; I never knew hemorrhoids could be such good news. I left with Joe, feeling very thankful for the help but a little disgusted with my abnormal life. Will I ever have a job with a nice income and family like these guys? The thought felt so elusive.

Joe and I had a great Chinese dinner and talked like old friends, even though I could barely taste my food and still felt tingly all over. His involvement with the youth in his church and with the Scouts gave us solid common ground for friendship and the night passed quickly. After dinner he dropped me off at the hotel and said to call if I needed anything. Feeling light-headed and wobbly, I feared the thought of spending another day in the hotel and hoped it wouldn't be necessary. I went to bed thanking God for taking care of me in so many ways in one day and praying for strength to ride the next morning. I couldn't help but think of Joe and Dr. Durham at home with their families as I drifted off to sleep alone in my hotel room.

Day 11
Tuesday, July 17, 1990
Globe, AZ to Safford, AZ
76 miles
6:15 a.m. - 12:00 p.m.

No Responsibility - No Dignity

I can't remember a time when I wanted to stay in bed worse than I did on Tuesday, July 17. As I slowly gained consciousness from my total coma of deep sleep in my big double bed, feeling weak and chilled with a plugged-up head, the last thing I wanted to do was pump up for a day's ride. If it had been a school day when I was young I would have moaned to mom and she would have let me stay in bed and taken care of me all day long. That's what I wanted; breakfast in bed, back to sleep, chicken noodle soup for lunch, a little TV in the afternoon, and then get up and see how I felt. Those were the days. But calling this day off and staying around Globe for an entire day, imposing on Joe, plus getting off schedule, changing plans with Ernie (my next stop in Safford), all drove me to get moving. The thought of listening to my body and taking care of myself for a day was a quiet whisper that didn't get much attention as I mustered up the strength to pack up my gear and get going. The drive to press on drowned out any opposing feelings or common sense that stood in the way. I prayed that the Lord would be my strength, and that he would get me through the day.

After gulping down my antibiotics and decongestants with a few glasses of water from the sink, and applying my Preparation H, I rolled my bike out of the hotel room feeling as if someone had draped a wet mattress over my back. The hotel was on top of a hill so coasting down the parking lot to the road was no problem. But when I pulled out onto the highway the grade turned upward and for the first time ever I had to shift down to first gear, rotating just enough to creep forward, head down, thinking hard about the situation I was in. After a mile or so of climbing, which seemed like forever, I finally reached the crest of the grade as the road flattened out and even began a slight downgrade. I thanked God for the relief as I methodically shifted into higher gears.

After ten miles or so I found myself faced with a new situation, one I had heard about while preparing for the trip but had not yet encountered. I had to go to the bathroom. I mean the real bathroom. But where? There was nothing but a two-lane highway cutting through the open rocks and brush in the Indian country of Arizona. I might as well have been on the fifty-yard line of a football field. I began talking with God in a very down-to-earth manner about my situation. "Dear God, I am so sorry, please get me out of this one, I don't know what to do." The situation was becoming desperate and potentially humiliating as I knew at some point I would have to pull over to the side of the road and do what I had to do, hoping a vacationing family didn't drive by for the show. How would dad explain that one to the kids?

About a quarter mile later I noticed an odd sight up ahead that, drawing closer, turned out to be a short, concrete bridge stretching over a dried creek bed with large bushes growing up from either side – a perfect setting for getting out of sight. I rolled onto the concrete slab and leaned my bike against the short guardrail, grabbing my little pack of Kleenex and following a dirt path ten feet down below the bridge to absolute paradise. With perfect privacy and everything I needed, I felt like a VIP in the luxury suite at the Hilton, with a perfectly placed branch as a handle to hold on to. Climbing up the path I couldn't help but thank God for simple and absolutely astounding blessings. I got back on the lonely highway feeling relieved in one department but still extremely weak and draining in my sinuses.

Just as I reached a comfortable cruising speed, and thinking I could zone out and plod along for the next twenty, flat miles, I was startled by another common biking problem that shot a jolt of fear right through my body. Across the open field to my left, at approximately ten o'clock, came the yapping sound of two frantic desert hounds charging full speed across the open field like two torpedoes locked in on their target. Instinctively, the inrush of fear and adrenaline supercharged my body and I began pumping and changing gears like a madman to beat them to the point on the highway where our paths would meet. With heart pounding and legs pumping I reached thirty-two miles per hour, watching and calculating as the missiles approached our intersection point. As our two trajectories met on the pavement my speed put me just five feet in front of their growling snouts as they pulled in right behind my rear tire and continued the chase. By that time their speed was no match for the maniac in eighteenth gear pedaling like a Tour de France racer. I gradually pulled away and outran them until they gave up and veered left back into the prairie.

The fear, adrenaline, drugs, and rapidly pounding heart made me forget how bad I felt as I slowed down to normal speed, panting, dripping with sweat, and trying to settle my rattling nerves. "What a nightmare," I thought, as I drooped my head down and eased back into my lethargic churn. But just as I got used to the monotony I noticed two people walking up ahead, apparently hoping to thumb a ride when a car came by. I knew I would have to ride right past them and for some reason my mind went wild with scary thoughts. "They could knock me out," I thought, "take my bike, and leave me dead behind a rock and nobody would know." Joe in Globe wouldn't know I hadn't made it to Safford, and Ernie in Safford wouldn't know I left Globe. I only talked once to Ernie the day before. If I didn't show up who would he call? I began to pray in the Spirit as I approached the two wanderers. "Protect me Lord," I whispered.

As I came closer they turned around and we made eye contact as I passed by in the middle of the lane, keeping my distance. My fear turned to compassion as I noticed a young boy and girl, around fifteen or sixteen years old, dirty, disheveled, and lifeless, moping along the highway with sadness written all over their faces. They looked like homeless people. I wanted so badly to stop and help them and even share Jesus with them but I pedaled on past. Was I acting like the religious people in the story of the Good Samaritan who walked past the man on the side of the road? What could I do for them? I prayed they would get picked up by someone who could truly help them out.

Gradually the empty, open prairie and scattered, rocky terrain gave way to flatlands and little shanty houses lining the road. Passing through towns like Geronimo and Ft. Howard tipped me off to the Native American culture I was entering. The scene became more and more depressing as the number of cheaply built houses lining the road increased, the yards littered with broken cars, plastic toys, and hanging laundry, displaying a culture of poverty and captivity that shocked me to the core. The haunting thought of being trapped in such a lifestyle touched a nerve so deep in my body it caused me literally to cringe. It was the total opposite of my upbringing and contrary to everything I longed for. Having grown up in nice neighborhoods with thick green yards, big shady trees, and two-car garages with basketball hoops, I knew what I liked, and even though my life in Ambridge was not like that, the thought of my privileged lifestyle suddenly became so cherished that every part of me wanted to flee the Native American scene as if I were running for my life.

That doesn't explain why, when I came upon a dirty little concrete block grocery store with a group of Native Americans hanging out on cars in the dusty parking lot, I decided to pull in. I guess after traveling through the open prairie and having the kind of day I had had, any hope of refrigeration and the prospect of getting something cold to drink seemed inviting.

I began to get second thoughts as I walked my bike across the dusty parking lot and leaned it against the building in front a group of older teens hanging out on the hood of a jacked-up Camaro by the front door. What could they possibly be thinking about this white guy in biker pants strolling into their convenience store on his way through their impoverished settlement? All I wanted was something to drink to go with my peanut butter sandwich left over from the day before. On my way in I prayed for angels to guard my bike while I was gone, and me when I came out.

Inside, I picked out some V-8 juice, apple juice, Gatorade, and plums and went outside and sat on the bench by the door to eat. Pretty soon I was talking with Fernando, a Native American with a ten-speed bike who also liked to ride. He was interested in my trip and asked if he could ride with me for a while when I took off. For some reason, the idea didn't sit well at all. Emotionally, I just didn't feel up to it, plus, I didn't know what kind of pace he could keep or how he would handle riding on the highway; I just didn't need a fluke accident to ruin the trip. I told him I didn't think it would work out and he seemed to understand. I felt bad as I rode off, but I knew it was the right decision.

I spent the remaining fifteen miles to Safford thinking about my conversation with Fernando and how he described the Native American situation in the area. According to him, the government had set up places for them to live and allocated money to keep them satisfied. The problem was nobody had to work and few had the incentive to better their lives, so they sat around, collected welfare, and looked for some kind of excitement in life. They had cars, music, beer, TV, and sex but no ambition or self-worth. It felt like a prison. I had always believed that God had a plan for every person, but applying that belief in the culture I had just passed through seemed impossible. Who would bring them hope?

Pretty soon I saw the Safford skyline and knew I was entering the big city. I pulled into the Wal-Mart and called Ernie from the pay phone outside the main door and he said he would be over to pick me up. After seventy-five miles of totally bizarre, hot, and emotionally intense riding, with a sick body full of drugs, I was ready to collapse on the half-empty palate of thirty-pound bags of kitty litter outside the store. I sat down on the lowest row of bags, placing my elbows on my knees and propping my head up with my hands. I really didn't know how I had made it. I also didn't know what I'd do if I didn't know Ernie was on his way; just looking out into the baking parking lot with the bright glare of the sun reflecting off the chrome and glass of the cars made me nauseous. I buried my head in my hands with my body in the fetal position and tried to be comfortable.

Ernie picked me up and we stopped at Taco Bell for lunch. All I wanted to do was put my head under the drink machine and pump five gallons of raspberry iced tea into my body but I threw in a few tacos for good measure. As we ate I shared in the best detail I could about the trip so far and the day I had just experienced. Ernie seemed genuinely interested and as we talked I thanked God that, once again, this was another providential connection. Ernie shared how he had lost his wife recently and how lonely he had been, and how happy he was to help me out. After lunch we drove up Mt. Graham, the largest mountain range in the area and took in the beautiful scenery. I was so tired and weak I could hardly see straight but was happy to at least be sitting and looking and not pedaling.

When we got back to Ernie's mobile home I was running on fumes. All I wanted to do was take a shower and lie down. That was a good plan except that Ernie had contacted the local newspaper and lined up an interview in town later that afternoon. The last thing I wanted to do was go anywhere but since Ernie had made the arrangements I couldn't say no. Plus, I thought it might be a good opportunity to talk about Jesus in an area that Ernie had told me was full of Mormons. Not that I had anything personally against Mormons, I just knew they didn't believe basic Christian doctrine and didn't like the way they masqueraded around as if they did. It seemed disingenuous to me and as I sat relaxing in my room I rehearsed how I might try to expose them for what they were.

Soon my hour nap was spent and I woke in a stupor and floundered around putting on my one pair of shorts, my flip-flops, and next day's clean T-shirt, ready to head back to town with Ernie. The Episcopal minister where Ernie went to church met us at the news office and joined me in the interview. Fr. Bud was a friendly guy, short and kind of thin, and his presence in the interview made me feel comfortable. As I should have expected, the interviewer was not at all as interested in the truth about Jesus and Mormons as he was in providing a public interest story about a guy passing through town on a cross-country bicycle trip. He asked the basic questions about who I was, where I was from, and why I was riding across country, and gave me good opportunity to explain all that God had done throughout the trip. I laid off the Mormon topic completely. My hope was that he would write something about how God had taken care of me along the way and give credit where credit was due. Ernie and Fr. Bud were glad for a few good plugs for their church.

Fr. Bud came over for dinner and we had a nice, relaxing evening like a group of old bachelor buddies. Of course, their level of faith seemed lukewarm compared to my revved- up attitude but the friendship and relaxation suited me just fine. I just hoped they would catch fire some day and get on with ministry to kids in the community. At some point my mind and body practically shut down and I excused myself for bed. When my head hit the pillow I felt close to comatose.

DAY 12
Wednesday, July 18, 1990
Safford, AZ to Silver City, NM
113 miles
6:30 a.m. - 7:30 p.m.

Where Does It Come From?

I woke up on Wednesday morning knowing that the longest ride of the trip and my entire biking life lay before me. I wrote the following words in my journal: "Today I tackle the longest leg so far. My throat is kind of sore and my sinuses still plugged. Lord, please be with me today. Keep me from any serious sickness."

Ernie took me back to the highway at 6:30 a.m. and assisted me in my routine of bike preparation. After securing the front wheel, attaching the panniers, and placing the three water bottles in their holders, I was ready to roll. Before I took off an early morning walker passed by on the sidewalk and I asked him to take our picture. Ernie and I had become good friends in our short, seventeen-hour relationship and I so much appreciated the way he had taken care of me. Having been a chef and hotel kitchen manager at Harold's Casino in Vegas, Ernie was well trained for the job and took great pleasure in feeding me and making sure I was comfortable

Ernie in Safford

during my stay; what a blessing he had been. We stood side by side like old buddies as the stranger clicked our picture. After a handshake and a short hug, I mounted up and pulled out of the parking lot, giving one last wave from the highway as I headed off, thankful, rested, and well-fed.

My route called for me to follow Highway 70 east out of Safford for about ten miles and then northeast on Route 666. I don't generally freak out over that number even though it is referred to in the Bible as a symbol for the devil, but when I turned onto that road, something inside me rose up in a way I can't describe. If I had been a cat, the hair on my back would have raised up. As I looked ahead at the long, straight, slightly rising strip of asphalt stretching ahead through the

Hwy 666 toward Mule Creek

wide-open, bushy desert, and disappearing into the foot of the humongous mountain range covering the horizon, I felt as though I were entering into Satan's very own territory.

Praying in the Spirit and focusing my mind on Jesus, I made my way through the flat desert and then pumped up the side of the fairly steep mountain range feeling somewhat satisfied when I reached the crest, only to have my jaw drop as I rounded over the peak and looked ahead over the immense valley down below, and an even more intimidating mountain range blocking the entire horizon. I felt as though I had climbed to the top of a large dog bowl only to discover I had to get to the rim on the other side, and the only way to get there was to coast down to the bottom and crank up the other side. Knowing what awaited, I hardly wanted to push off to begin the long coast downward, but figuring I might as well enjoy a good time while it lasted, I pushed off. I flew like a bird, coasting down the winding road and taking in the awesome scenery of vast mountain peaks and huge, grass- covered rock towers standing right across the bowl from me. If only I could pull on the handlebars and soar to Mule Chute Pass on the other side. "E.T. call home!" I shouted as I flew down the mountain with the wind blowing across my face.

The air blew across my body the whole way down until I glided to the foot of Mule Chute Pass without pedaling a stroke. It was nine o'clock in the morning and other than the downhill, my morning had already been a fairly tough thirty-four miles. At the base of the mountain, the road split into a three-way junction: Route 666 turning north, Highway 78 heading straight ahead (and up) to Mule Creek, and Highway 75 turning south. I pulled into the 3 Way Market, a small country store with a dirt parking lot servicing the mountain travelers, to get some Gatorade and a banana. The lady behind the counter was exceptionally friendly as she informed me

To Mule Creek

that the next ten miles through Mule Chute Pass were "straight up, and Silver City is another eighty miles after that." Stunned, I asked, "Are you sure?" Two young women with their truck and horse trailer in the parking lot preparing for a pleasant ride in the mountains stood beside me at the counter and verified the information. Ninety more miles with ten straight up, on top of the thirty-four I'd already done? I tried not to panic as the "butterflies" swirled in my stomach and I searched for the calmness to walk out the door.

The good thing was I didn't have many options to confuse my decision making. I basically had two choices, hang out at the "3 Way Market" or mount up and climb the mountain to Silver City. Nerves, adrenaline, and desperation kicked in and up the mountain I went.

It was the toughest climb of my life, taking over two hours to climb seven miles. At one point, when the pleasant morning sunlight had turned to a hot, pounding heat lamp, and my body approached exhaustion, a thick, gray cloud moved overhead and shaded me through the remaining switchbacks to the top of the ridge. Not only was the blocked sun a relief, the very presence of the cloud gave me inspiration to keep pedaling as I grinded along at walking speed toward the peak. Once on top of the rim I looked back over all of the terrain I had covered: the immense valley below, the first mountain range beyond that, and the desert flatlands of Highway 666; I could see it all from my elevated view as I stood there and thanked God that I had made it. The road now began to weave gently through a peaceful pine forest on the edge of the mountain range and I felt I had entered into a different world; one of trees and scenic cruising instead of the desert dog bowl.

Approaching the border of New Mexico, I stopped at the Smokey-the-Bear-looking welcome sign to get a picture. I had to get some memorabilia of the victory, thinking I'd never be this way again. When I got off my bike and walked over to the sign I noticed a car parked in the picnic area back through the pine trees. Rather than take the picture I decided to wander over to the tables and see

who was there. My real motive was my empty stomach; I had not brought enough food for the long day and was absolutely famished.

I walked toward the picnic table rolling my bike at my side, and gave a friendly "Hi there" to the family when I got close enough. Sitting at the table was a man in his forties, his wife and their son, around ten. We started talking and soon discovered we were all Christians. They asked if I were hungry and invited me to sit down at

Lunch with Jonathan, Julie, Barry

their table where they lavished me with sandwiches, fruit, cookies, and Coke until I was completely full, then gave me extra snacks for the road. During the feast I didn't know whether to burst with excitement or cry with thanksgiving to God for another incredible miracle, but I kept my composure and simply shared the miracle without going overboard. There was no way they could understand how miraculous our meeting was to me. Jonathan, the son, walked back over to the border sign with me and we took some pictures, then it was time to depart, me to Silver City and them to Safford. I forgot to get their full name and address but let me take the time now to say thanks to Barry, Julie, and Jonathan for being Christ to me at a critical time. I'm sure we will meet again some day at another divine appointment.

Barry had estimated I still had a pretty tough sixty miles to Silver City—hills, prairie, and basic boondocks—so the day was long from over.

When I reached what, on the map, was supposed to be the town of Mule Creek, I was out of water and no town could be found, only a rundown farm on the side of the road with a little wooden shack **After-lunch photo op** with a sign over the door that read, "Post Office." Not wanting to waste my time in such uninhabited woods, I initially passed by the shack thinking I would find something better up ahead, but as I pedaled past the overgrown little farm set back behind the Post Office shack, something compelled me to turn around.

Dismounting and walking past the 10 x 10-foot wooden shack with no one inside, I continued to walk down the little dirt driveway toward the overgrown farm, passing old cars under the trees that appeared to be under repair, at least were at one time. Not knowing what I would find, I slowly approached the farmhouse until I noticed **Mule Creek PO** two little children, a boy and a girl, quietly playing with the hose on the other side of a wire fence in the backyard. They noticed me and came running up to the fence and began talking with me. As they talked, with the hose in the boy's hand streaming out fresh water, the miracle came into view. They got a thrill out of filling all three of my water bottles and getting their picture taken. After a refreshing splash on my head and face I walked back to the road and pushed off.

Chrissie & BJ sharing water in Mule Creek

The already long day began to get longer, hotter, and more tiring as I covered the next thirty miles without a hint of water. I began thanking God for the little children in Mule Creek as I burned through my last bottle. What would I have done? At what point would dehydration have kicked in? "God, please get me through this day," I thought.

Riding in the prairie once again, I couldn't believe my eyes when I noticed a huge storm up ahead rumbling with deep thunder, streaking the sky with intense lightening, and pouring out sheets of rain into the open fields. The headwinds drove into my face, making my exhausted body push even harder. It was Gila Bend all over again, except this time I was completely worn out and in no mood for a fight. Once again, with no place to go for shelter and being out in the middle of nowhere, my only option was to plead with God.

In the same Gila Bend fashion, as I prayed and continued to ride toward the blackness, the storm moved slowly across the horizon, leaving wet roads, streams alongside the desert, and thick clouds overhead shading the hot afternoon sun. The relief was too wonderful for words. I rode in calm, peaceful silence, unable to express my thanks to God for his goodness.

In the town of Cliff, New Mexico, I stopped at a little grocery store to rest and try to take it all in. What a day. After three bananas, two oranges, a bag of peanuts, and a fig bar I was ready to tackle the remaining thirty miles to Silver City.

Hwy 180 to Silver City

In Riverside, a small, unmapped town twenty miles up the road, I stopped in another quiet, country store to make a call to my contact in Silver City. As I entered the dimly lit, empty, wooden structure, two teenagers broke their embrace in the back room and emerged to wait on me. I asked if they had a pay phone in the store but no such luck. They thought maybe the gas station down the road had one. I thanked them and turned to walk out when something like a brick wall stopped me dead in my tracks. Turning around and looking compassionately into their young eyes, I began to fumble out some words. "This might sound strange," I said sincerely, "but Jesus Christ wants you both to know how much he loves you and wants to be the at the center of your relationship...Does that make any sense?" The conversation that followed was remarkable as they explained how they used to go to church when they were younger and really liked it but now it just wasn't very exciting. They knew of some friends that were involved in a big youth group but their church didn't have one. I encouraged them to check out their friends' group and see if they liked it. As I turned to leave I realized what a bizarre encounter we had just had. Would they think that maybe God had arranged our meeting or would they consider me the weirdest person they had ever met? As I mounted the bike to ride off I figured both were probably true.

After being on the road nearly twelve hours the final ten miles uphill to Silver City seemed like a blur. Feeling somewhat delirious, I talked out loud to myself and mooed at cows as I passed by, even talking to them at times. "Hey, what's up? You guys look busy today. Nice ears. Yeah, just passin' through. You take care now." Something was wrong with me but I didn't know what. If nothing else, at least I was amusing myself.

As I moaned and mooed up the final grade toward the Continental Divide I noticed a large buzzard circling overhead. Did I look that bad? "Get lost, you bum!" I shouted. "Jesus, please get me there." Finally, He did. I crossed the marker for the Continental Divide and began a heavenly coast into Silver City. Once in town I called the home of the Episcopal priest and his family who had invited me to stay at their house and followed the simple directions and pulled up to a nice, two-story house. I felt like kissing their front yard. Just like all the good folks so far, they showed me to my own room, treated me like a family member, fed me a home-cooked dinner, and all the rest. I fell asleep wondering if I would ever wake up.

Continental Divide

Day 13

Thursday, July 19, 1990

From Silver City, NM to Las Cruces, NM

132 miles

8:00 a.m. - 6:30 p.m.

Grace is Greater

I could hardly get out of bed Thursday morning July 19; my body was on strike. After the marathon ride the day before, my muscles, bones, and tendons had a meeting and decided they just couldn't take another day like that one so soon. They had never come close to climbing mountains like Mule Creek Pass, or ever ridden 100 miles in one day, let alone doing both in one day, and they were not ready to do it again. A day off was in order.

By the time I moseyed into the kitchen it was later than my usual departure time and my hosts Randy and Mona were ready with steamy pancakes. After a hefty feed and some friendly conversation I went back to my room to begin negotiations with my body about riding. The machine simply did not want to tackle the 135 miles back down to the hot desert and over to Las Cruces. It was already 7:30 in the morning, the sun was bright, the ride exceptionally long, and everyone was beat from the day before. I agreed; it just didn't seem possible to expect the body to continue functioning under those conditions. End of discussion. I went back up the basement stairs to the kitchen and shared my situation with Randy and Mona, proposing the possibility of resting for the day and getting an early start in the morning.

Mona's gentle but somewhat startled response was, "Well…uh…I guess if you need to rest…that would…uh…be alright." My ultra-sensitive interpretation of the statement went something like, "We could probably make this work if we have to, and we can't say no because we're a priest family, but our life would be simpler if you could make the ride." Randy, tuning into Mona's frequency, upped his response to the persuasive level by selling the idea that the ride to Las Cruces was the ultimate pleasure cruise. "Lots of nice places to stop for lunch and refreshments," he touted, "and the desert is nothing like around Yuma." Then the final sales pitch, "I've always wanted to make that bike trip myself." And in the same breath he cheerfully instructed Mona to pack up the bananas we had talked about earlier for the ride and, before I knew it, we were all holding hands while Randy prayed for a safe trip.

Overriding all of my body signals and feeling I really had no choice, I persuaded myself it wouldn't be so bad after all, and returned to the basement to gather my things. My body spoke up, "I thought we decided it was too late to get started and we were too tired to ride." "I know," my mind replied, "but Randy said the ride was easy and would be enjoyable, plus, they really don't want us to stay. We're going for it, that's it." I packed my gear, loaded up my bike, took a happy picture together in the driveway, and headed off for Las Cruces at 8:00 a.m., the sun shining bright in the perfectly blue sky.

After a few small hills, Highway 180 smoothed out and maintained a slight downgrade, allowing me to speed along the two-lane asphalt stretch in the low twenties checking out the wide-open, New Mexican prairie. I pedaled thirty-five non-stop miles before pulling into a rest area, the first pull-off of any kind I'd seen since Silver City.

I needed to stop for a number of reasons but one was I had left the house without applying the various ointments necessary to protect my critical areas. One full day without sunscreen, lip balm, and Preparation H (in that order) and I'd be toast.

After taking care of the other reason I really needed to stop, I was standing by my bike when Jim, a soft spoken, sixty-five-year-old gentleman came up and started asking me about my trip. With a distinctive southern drawl he proceeded to tell me how when he was a teenager, he and four of his buddies decided to ride their one-speed Western Flyers from Miami, Florida, to Mobile, Alabama. When they crossed the Florida line they ran out of money so one of the boys sold his bike for fifteen dollars and the group alternated towing one another the rest of the way. He didn't say how they got back.

Jim went back to his car as I rolled my bike under one of the picnic shelters and sat down on the table to do some writing. "Hey, the ride is going to be a breeze," I thought "No need to hurry, I'll take my time." I decided to get a picture of Jim because I enjoyed his story and wanted to remember our meeting. I walked up to his car and asked if he would mind taking a picture with me. To my surprise he declined, saying he was just an old man and didn't care much for pictures. I went back to the shelter and began writing some more in my journal.

A few minutes later Jim walked up and apologized for turning me away at his car window. "You see," he explained with difficulty, "I had cancer in my inner thigh eight years ago and the surgery left me with a large hole on the inside of my leg. When you came up to my car I was cleaning and repacking the hole with gauze."

Swallowing hard and trying not to show my queasiness, I accepted his apology and tried to sympathize with his condition, not knowing how he felt but certainly knowing and feeling my own deep-seated uneasiness toward such permanent disabilities and chronic illnesses. As we were talking, Jim's daughter walked up and took our picture, and after exchanging addresses, they took off. Waving good-bye, I pondered how two strangers could have just shared such intimacy.

Still thinking I had nothing but a dream ride ahead, I wrote some more in my journal and talked with another stranger who had recently been hit by a car while biking and had the scars to prove it. He had decided to take up mountain biking. Thanks for sharing, I thought. I packed up my journal and headed for the highway, not worrying about filling my two empty water bottles because of the "many refreshment places" awaiting me up ahead.

The wind pushed steadily against my body and I could feel the elevated temperature as I turned left from Highway 180 onto 26 to Hatch. So far the route had covered 52 miles without one gas station, convenience store, or café of any kind, and now the sun beamed straight overhead. Highway 180 had been well-traveled because it intersected I-10, but Highway 26 to Hatch turned into a tumbleweed wasteland without a car in sight. A feeling came over me that I had

left the watchful eye of the travelers on 180 and was now on my own, totally at the mercy of the elements. What if a bug flew in my mouth and choked me to death? Months later they'd find a white skeleton on the side of the road sitting on a bike with a white Nike hat and a big smile on his face "enjoying his ride to Las Cruces." I was beginning to get mad.

All day scenery to Las Cruces

My last water bottle was nearly empty when I turned onto Highway 26, and even though the road ahead looked like Death Valley I held on to the hope that "lots of nice places to stop" still lay ahead. With that hope in mind I almost passed by the ghost town-looking church building standing off to the side of the road baking in the late morning sun. The grounds were barren and dry and the parking area dusty and rocky with big clumps of brown weeds posing as landscaping. As uninviting as the vacant property looked something told me to pull off the road and check it out. Walking my bike up the dirt driveway, I looked for nasty thorns that might pop my tires as I investigated the building.

Alongside the baked brick structure, underneath a boarded-up window I discovered a water faucet and decided to give it a try. Surprisingly, it worked and after letting it run for a little while, the clear cool water flowed and I filled my three empty bottles and splashed my face and neck with the refreshment. After over 50 miles of riding my body needed a little fuel so I sat down on the concrete by the back door under the shade of the overhang and ate my three bananas and box of raisins. It wasn't much but I thought it would tide me over until lunch, whenever that might be.

I walked my bike back to the road in the blazing sun fully dressed in my self-designed desert garb. I looked like the Sheik of Hatch with my handkerchief flowing out from under my baseball hat, a long-sleeve white T-shirt and fingerless riding gloves, shades, sunscreen, and lip balm. Sunburn, anyway, was not my problem.

After about 25 more miles of non-stop midday riding I was tired, hungry, low on water, and mad as hell. Where were all these places to stop? I had not seen one in 75 miles and I was fuming, not to mention desperate. Up ahead, on the opposite side of the road, in a sparse, uncovered, roadside pull-off, I noticed a car parked next to a roadside table with the hood up. Getting closer, I noticed an elderly lady, another woman, and three girls standing around the car. Figuring they were stranded, and we could all die together, I decided to pull in and see how they were doing.

They greeted me kindly and explained how they had stopped for lunch and when they got ready to leave, the battery was dead and the car wouldn't start. I asked them to try it again and sure enough nothing happened, only a click. Someone got the idea to try to flag down a car so I walked over to the highway and waited for one to finally drive by. They pulled over but neither car had jumper cables so the driver said he would send help when they got to Hatch.

Back at the car we hung around and talked until I got up the courage to ask if they had an orange or something I could snack on. "We don't have any oranges," the older lady said, "but we have plenty of lunch meat if you'd like a sandwich or something." Opening the lid to a big, red, Coleman cooler stocked with ham, turkey, cheese, bread, lettuce, tomato, apples, drinks, and even ice, she proceeded to fix me a feast I could only have dreamed of a half hour earlier. After a beautiful sandwich, chips, veggies, and even an ice-cold Coke there was no way to communicate the feelings going on in my mind. How could these people possibly comprehend the miracle they had just participated in? When the feast was over, I tried to express my gratitude to them for being so kind and to the Lord for bringing us together. That prompted a conversation about God and his provision, which led one of the young girls to talk about her faith and how we should ask God to start the car. It was getting near two o'clock and I knew I had to get going so I agreed with the idea and offered up a "Please God, start the car" prayer. The mom climbed in and it started up without hesitation. We all cheered and thanked the Lord, then they filled up my water bottles and gave me some bananas and peanut butter crackers for the road, and we took off in separate directions.

The excitement and joy of such a divine appointment inspired me as I battled the wind and heat on my way to Hatch. Despite the conditions, I was in orbit over the biking adventure I was on and overwhelmed with the fact that I was actually out in the middle of nowhere, totally dependent on my bike and my body to move me along the highway towards my destination. Out in the middle of nowhere for endless stretches of deserted highway, I would hang my head down in perfect peace with no distractions and just stare at the pedals and wheels turning round and round as the faint white line on the edge of the road kept my bearings. The uncommon serenity combined with the incomparable thrill and adventure of the journey I was on temporarily masked the exhaustion that was beginning to set in.

By the time I reached the dusty, disenchanting little town of Hatch, I had covered 97 hot, dry miles without one civilized pull-off -- and my anger was back to the boiling point. How could a person be so wrong about this route from Silver City to Las Cruces? It was now 3:30 in the afternoon and I had another thirty-five miles to go. I thought about taking a break in Hatch but the town was so dirty and the main road torn up and detoured around the back side of town, adding to my already fuming attitude, I didn't bother. Surely there would be something ahead. Besides, this part of the trip was supposed to be

All those stops

downhill and scenic all the way to Las Cruces and I wanted to get on with it, so much so that I didn't even fill my water bottles. I was supposed to call Ralph Chamblin, my contact in Las Cruces, from Hatch but decided to even do that later.

The terrain did change, but not as I had been told. The flat prairie and open plains changed into taxing rolling hills and dried-up river washes that made their way from the mountains on my right toward the famous Rio Grande running alongside my left. The problem was whenever the rains came, the water washed toward the river either under the road through strategically placed drainage pipes, or right over the road where the volume of water couldn't be contained, leaving a path of dirt, rocks, and desert branches on top. On two occasions I had to get off my bike and walk across the dried-up pile of debris to keep from wiping out. When I got off the bike the second time, a blanket of heat closed around me like an overheated sauna and my whole body began to throb, especially my head and face, as if I had just sprinted the home stretch of a 10K race. As I walked my bike across the dirt- and-rock path covering the road, my head got dizzy and I began to lose my balance. Putting one hand on my knee and holding my bike with the other I tried to steady myself and regain my senses. As my vision cleared and my balance returned, I desperately mounted the bike to get moving and allow some kind of air across my throbbing body to cool down. The fear of heat exhaustion flooded my mind. With no place to get out of the heat, I realized I had to keep moving in order to keep my temperature down but I needed to conserve enough energy…so I could keep moving. After ten miles of hills and river washes I was out of water and deliriously depleted. Soon small houses began to pop up along the road and the only question was, "Which one?" The run-down shacks with broken cars in the side yard and "Beware of Dog" signs on the chain link fences were not inviting, but I was getting desperate.

I came to a house with horse stables in the back property and a young Hispanic guy working in the side yard. Rolling to a stop and walking my bike across the front yard, I called out to the man so as not to startle him, "Excuse me. Do you happen to have a hose and some water I could have?" "Sure," he said, "come on around back." I followed him to the stables where he turned on the hose and presented me with the most refreshing water I had ever felt in my life as I drank it, held it, splashed it on my face, and finally sprayed it all over my body. As I filled my three empty bottles one by one, snapping the plastic lids back in place and placing them in their respective metal holders, we talked about his band and the conflict he had between playing gigs on the road and trying to be with his family. It sounded like it wasn't working out very well and the relationship with his wife had become strained. My guess was his wife felt he loved the band more than her but I wasn't going to get into it. "That sounds tough," I told him. "I'll pray that God helps you find a good balance between your band and your family." I thanked him for the water and took off.

Down the road I passed through a pecan orchard with trees that lined the road on both sides creating a shady tunnel for about a half mile. Riding through under the shade was so refreshing and cool compared to the rest of the day I spontaneously broke out in thankfulness to God, speaking words of thanks and praise out loud. Ten miles remained to Las Cruces and I knew I was going to make it.

At the outer edge of Las Cruces I pulled into the Circle K to call Ralph and flood myself with refrigerated Gatorade. Sitting on the curb in the shade of the building at 6:30 in the afternoon, drinking my ice-cold electrolytes, I reflected on the day: Ten hours and 135 miles – my second record-breaking day in a row – and I felt every mile of it. Ralph pulled up in his Chevy station wagon and loaded me up like a Red Cross worker. We went straight to his house and after meeting his wife Isabel and taking the most refreshing shower of my life, I sat down at the dinner table as Isabel served up the meal of a lifetime. They had already eaten but joined me in conversation and watched in amazement as I consumed the better part of an entire lasagna casserole. I have no recollection of anything after that.

Day 14
Friday, July 20, 1990
Las Cruces, NM
Rest Day

The Mall

Today was a rest day, period. Ralph and Isabel gladly agreed for me to stay an extra day and even left me alone in their house after breakfast and ran errands until noon so I could lounge in peace. And that's what I did: Hung out inside, ate, drank, and rested until they returned to fix lunch and take me to the mall. Gee, I felt like a teenager all over again.

One reason for going to the mall is that my back wheel had picked up a wobble and I wanted to get it taken care of while I was in the city and could find a bike shop qualified to do it. The thought of having bike trouble on the open road was nightmarish; had it happened the day before I would have been a goner. When I called the bike shop and told them my situation they quickly agreed to squeeze me in and do the work while I waited. Ralph offered to drop me off and pick me up in a couple of hours to save me from riding. Thank goodness; the thought of my rear end even touching that seat made me quiver.

We pulled around back of the mall and unloaded my bike at the back entrance to the bike shop. Ralph took off and I wheeled into the service area and introduced myself. After the twenty-something-year-old mechanic had clamped my bike on the rack and got started on the work, I made my way inside the mall to rejoin the civilized world and be normal for an hour or two. Two weeks on the road had me feeling like a complete alien and I needed a taste of everyday life. Grabbing a bag of trail mix from the nut stand in the middle of the mall and slowly meandering toward J C Penny at the other end, I strolled along casually, paying attention to everything and everybody. I noticed the elderly couple sitting on the wooden bench next to the new car display, the young woman looking at clothes on the sale rack just inside the glass storefront, and the moms pushing baby strollers while their other kids walked along quietly. And then there was me, walking alone without a friend within a thousand miles, and even there, no one close like a spouse, or even a girlfriend. How wonderful would it be to have a person by my side, holding hands, talking, and sharing my thoughts and feelings? Maybe we could go to the food court and sit down across from each other and share something to eat. Why was that not happening? Why was I content going to high school football games and ice skating with teenagers instead of going out on a date? I began to feel as though I was walking inside a big bubble, close to people but insulated from them in my own world. Would I ever break out and participate with everyone else in the human race, or would I continue to keep my distance and play it safe? What would it take? The bike was probably ready by now.

Ralph came back and picked me up at the back door of the bike shop and after a quick stop to get a hair cut from some military sergeant who gave me the new-recruit, buzz special, we headed home and enjoyed a special dinner that Isabel had prepared just for the occasion.

Breakfast with Ralph

After talking about some Episcopal Church issues and in particular, a notorious liberal bishop, John Spong, whom Isabel thought was a wonderful teacher and I absolutely loathed, I excused myself to take a shower and go to bed. It had been a perfect day off, and then some.

Day 15

Saturday, July 21, 1990

*Las Cruces, NM to Alamogordo, NM
to Carrizozo, NM*

69 miles to Alomagordo, 57 to Carrizozo

6:45 a.m. - 1:00 p.m., 3:30 p.m. - 5:30 p.m.

Overreaching

I rolled out of Ralph's driveway at 6:45 a.m. anticipating a laid back, uneventful ride to Alamogordo. It was only sixty-nine miles so I could take my time and enjoy a nice Saturday morning cruise. Ralph and I had had a leisurely pancake breakfast together followed by a few pictures in the driveway and a more emotional good-bye than I expected. He and Isabel had become like longtime friends and saying good-bye caught me by surprise as I fought back tears and rolled out of the driveway. The truth is they had practically saved my life. God only knows what I would have done on Thursday, pulling into town in my condition without someone to help. This nice couple had taken me in, fed me, cared for me, and been friends to me having never met me before. Little did I know back in May when my buddy Dave gave me Ralph's address on a little scrap of paper that my stay in Las Cruces would be so critical. Now, here I was, fully recovered and peddling smoothly on a quiet Saturday morning toward my next destination.

I was familiar with the road because Ralph and I had driven that way to the mall the day before. The workday traffic had been intense but now the streets were quiet. Thank God for weekends.

As I made my way out of town and settled into the rhythm of the open highway, my mind began to churn, as usual, over the events and emotions of the ride. Nothing in my life could compare to this experience and I spent countless hours pedaling and processing the data. The topic for the morning had to do with the dinner conversation the night before about the controversial Episcopal bishop. Ralph and Isabel had lived near his parish before he was made a bishop and Isabel found him to be an interesting teacher. My view was completely opposite even though I had never heard him speak in person. That didn't matter though, since he had publicly denied the basics of the faith in his writings and every time he went on TV. He represented the antithesis of all that I respected in a clergyman, and if the truth be known, I considered him a complete loser and a disgrace to the church. But, out of respect and appreciation for Ralph and Isabel, I kept my opinion to myself, and, maybe for the first time, listened more than

I spoke. But the thought of Isabel and so many good people being led astray by such deception made my blood boil.

Now, on the open road, I had the opportunity to let it out and I was steaming. "You took vows before God and man!" I shouted, "to uphold the scriptures and the doctrines of the Church as they had been handed down to you! And now what, you've changed your mind?!! Or were you crossing your fingers during the ordination service?! People died for what you promised to uphold, and now you want to teach something else?! You're a disgrace!!" The ranting went on for miles. People in the houses along the road must have thought a revival meeting had come to town. I didn't care, I was on a roll and it felt good to get it out.

Just as I was belting out the altar call for all wayward bishops to repent of their sin and turn to Christ for the salvation of their souls, an unsuspecting biker, apparently out for a nice Saturday morning ride, approached from behind just as I finished the punch line, "Repent of your sins and turn to Christ!" I wasn't sure how long he had been following or how much he had heard as he approached but what he did hear was probably more than he expected when he left the house that morning. I was a bit surprised myself and gave him one of those Snoopy smiles and a nice, "Good morning" as he passed by. Oh well, I thought, I'm not going to apologize for speaking the truth. These bums get a free pass for speaking their nonsense to all kinds of unsuspecting people; I'm not going to feel embarrassed for calling a spade a spade. Settling down and feeling a little lighthearted about the preaching incident, I switched my focus to the beautiful mountain up ahead and began enjoying the ride.

The mountain looked fairly steep as I approached but after what I had been through the past two weeks I wasn't all that worried. As it turned out the climb proved effortless and as I approached the top, an intense feeling of accomplishment and victory flooded my mind. Not quite Rocky on the top of the steps, but a genuine emotional boost, and along with it a determination to finish the trip like I had never felt before. I wasn't sure if from the beginning I really believed I could finish, but now a resolve set in that had the end in mind.

Confirmation came as I rounded the peak of the mountain and caught sight of the expansive scenery that stretched out towards the horizon. The view was so magnificent I pulled off the highway to an observation point for a picture. To get to the edge of the overlook I had to lift my bike over the narrow gate and carry it up a dirt path, but what a sight. Out there, as far as I could see, was the White Sands National Park and military testing grounds. I sat there relaxed and motionless, trying to take it all in. Was I really alive? Was this really me out here overlooking half the country? I knew a picture wouldn't capture what I was experiencing but I took one anyway and headed back toward the highway, looking forward to the free downhill ride towards White Sands. I was going to enjoy this one.

Going down mountains usually isn't enough payback for all the effort getting up but flying down this one was worth every stroke. The thrill of speeding along at thirty-two mph without a bit of effort, surrounded by beautiful scenery on all sides, brought out the kid in me as I shouted and whooped it up the whole way down.

At the bottom of the mountain the road leveled off into the most wide open desert I had ever seen, but with the National Park just up ahead and plenty of tourists passing me by, the concern for survival was minimal. I just cranked my way to the park entrance and pulled in like the rest of the tourists. So far, it had been a satisfying sixty miles.

Surprisingly though, as I dismounted in front of the gift shop and information center, leaning my bike against the building and walking inside, I felt like a Martian again who had just descended to planet Earth. Surely it was all in my mind but the feeling of alienation segregated me from everyone in the building. I browsed around the gift shop looking at the coffee mugs and trinkets from White Sands but just couldn't get into the tourist mode. I decided to go outside and sit on a bench by the front entrance and watch the people.

Sitting on another bench nearby were two women in their late thirties who didn't seem to be much into the tourist scene either. Instead of shorts and flip-flops they wore jeans, and instead of cameras and purses by their side, they sported black leather jackets, probably to go along with the humongous Harleys in the nearby parking space. Attracted to their alien existence, I struck up a conversation and discovered that one of their motorcycles was having problems and some of their friends had gone to the next town to get some parts. I also discovered that underneath that "Harley" image were two caring women who worked with juvenile offenders in a rehab program. They told me about their camping program and how most of the kids they dealt with didn't act like criminals when they got away from the influence of the city and out in the mountains camping. The kids usually shared their fears and problems and opened and cooperated with the caregivers who showed them love and attention.

As we were talking, a teenage boy with his dad walked out of the gift shop and, seeing my bike against the wall, struck up a conversation. Jason was a biker himself and could hardly contain himself over my trip and the discovery that I was a Christian. He had taken a bike trip with his youth group last summer and was hoping to do another one this year. He just couldn't wait to get home to Wisconsin and ride. We exchanged addresses, took a picture together and he took off. How uplifted I felt connecting with people and not feeling like an alien. Alamogordo was just up the road and I was feeling pretty good about the day, except for discovering my front derailleur cable had frayed on the frame guide and was holding on by one thin wire strand. I would avoid shifting the front sprockets as much as possible and look for a bike shop in Alamogordo. The first thing to do when I got there though was to call the pastor who had agreed to house me and let him know I was in town.

It was a bright, sunny afternoon when I reached the outskirts of Alamogordo at around 1:00 for one of the easiest day's rides so far. Away from White Sands the peaceful scenery had quickly changed into busy weekend traffic with potholes and roadside businesses, but the day was young and as soon as I could make contact with my hosts and get my bike fixed, I was sure I could find a nice pool to jump into.

Pulling into a mini mart I called the pastor's house and after getting the answering machine, left a message that I was in town and would call back. I then hunted down a bike shop in the Yellow Pages, got some directions and hit the road.

The bike shop had the cable I needed and let me work on my bike right in the shop. I called the pastor's house again and got the answering machine, this time leaving a message that I was at the bike shop and the number they could call when they got home. Without anything else to do, I took my time working on the bike,

Jason in White Sands

eating my peanut butter and honey sandwich, and talking with the guys in the shop. The swimming pool idea was sounding better and better and soon, I thought, I'd be on my way. I finished the bike and waited. When are they going to call? I started getting restless around the bike shop. I wanted to do something. I could go to a pool and hang out and relax. Or—a wild thought entered my mind...I could call my contact in Carrizozo, the next town up, and see if she could take me tonight. It was three o'clock in the afternoon and Carrizozo was fifty-seven miles away. I could make it before dark if everything went well. No way. A few more minutes of waiting.... Why not? I decided to call.

Rene Burton was one of the few people who had responded to the postcard I sent back in May requesting housing. Her church didn't have a full-time pastor but she indicated in her reply that she would be glad for me to stay. Rene answered the phone and I explained my situation and told her I thought I could make Carrizozo before dark. She reluctantly agreed. It was now 3:30 in the afternoon and I told her to look for me around 8:00 p.m., although that might be pushing it. The guys at the bike shop gave me a back route out of town and I bid them farewell.

On my quiet back road out of town I passed a teenager watering plants in front of a juvenile rehabilitation facility. I thought of the Harley riders back in White Sands and since I needed to fill my water bottles, I pulled into the parking lot and introduced myself. His name was René and he had gotten himself into trouble and was sent to this facility to straighten out. Having recently accepted Christ into his life, he was now trying to grow as a Christian and find direction in his life. We seemed to connect right away and after talking a while he invited me to his baseball game later that afternoon. Just then a lady in a car pulled up in the circular driveway and asked who I was. I gave her the short version and she asked René if he was okay talking with me. He said he was and she drove away. I regretted not being able to stay for the game but I had to get going. We filled my water bottles and called over a friend of his to take our picture. I wished him well and took off thanking God for the opportunity and hoped I had been some kind of encouragement to him. I prayed for him as I rode out of town.

Pretty soon I was on the open road between Alamogordo and Carrizozo, and I mean open road. I'm talking wagon train. New Mexico had every kind of landscape imaginable and right now I was on the lone prairie. I was flanked with mountains on my right and could see huge mountains in the distance to the left but down on the two-lane strip of rough asphalt there was nothing but wide-open space. It was late in the hot, quiet, afternoon and I felt very alone as I cranked away.

René at Youth Ranch

As I pushed along the cattle trail-made highway, I noticed huge, ominous black clouds stretching above the mountains straight ahead. They completely covered the sky and seemed to be heading my way. Like a bad dream, long, streaking bolts of lighting flashed above the mountains and the wind blew with a chilly feel that said moisture was on the way. I had come too far to turn back, and since there was absolutely no shelter to get under, I just continued to pedal and pray, seriously regretting my decision to make this run. If only I had stayed in Alamogordo.

Up ahead, across the open prairie, I saw what looked like a wall of rain heading my way. The lighting and clouds were still some distance away and as the wall approached I realized it was not rain but a swirling mass of sand and dust whipping up from the leading edge of the storm. I felt as helpless as ever. I began confessing to God that I had made a poor decision and begging for forgiveness. Subtly, a peace came over me and I decided to pull off the road and prepare for what was coming. Digging into my packs, I pulled out my lightweight, hooded rain jacket and slipped it over my head, laying my bike on the ground and squatting down, prepared to take my licks. I looked around for trees or poles or anything that might attract the lighting somewhere else, but there was nothing. I was the tallest lighting rod in the desert. A hot wave of fear flooded my body as the reality of death entered my mind. Occasionally a car would speed by and at first I didn't consider getting a ride because I didn't want to ruin the trip, but as the wall of sand approached with the rain and lightning right behind I decided to walk closer to the road and try to get a ride back to Alamogordo. Cars heading in that direction coming out of the storm toward Carrizozo were wet and had their lights on and didn't stop. I understood why – they were outrunning a storm and didn't know what to do with a stranger and his bicycle – but at the same time couldn't they see I was in trouble? I began to pray desperately as the wind picked up and light sand began whipping around, "Lord, I am so sorry. Please get me out of this mess." At that point I decided to take a ride in any direction I could go; I just needed to get in a vehicle before I got covered over by this storm.

As I watched the road coming out of the storm toward Carrizozo, all of a sudden, a van pulled up from behind and stopped abruptly right alongside of me. A girl hopped out of the passenger door giving a hurried greeting as she opened the sliding door so I could load my bike inside. Since there were no seats in the carpeted living space there was plenty of room for me and my bike so I quickly lifted my bike inside and leaned it against the side and plopped down on the floor behind the two front seats. As the sliding door slammed and the inside calm replaced the outside chaos, a feeling of relief and thankfulness came over me, mingled with a hint of remorse for getting a ride. My plan had always been to ride the whole way, now there I was in the back of a hippie van with a guy and his girlfriend, hitchhiking my way to Carrizozo.

Of course they knew nothing of that as I thanked them for saving me from the storm. Actually, they weren't hippies at all but kids from South Africa with one-year visas, just cruising around the U.S. They were intrigued by my trip and as I explained my motives and my faith in God, the girl began asking me questions. "Do you really believe God exists?" "Do you think heaven and hell are real places?" She gave me an opportunity to explain what I believed and we had a reasonable conversation.

She had grown up in a strict church as a child and knew nothing but rules and regulations and was basically turned off to religion. I was turned off to phony religion too and was quick to explain the difference. "What I'm talking about is a relationship with a loving God who died on a cross to forgive the sins of his people," I pleaded. "That's a lot different than churchy religion." "We believe in God," she said. "We just don't think you have to go to church and all that." I wasn't sure what "all that" meant but they had told me earlier that they weren't married but were just friends traveling around the country together and I figured maybe that was part of the problem. I wasn't all that serious about God either during my college days of sleeping around and doing things I knew he didn't like. But I wasn't going to get into that now. I just wanted them to hear the truth and be blessed in their relationship. I figured it would help.

We had driven about thirty miles and the storm was gone so I asked if they would let me out so I could ride the rest of the way. We said good-bye and I pedaled on to Carrizozo, taking some consolation that God had used the situation for his good. I'd worry about the riding part later.

When I called Rene from the pay phone on the main street in front of the Jiffy store she was surprised to hear I was in town so soon. I told her I was really fast but she didn't buy it. She had been worried about me in the storm and had driven almost all the way to Alamogordo looking for me and was glad I was okay. She lived close by and said she would be right over to show me the way to her home. After a short ride following Rene, the wild day was over. I showered and changed into my shorts and next day's riding shirt and we talked in the kitchen as she finished preparing the dinner she had started before Mr. Impulse called and invaded her life. We ate dinner and had a good time talking and getting to know one another. I was grateful again that God had led me to such a nice person.

Day 16

Sunday, July 22, 1990

Carrizozo, NM

35 make-up miles

Perfectionism Rules

I woke up Sunday morning feeling guilty about the van ride. The thought of a gap in my route ruined the trip. Rationally, I understood I could have died in the storm and getting a ride was the best option, but mingled in the rational thought was this haunting worry that I had waffled in my faith and let God down by not trusting Him through the storm. It didn't make sense but the feeling was real. Had I removed His hand of blessing by breaking my vow to ride the whole way? Was God or other people going to think less of me now that my trip was blemished? Theologically I knew that was not true. God (and most people) doesn't abandon people when they make a bad decision. But knowing that somehow did not eliminate the worry. I had told a thousand teenagers that bad choices often bring about bad consequences, but our relationship with God was secure. Had I compromised my relationship with Him by my bad decision? Was it even a bad decision? Even if it was, Jesus would not love me less for trying to save my life. So why the struggle? Why not just thank God for my safety and enjoy the Sabbath? Sounded rational but something in me could not live with that gap in the ride and I had to do something about it. But first, it was off to breakfast and church with Rene.

Rene was a nice Christian lady from St. Mathias Episcopal Church who had responded to the card I sent to the church back in May asking for housing. From her reply I could tell she had a sincere love for God. That was one of my reasons for wanting to get to Carrizozo so badly the day before. Having met her, I knew she would be supportive in helping me work through my nagging feelings.

We went to breakfast at a nearby diner where the patrons chatted with one another like family. Rene introduced me to a few friends and, sure enough, we struck up a conversation and talked casually across the tables with no reservation. Naturally, when it came time to order, I chose the rancher's special, which had two of everything on the menu.

After a satisfying breakfast, we had a little time to kill before church so we took a drive out to the Valley of Fires, a huge valley covered with lava. On the drive out we ran over a rattlesnake and I turned around and watched it flip around on the road. I thought what a drag it would be to run over one of those things on my bike. I got this picture in my mind of lifting my feet high off the pedals and bouncing over the fat serpent as he tried to bite me. What a horrible way to go. At a roadside pull-off to look at the lava valley we met an old homeless guy with a bike loaded down like a gypsy caravan. "My name is Lebo, glad to meet you," he said, explaining he was a Frenchman on his way to California. We talked a little about biking as he explained how he took up the sport after he canoed across the U.S. He agreed to take a picture of me and Rene standing next to a huge blob of lava; then we said good-bye and headed off for church. On the ride back I thought about Lebo, a fellow biker on a journey of his own. I felt sorry for him. How did he get that way? I concluded, "There, but for the grace of God, go I."

St. Mathias was a small building with an even smaller congregation. Five of us plus the pastor made up the Sunday attendance. The organist was out of town. Even still, a good spirit was there among the people and we had a nice time of worship and a refreshingly solid Christian message followed by the traditional Episcopal coffee hour of visiting and snacks. The pastor, who worked full time in his own business, had studied in California under a popular radio bible teacher and was ordained by the diocese under a special canon to pastor that specific church. The other three people attending were from the Spencer family: Mrs. Spencer, the grandmother; Spencer, her son; and Spence, the teenage grandson. What one might call a family church. The Spencers went way back to the early ranching days and still lived on the original ranch that was pioneered over a century ago. I was hoping to get a chance to visit the ranch but the first item on my list, which had developed during the church service, was to make up the mileage from the van ride. Regardless of where

Rene Burton

the motivation was coming from, I felt strongly about making up the mileage and even concluded it might be a good way to spend a quiet, relaxing Sunday afternoon.

Rene agreed to take me back to where I had been rescued from the storm and let me ride back. The idea excited me and I could hardly wait to get started, but only after a quick call to Josie back in Ambridge to let her know how things were going. She was glad to hear from me and get a first-hand report but also had some news of her own: her teenage daughter, who actually had brought the family to the Church of the Savior in the first place, had made a bad decision herself and was now pregnant. What a shame, I thought; a pretty young girl with plans of dancing and modeling, and all of a sudden life changes. In my head I knew God's love for Dana did not depend on her decision making any more than it did on mine, but I wondered how she might be feeling about her situation. Hopefully, she would know the love and forgiveness of God in the midst of her new challenge and not be buried by the guilt or condemnation associated with her failings.

I loaded my bike in Rene's little pickup, panniers and all, and we headed back to the storm sight. I couldn't believe how long the drive was back to my spot. We finally reached the rescue sight where she dropped me off with her blessing for a safe ride home. Standing in the same place I was the day before in perfect silence, with blue skies and wide-open scenery in all directions, felt like a dream. The serenity was only matched by the peace I felt in my insides. All I wanted to do was start pedaling and take it all in.

Make-up to Carrizozo

A gentle breeze blew across the road and with the easy cruising I would be home in a couple of hours. As I pedaled along, my mind naturally began to churn about Dana, decision making, and God's promises. How much power did people really have to alter God's plans? I thought. My mind went to Abraham and Sarah in the Bible and the promise God made that they would be the parents of many people. They were old and lacked the faith to trust God and decided to use the servant girl Hagar to have Abraham's babies. That was a bad decision, I thought, and not what God had in mind and the result was the rebel Ishmael, who has been warring against his brothers ever since. But God proved himself to be faithful by bringing about his promise anyway, and Sarah had Isaac and the promise was fulfilled. So, I concluded, Abraham and Sarah really didn't alter God's plan by their bad decision, they just continued to trust God and his plan was worked out in their lives, even if it was a little messier than it could have been. "So it will be with your make-up ride and Dana's different life," I preached out loud. "God's promises are true and his plan will be carried out for both of you regardless of how you've messed up! Just continue to trust in Him!" I prayed Dana would continue to trust Him.

As I finished the prayer, I became increasingly aware that the breeze that had been blowing across the road when I first began was now a punishing wind blowing right into my face. The first fifteen miles had been fairly easy, cruising along at about twenty mph, but now, with this force against my body, I was using my low front sprocket and barely pumping out eight. At this rate the remaining twenty-three miles could take two and half hard hours, I figured. With my head down and my body crouched low to lessen the drag, the going was still tough and the road below just crept by. Plus, where did all these hills come from? I didn't notice them on the drive in or out, what a pain. Was this a test? Was it extra hardship to make this ride really count as make-up? "It can't be either," I determined, and began singing "What a mighty God we serve" and thanking God for his goodness and love as I pressed on with even more resolve to make it back.

Then a disturbing thought crossed my mind. I had eighty barren miles like these on my way to Vaughn the next day. With a wind like this in my face, and a whole day of intense heat, it would be nearly impossible for me to make it. I decided to save that worry for the next day and just keep pumping.

Rene, Marian, Spencer, Spence at Ranch

When I finally huffed into town I felt as if the mission had been accomplished. God had given me the opportunity to satisfy my desire to make up the uncovered miles and had taught me a little more about his grace and love in the midst of my poor decisions. What a great feeling I had riding into town with the assurance of God's love.

When I returned to Rene's house she told me she had arranged for us to go to the Spencers' ranch for dinner. With the excitement of a kid going to Grandma's house, I hopped in the shower and happily washed off thirty-seven miles of wind-dried sweat and desert dirt as I prepared for a good time with friends and a good dinner at the ranch. "Could it get any better than this?" I thought. Cleaned up and dressed, I relaxed for a while and checked out the Genesis 17 passage and then we headed for the ranch.

The sun was still bright but dropping low in the horizon as we pulled off of the highway through the open gate leading to the main house. The long, dirt road wound around the scattered trees while the wide-open land stretched out endlessly on all sides. In the distance stood the ranch house among a towering mass of trees like an oasis in the desert. Along one side ran the only running stream I'd seen in the last one thousand miles. Scanning the property I could tell it had been around a long time, and in some odd way had become one with the land. Inside you could almost feel the history: the wood plank floors, the stone fireplace, the well-worn furniture—all had stories to tell. After visiting for a while in the large living room and watching the tale end of a Walt Disney movie with Mrs. Spencer, Spencer, and Spence, we were given the grand tour. Spencer, the grown son who managed the ranch, took me for a walk around the outside and showed me the corrals and barns. The sun was beginning to set in the orange horizon and the dry wind blew steadily across the landscape, creating a majesty and peace that autographed the moment. I wanted to press the hold button and stop life right there.

Eventually we went inside and gathered in the large kitchen for dinner. Mrs. Spencer explained that this was the same kitchen where as a young woman she used to serve up breakfast for twelve hungry ranch hands before a long day on the range, and then dinner at the end of the day. We were eating at the same wooden table where those strapping raw hides dug into some serious vittles. Now she was talking my language, and followed it up by serving us a delicious steak dinner with all the fixins. I think she got a little flashback after my third piece of pie. After a wonderful evening Rene and I headed home and talked a little about God's goodness before retiring for the night.

Day 17

Monday, July 23, 1990

Carrizozo, NM to Vaughn, NM

81 miles

6:45 a.m. - 2:00 p.m.

Good-byes and Hellos

Mornings were generally tough. Monday mornings were always tough. Thoughts of the weekend, reluctance about leaving newfound friends, nervous feelings about the unknown ride ahead, all contributed to a swirl of anxious emotion. Everything and everybody was new. There was no everyday routine like getting up and going to work, and, worst of all, no everyday people that I could count on seeing and talking to. Every morning was saying "good-bye" without knowing what the next "hello" would be like.

After my ride into Carrizozo on Saturday and the make-up on Sunday I woke up Monday morning feeling a little gun-shy about riding even though things had eventually worked out. The truth was those days were scary and I found myself a tad reluctant to go through more of the same. I prayed, as I usually did in the morning, asking God for his will to be done and for his Holy Spirit to fill me and guide me. After some scrambled eggs and toast I said good-bye to Rene and headed off.

Much to my surprise, the early morning air had a bit of a chill to it and for the first time during the ride I had to put on my windbreaker to keep warm. At least for a while, my concerns about the heat were settled. The road was also pretty decent and the traffic was light, making for a pleasant and even enjoyable morning ride once I got into the groove. I passed by the Spencers' ranch on my way out of town and wondered what it would be like to live there permanently. Part of me was drawn to the stability of the third-generation ranch and wanted to pull into the long driveway and relive the good memory of the day before, but reality called and I needed to press on across the great "Land of Enchantment."

New Mexico really was enchanting. The landscape was unspoiled and the road I was riding on seemed to be the only sign of civilization within a hundred miles. I peddled over beautiful green hills and cut through jagged rocky cliffs, sighting herds of deer grazing in the fields and running through the trees. At one point I surprised a herd of antelope grazing in the brush by the road. A few of them bolted in the opposite direction while two huge mamas galloped across the road ten feet in front of me, their hooves thudding on the road and their snorts huffing in my ears. The untamed speed and power in their gallop frightened and energized my body as I entered so closely into their wild world. For just an

Sunrise in Carrizozo

instant I was right there with them. I just hoped they didn't flip out and stampede me, but they leaped and soared across the road and disappeared into the woods. I never saw such large animals move with such spring and power.

The rest of the ride was a panoramic, scenic tour with small white puffs of clouds shielding me from the sun and the temperature on my bike thermometer staying in the mid seventies. Around noon I pulled over and enjoyed a peaceful, roadside lunch that Rene had prepared, and then pedaled into Vaughn.

I didn't know anyone in Vaughn and as I approached the rather unattractive town I was happier than ever knowing that my friends from Albuquerque had offered to meet me and take me to their house for the night. Not that Vaughn was a total eyesore or anything, but some towns felt good when I pulled in and others gave me the creeps. Vaughn gave me the creeps. It sat on a hill in the middle of nowhere and was basically an overgrown truck stop. I wish I could say that was the only reason I was uncomfortable but it wasn't. Something in my spirit was uneasy about the place. The plan was to meet an old friend, Hazel Kelshaw, the wife of Episcopal Bishop Terry Kelshaw, and a former professor at the seminary, at the first restaurant I came to. The first building was sort of a cross between a truck stop and a restaurant and had a "Restaurant" sign out front so I pulled in.

The attendant sat outside in a chair leaning back against the building under the shade of the roof covering the gas pumps and I wasn't sure if he was asleep or dead. I didn't blame him; what else was there to do in Vaughn, New Mexico, at two o'clock in the sweltering hot afternoon? I leaned my bike against the building and asked him if I could use the men's room. He kindly directed me through the gift shop to the hall on the right side of the room. I gathered the clothes I needed out of my packs and went inside. Actually, the place was pretty nice and the AC felt like heaven. The facilities were clean with no people around, which helped since I was basically going to bathe in the sink and put on my street clothes and wait for Hazel. I had a couple hours before Hazel was supposed to meet me so I planned to relax in the empty restaurant, drink Gatorade, and catch up on my journal.

I emerged from the men's room with my shorts, T-shirt, and flip-flops, feeling perfectly accommodated. I walked outside to hang my wet riding clothes on my bike and roll the trusty machine in front of a window so I could keep an eye on it while I sat inside. The heat outside was punishing. The cloud cover that had been with me most of the day was gone and the only place to put my bike was in the direct sun next to the building; I thought the rubber would melt. I draped my washed out T-shirt, socks, and riding pants over the seat and handlebars and went inside.

The attendant offered one of the diner-style tables and said I could help myself to the cold water fountain. What a set up. I could relax, write, and wait for Hazel. "Thank you Lord," I said, as I settled in for some downtime.

As I wrote in my journal I hardly noticed the guy who walked through the gift shop and wandered into the restaurant section where I was sitting. That is, until he pulled up a chair at my table and, out of the clear blue, asked me if I were a minister. "Who me?" I said, looking around at the empty booths. "Well, uh, sort of. What's going on?" He proceeded to share openly about his life and the hardship of having been born crippled. In an openness that astounded me, he expressed the inward pain of such a life, not only missing out on the normal activities of running, swimming, and playing sports like most kids, but being lonely and wanting a wife and kids someday. Forty-five years old, crippled, overweight, and living in Vaughn, New Mexico. "Why did God make me this way?" he said sadly, looking into my eyes.

I'm not sure if he noticed my jaw slightly drop and the blank look come over my face but the pause in my reply seemed like minutes. All I could do was pray silently and trust God for the right words. "Phil, I don't know why God made you the way he did but I do know it wasn't because he's mad at you. When Jesus was asked a similar question about why a man was born blind he said it was so that God could be glorified through him. I know that Jesus loves you a lot and has the power to heal your body in an instant but he's even more interested in drawing you to Himself and showing you His love. It could be that God has led you to this moment to remind you of the great news about his Son Jesus. Have you ever heard the Bible's teaching about Jesus and His sacrifice on the cross for the sin of the world?" "No," he said sincerely. "The good news of the gospel," I explained caringly, "is that out of great love for you and me, God sent his Son to die on the cross to pay the penalty for all our sin. Now, by believing in Him, we are forgiven and made his friends. Does that make sense to you?" "Sort of, but why did he make me like this?" he sighed. "Phil, I'm sorry, I just don't know," I said honestly, "but I would be glad to pray with you and ask God to give you some peace about it." He agreed and we said a brief prayer together.

Phil's legs weren't healed and the love of his life didn't walk through the door, but his prayer was for Christ to become his Savior and bring him peace and I believe it happened. We laughed and talked some more and were soon joined by the daughter of the station owner who had some concerns of her own.

She had asked the Lord into her life the year before in another town and was excited about the Lord until she moved to Vaughn. She fell out of fellowship and she and her husband hit the party scene and she felt guilty. She could hardly talk about God because she felt so ashamed. We prayed that she might be set free from the bondage of the devil in this town and find Christian fellowship to support her in her walk with God. Two of her friends walked in and we talked about God's plan for marriage and how Jesus needed to be the center of the marriage relationship for it to work. One of the women already knew what didn't work.

By then it was getting late and Hazel still hadn't arrived. I asked Phil if there was another restaurant nearby that my friend might have gone to and he knew of only one. He drove me 100 yards down the street to take a look and sure enough, Hazel was there waiting at a table for me. She followed us back to my counseling office/truck stop where we loaded up my stuff and said good-bye. "So, how was your ride?" Hazel asked, as I waved good-bye to Phil through the window. I didn't know where to begin, but she graciously listened to the whole story as we drove to Albuquerque.

Bishop Terry was home when we arrived around 7:00 p.m. I visited with their teenage son and his friend while Terry manned the grill and Hazel prepared food in the kitchen. We shared a great meal together outside on the deck as the colorful sun disappeared behind the beautiful mountains in the distance. Some teenage girls came over and joined us for a while, then went inside to the living room to watch a movie with the

My friends the Kelshaws

guys. How refreshing it was to be with such a godly family, especially with such a solid bishop of the church who actually believed the Christian faith and could understand my encounter with Phil.

The evening drew to a close and I retired to my room ready for a good night's sleep. The spiritual intensity had been draining. How comforting it was to be sleeping in such a spiritual refuge with such a wonderful family.

Day 18

Tuesday, July 24, 1990

Vaughn, NM to Taiban, NM

73 miles

10:00 a.m. - 4:30 p.m.

A Very Quiet Place

Bishop Terry took me back to the truck stop and sent me on with his blessing. And what a blessing it was. The ride took me to the most absolute, quietest, coolest situation I think I had ever been in, ever. The only problem was there was no one around to share it with. Oh, I thought, for just one person to sit and marvel with. Anyway, I knew I'd never be able to describe the experience but thought that maybe by capturing it in my journal on sight I might at least communicate a glimpse of the experience. The following is what I wrote sitting on the side of Highway 60 in the middle of New Mexico.

Total silence

I'm taking a roadside break that has been the most peaceful experience of my life. A very slight breeze is drifting gently by while a puffy white cloud provides shade overhead. There is not a sight or sound of civilization in existence. I mean perfectly quiet. To the left I can see nothing but pasture stretching all the way to the horizon with a ribbon of road running straight as an arrow to the end. The main reason I stopped was because I needed to go to the bathroom and this was the only clump of trees I'd seen for miles. God leads us to quiet places sometimes. I need to stop riding so hard and take more breaks. I like to push and push but it really isn't good for me.

That was all I wrote about that day. The peace by that roadside was so unlike anything I had ever experienced I decided to leave it at that.

My accommodations with Art and Sue, a sweet couple and friends of Fr. Louie Cochran Ashley, a graduate of the seminary, worked out perfectly; a peaceful end to a peaceful day.

Day 19
Wednesday, July 25, 1990
Taiban, NM to Tucumcari, NM
67 miles
8:30 a.m. - 4:00 p.m.

Happy Trails

Art and Sue hugged me and said good-bye as we stood alongside their station wagon at the junction of Highway 84 and "Old" Highway 252 out of Taiban. I guess the word "old" should have tipped me off. Talk about Nowheresville—this road made Highway 60 out of Vaughn look like the LA freeway. A sign said "Billy the Kid Gravesite 15 miles." I could only imagine what that hot spot was going to look like. As I pedaled along the vacant stretch feeling like the only human being on earth, I started laughing as I remembered Art telling me to watch out for the traffic. I didn't get it at the time but that was funny. The only thing to watch out for along this road was the free-roaming cows.

That morning Art, Sue, Louis, and I had had breakfast together and talked about the early Methodist circuit riders. These brave and committed ministers had traveled on horseback through the sprawling countryside preaching and ministering the gospel to the people scattered in towns across the prairie, the same prairie I was pedaling across. All of a sudden my imagination ran wild as the clock turned back a hundred years. The asphalt road turned back to a dusty wagon trail, my bike turned into a

Art & Sue

strong, slow-walking horse, and I started rocking back and forth in my seat and singing "Happy Trails" and talking like a cowboy to the cows in the open field. Aside from some military satellite, I was positive no human being could hear or see what I was doing.

I had twenty-two lazy miles to House, New Mexico, one of three towns on the way to Tucumcari, and I wondered if I would see one car or any sign of human life the whole way. Just outside of House a big Lincoln drove by with four, nicely dressed elderly folks inside. They had to be lost, I thought. What would four elderly people be doing way out here? They were probably wondering the same thing about me.

As I passed by the plain, white welcome sign to "House, New Mexico" I

Church in Taiban

noticed a cemetery with about 200 gravestones in it and no sign of life anywhere. Is that House? I wondered. Where's the town? I pictured a ghost town up ahead with flapping wooden shutters and tumbleweeds rolling down the dirt main street. Then I passed a farmhouse that looked habitable and figured people must be close by. Finally, I approached what looked like an old-time gas station, now hardware store, mini market, and general meeting place. It had a friendly look to it so I pulled in and leaned my bike against the windowsill alongside a pick-up with a local guy loading his newly repaired tractor tire in the back. "Where ya headin'?" he asked in a friendly tone. "Pittsburgh," I said, knowingly setting myself up. "Pittsburgh? "Where ya comin' from?" "San Diego." "Whoa, what for?" "Uh, to raise awareness for youth ministry."

Sometimes that explanation goes over like grits in New Jersey but this guy latched right on and proceeded to tell me about the Cowboy Camp Meeting starting the next day and the youth tent they were having for the first time this year. "Maybe you should check it out," he suggested, as kind of an invitation. "That sounds good," I said sincerely, "but I've got to keep moving. I hope it goes well." I thanked him and went inside.

Over near the steel pipe section was a teenage girl straightening some items on the rack. I asked if I could get some water and she showed me the sink where we talked as I filled up my bottles. Her name was Jacque. She was a nice girl who attended the local high school and stayed busy with friends and job and church like any normal teenager. Her relationship with God was important to her but not with a lot of her friends and that didn't seem to matter. We talked a little about the camp meeting, which she didn't think she would be attending, and then I took off. The conversation was refreshing and I realized how badly I needed some company.

Pedaling down the lonely road, I started thinking about how many friends I really had. Not the many acquaintances all around, but the real friends who knew and cared about my life. Who were they? Who would I share my deepest feelings with? Who would listen to my loneliness right now? Did it matter if they shared my faith or went to church? For me it did. My faith was who I was in the deepest part of me and I needed the connection. I thought of three guys, Joe, Langley, and Bob, and wished I could somehow share with them what I was feeling right now. I needed people. It was forty-five miles to Tucumcari and I hoped I would find some company there.

The noonday sun shone bright as I rolled along through the quiet countryside, now scattered with an occasional farm. The humidity was low and temperature moderate, making for an enjoyable and peaceful ride. After fifteen miles or so of basically the same wide-open scenery I began to look for a decent place to pull off and eat the raisins, peanuts and banana I

Jacque in House

had saved for lunch. Nothing along the route looked inviting so I decided to wait until Ragland, the next town on my way to Tucumcari.

When I reached the junction of Old 252 and Highway 209 to Tucumcari I found everything except the town of Ragland. That might have been disappointing except when I hung a left onto 209 it was as if I entered into a whole new world. I couldn't believe the sudden change of scenery. The endless flat prairie still stretched out in all directions but now the flat land was cut up with deep, jagged canyons cutting through the earth and carving out deep valleys down below.

As I gasped over the new scenery on my right, I passed an old, boarded-up gas station on my left that looked perfect for a lunch stop. Sitting on the concrete curb in front of the dilapidated front door shaded by the weathered wooden roof over the rusty gas pumps, I had a perfect view of the beautiful Quay Valley stretched out in front of me. I pulled out my gourmet lunch and settled back to enjoy an exquisite dining experience. No cars, no phone, no pressure, just hanging out in a boarded-up gas station in Ragland, New Mexico overlooking the Quay Valley. What a day. What a moment.

When I finally decided I couldn't stay there all day, I threw my raisin box, banana peel, and wrappers in the old, rusty trash can that hadn't been used in years and headed out toward the canyon. The road dipped gradually and I began coasting down into the valley. The remaining twenty-four miles to Tucumcari were spent in the valley where the temperature increased noticeably but I didn't mind; the change of scenery was worth it and I knew I could survive the twenty-mile home stretch. Along the way I passed a landmark sign about a famous train robber but it was too hot to stop and read and I was anxious to get to my hosts in Tucumcari and make some friends.

Gay Wellborn was another lady who had responded to my card requesting housing and she and her husband were waiting for my call at their family-owned pharmacy in Tucumcari. I knew I was in town when I passed the Golden Arches. The unmistakable aroma smelled so good I pulled in to scarf down a Quarter Pounder meal, but when I stepped inside the door the "alien" syndrome hit me so hard I felt like a man from Mars and quickly turned around and hopped back on the bike—people without relationship just would not do. Down the road I found a phone booth and called the pharmacy to tell the Wellborns I was on my way. I so ached for a home-cooked dinner with people I could talk to.

When I got to the glass-front pharmacy and walked inside, the nice girl at the front counter greeted me with a smile and went to the back to tell Don and Gay I was there. They all came back together and welcomed me with an ice-cold can of Coke. Gay asked if I minded if they had called the local newspaper to do a quick story. The reporter would be right over for an interview if I didn't mind waiting. I didn't mind. I welcomed any opportunity to talk about how incredibly God was taking care of me on the trip. When the guy arrived I gave him the whole scoop and he ate it up. When we finished, Don and Gay gave me directions to their house and told me their son Joe would be there to get me situated. "He's a lifeguard at the pool," they said, "and should be home by now." Did someone say "pool?"

Joe was there to welcome me and show me my room. I got showered and stretched out on my own bed for a quick nap. Don and Gay got home and we all gathered for a great family dinner together with lots of happy conversation and thoughtful interaction. Talking around the table and sharing stories together made me realize how God had more than answered my prayer for friends, He had brought me into a Christian family and instantly made me a member. My needy soul could hardly take it in. Before bed we all agreed that a day off tomorrow was in order.

Day 20

Thursday, July 26, 1990

Tucumcari, NM

Stay over

Silent Men and Dominant Women

Because I was used to my early morning routine, getting up and joining Gay and Don for breakfast before they headed off for work was no trouble. Joining anyone for breakfast was no trouble. My metabolism was revved up so high, when I wasn't riding I was either resting or eating.

When I walked into the kitchen Gay was ready with eggs, bacon, toast, cereal, fruit and anything else I wanted. Don had his toast and coffee and the three of us talked casually around the kitchen table. As it turned out, Gay was a Canon 9 minister at her Episcopal church just like Rene's minister in Carrizozo. She worked with Don at the pharmacy but doubled as the minister at St. Michael's Episcopal Church on Sundays. The minister role was obviously the more exciting one as she and I dominated the conversation with church talk while Don sat silently, offering an occasional comment here and there. My preference would have been the other way around as I occasionally tried to draw Don into the conversation but with little results. As this dynamic of Gay's dominance and Don's silence continued I found myself increasingly irritated deep in my gut. Why was Don so silent about his faith? Why were men, in general, so silent, or even absent from the discussion about God and His Church? I wanted, I needed, solid Christian men to be involved in the Church and in my life, and it wasn't happening.

We still had a nice breakfast together and soon it was time for them to head to work and me to go back to my room and chill out a little. The only two items on my agenda for the day were to work out my housing for my next stop and hit the pool. Earlier in the week my friend Langley had given me the name of a friend of his in Amarillo whom he hadn't seen in ten years but might be able to help. Amarillo was too far off my path for an overnight but I decided to give the guy a call and see what turned up.

Heading out to the living room I punched out the number and took a deep breath as the digital tones made the connection. "First National Bank, may I help you?" the nice Texas lady said with an accent that made me want to melt. "Yes, is Mark Osborne in?" "May I tell him who's calling?" she asked so nicely. Oh brother, I thought, do I have to go through my whole deal with this nice lady? Another idea came to mind. "Uh, I'm a friend of Langley Granbery just passing through town." Good move. There's no way he would have picked up the phone if I had told her who I really was. I still hoped.

"Hello, Mark Osborne," the man said in a professional banker tone. "Hello Mark. My name is Joseph Martin and I'm a friend of Langley Granbery." "Oh yeah? How's Langley doing?" He said with a lighter tone, as I knew I had broken through the barrier. We talked casually for a while then moved into the bike trip issue and my need for housing somewhere between Tucumcari and Liberal, Kansas. He seemed intrigued by the trip and after a few questions about my route volunteered his friend Ron, a banker in Stratford, Texas almost halfway between Tucumcari and Liberal who he "knew would be glad to accommodate me." He told me to just show up the next day at the bank in Stratford and tell Ron that Mark Osborne told me he would be glad to put me up for the night. I thanked him and hung up excited that something had worked out but feeling a little shaky with the idea of just showing up without contacting Ron first.

As I thought about Mark's lighthearted attitude on the phone I began to wonder why he wanted me to just show up at the bank. The idea, together with Mark's fraternity brother-type personality made me think this could be the makings of the funniest joke Mark ever played on his friend in Stratford. I pictured Ron calling Mark after I left the bank. "Real funny, jerk." And Mark howling over the phone. I thought of the time a couple of us were walking back from class and discovered one of the fraternity brother's car parked in front of the fraternity house with the motor running. We instinctively hopped in and drove the car around to the back parking lot and left it there and went up the back steps. Our friend, who had run inside the fraternity house to get something, returned to find his car missing and started freaking out. We watched him from the second-story window and thought it was hilarious. I decided to call Ron.

Laboring through the phone maze I finally reached Ron's secretary who put me through. "Hello, Ron Johnson," he said bankerly. I felt like a goofball explaining my situation one more time but finally got through. As we talked I could tell he was a bit uneasy about the predicament his friend had gotten him into and finally decided that with family coming over and the lack of space in his house it just wouldn't be possible to put me up, but he knew a retired banking friend who had a nice house and would probably be glad to help. I hung up the phone a little disappointed but understood how strange these calls must be for most people. I pictured Ron hanging up the phone and staring blankly across his desk. "What was that all about?" He probably made a call to Amarillo.

I took a deep breath and called the number for the retired banker, Mr. Oquin. His wife Judy answered the phone and after listening to the nicest version of the story I could muster, said she would have to wait for her husband to get home before she could give me an answer. "But I'm a really nice guy," I thought. "I grew up in a nice family and even worked in a bank." I guess I'd have to wait. She told me to call back the next day from Dalhart, the last town on the ride to Stratford and she'd let me know. Not exactly a done deal but it was the best I could do.

Plus, I wanted to get to the pool.

I spent the afternoon swimming at the pool and lounging on a beach towel. What a perfect day. When the pool closed, I hung around with Joe and the other lifeguards and swam some more until I started to prune out. On the way home Joe and I dropped by the video store and grabbed a couple of movies for the evening chill with the family. Don and Gay came home from work and we spent a great evening together having dinner and talking. We never got around to watching movies. I went to bed overflowing with gratitude.

Day 21

Friday, July 27, 1990

Tucumcari, NM to Stratford, TX

126 miles

6:00 a.m. to 4:30 p.m.

Unconscious Grace

The morning was quiet and cool at 6:00 a.m. as I pedaled slowly away from the Wellborn's neighborhood toward Highway 54. Not much activity in Tucumcari at six o'clock in the morning, which was fine with me since my body and emotions were not quite ready for normal speed. After a full day of resting and two good nights' sleep, I needed time to get back into riding mode and for now, cruising gently on the quiet back streets as the sun rose over my right shoulder was just right. My destination was Stratford, Texas, 125 miles, straight as an arrow northeast, but I just wasn't ready to think about that much riding.

Once I hit Highway 54 with the wind at my back and a slight downgrade I covered the first twenty-three miles to Logan by 7:30 a.m. "What a breeze," I thought, continuing on for the next twenty-four non-stop miles to Nara Visa. It was only 9:00 a.m. Never had riding been so easy. Crossing the Texas border and into the central time zone, I polished off the barren forty-six-mile stretch to Dalhart by 12:15. The time change made it 1:15, putting me well within striking range of Stratford, only thirty-one miles away. Without a doubt it had been the easiest ride of the trip so far – ninety-four miles in six hours and I didn't even feel it.

Once in Dalhart, it was time to face the moment of truth and make the call to the Oquins to see if they would take me in. This was the first day of the trip when housing had not been lined up at least one night ahead, and all morning I had been thinking about it. My level of trust seemed to be increasing but the "what if" still lingered in my mind. I did have a contact in Liberal, Kansas but that was another hundred miles away; no way, not this time.

Located at the intersection of Highways 54, 87, and 385, Dalhart was the hub of the desert and crawling with eighteen wheelers. Ready for a lunch break and needing a phone to call Mrs. Oquin, I spotted the Wagon Wheel restaurant and rolled into the parking lot, dismounting and parking my bike against the windowsill so I could see the handlebars from the inside. Lunchtime was winding down and the place fairly empty as I walked in feeling a little self conscious in my biking gear as country music played in the background. The man in blue jeans, boots, and a light, cotton, plaid work shirt sitting quietly with his young son in the booth by the window looked more like the normal customer. But, having no other choice, I walked through the dining room feeling like I had a big bull's-eye on my shirt and took a seat by the salad bar where I could see my bike.

Having a sandwich from the Wellborn's, I asked the waitress if I could order a Coke and a side of coleslaw to eat with my sandwich. "Sure can," she said, in her straight-talk, friendly attitude. After ordering, I took the little piece of paper with the Oquin's phone number on it and went back to the phone by the front door to make the big call. The lady behind the cash register didn't have any customers so I figured she'd be listening. It's not every day a guy comes into the Wagon Wheel in biking pants and a "Wise Men Still Seek Him" long-sleeve T-shirt. Why wouldn't she listen?

Mrs. Oquin answered the phone and said her husband was not home but they had decided I could stay at their house and I could call for directions from the first mini-mart when I reached town. "Thank you so much," I said, holding back the celebration. "I'll call you when I get there." Completely elated, I almost gave the lady at the cash register a high five as I walked back to my table, sitting down in total relief, ready to relax and enjoy my hodgepodge of a lunch. With my coleslaw and large glass of icy Coke sitting on the table, and the Oquins waiting for me in Stafford, life was peaceful and I thanked God for his goodness.

The ride from Dalhart was just as smooth as the ninety-four-mile cruise from Tucumcari. I breezed along between twenty and twenty-five mph almost the whole way enjoying the speed. Passing through Conlen, Texas, ten miles outside of Stratford, I was awestruck by the enormity of the grain elevators that towered over the otherwise flat and nonexistent town. At first I passed by because I was cruising so steadily and didn't want to break my pace, but then decided to take a scenic break and check the huge things out. I only had to back track about fifty yards or so.

When I turned around to head back in the opposite direction toward

A view from the top

the elevators I was shockingly confronted by a wall of wind and an upward road grade that made riding an absolute killer. I had to drop down to low gears and pump hard just to get ten mph as opposed to the effortless cruise at twenty to twenty-five mph I had had all day. I couldn't believe how hard it was. There was no way I could have traveled all day like that. I realized what total grace I had been operating under all day long without realizing the magnitude of it.

When I pulled off the highway and began walking my bike toward the towers, a pickup truck pulled alongside with the window down and the driver's tan arm resting on the edge. "What's going on?" the young Hispanic guy asked in a friendly tone. "Just passing through and wanted to take a look at these huge towers," I said. "Let me park this thing and I'll show you around." He introduced himself as Eddie. He was the plant manager and along with showing me around the ground level he offered to take me up the service elevator to the top of the 150-foot structure. He manned the hand-operated, open, steel cage that took us to the top and then led us out to a steel platform on the very top that seemed to overlook the entire world. I felt like I could see San Diego to the west and Ambridge to the east, the road stretching out in both directions and dropping over the horizons. I couldn't believe how far I'd come. I stared out over the endless view as the wind blew steadily in my face.

Eddie knew how awestruck I would be and took pleasure in my excitement, but there was no way he could know what a double blessing he had provided. The view was one thing, but to connect a view of the landscape with the experience I had had so far was incomprehensible. After a look at the conveyor systems across the top he showed me how to operate the elevator and sent me down alone. All I had to do was hold the lever down until I got to ground level and then line the bottom up with the floor so I could get out. What a rush. I could look down and see the daylight coming through the loading dock doors on the ground floor as I approached. I turned the lever at the right time and got out just as a huge eighteen wheeler was pulling under the shoot to fill up with millet. He pulled onto the scale inside the enclosed filling station and in about five minutes was filled to the top by a massive overhead pipe. At first he didn't line up just right and grain ricocheted off the top of the truck all over the floor but that just gave Eddie and I a chance to talk as he swept up the loose millet and told me about his Christian life and his desire to share his faith with his fellow employees. What a super guy. I thanked him for the tour and the conversation and said good-bye. What a great way to end a great ride, I thought, as I mounted up and headed for Stafford. I

Eddie up high

couldn't wait to meet the Oquins and settle into some more Texas hospitality.

About a half mile outside of Stratford I noticed a nice Lincoln Town Car parked off the road with a man looking out of the window. I knew it had to be Harold so as I got closer I waved and called out his name. He waved back and signaled with his finger to keep going straight and then pulled the car out after I passed by. He pulled alongside and gave me instructions through the passenger window to meet him at the quick mart right up the road. "See you there!" I said, sincerely ecstatic.

We met outside the store and shook hands then went inside to get something to drink. Inside were a few booths along one wall where four men sat as if they were expecting us. Actually, they were. They were friends of Harold who had been invited to meet us there. I figured it was kind of a double meeting, one to meet a guy bicycling across the country, and the other to make sure Harold wasn't getting involved with some kind of a kook. They were great old guys and the six of us had a fun time talking. I guess after I passed the test, Harold excused us and we headed for his house.

Texas

I followed Harold off the main road and back into a beautiful neighborhood of well-kept yards and stately ranch houses. As we pulled into the driveway of his home surrounded with large, shady trees, I whispered, "Thank you Jesus," feeling honored to be welcomed into such a deep-rooted, traditional home. Inside, the décor was immaculate and classy with a nostalgic family feel, telling of many good years of kids growing up with lots of unforgettable family memories.

Judy came out of the kitchen and greeted me warmly like a mother who had raised kids about my age. We talked about my schedule and what I wanted to do about showering and having dinner and then Harold showed me my room.

The rest of the evening was a total delight as Harold grilled steaks outside on the patio in their large, well-manicured backyard as we talked and looked at the many fruit trees and vegetable plants that he and Judy grew instead of flowers. After a wonderful dinner we took a drive around Stratford looking at the feed lots, packing houses, and the prize of the town, the golf course. The sun was setting and a gentle breeze blew through the trees as we walked around one of the perfectly manicured greens talking about the town, the cattle industry, and other Stratford trivia. Afterwards we went home and sat around the spacious, beige-carpeted living room as Judy served up milk and homemade chocolate pie. We talked until around 11:00. Saying goodnight, I went to bed in the comfort of home, wondering if I would ever have such a life.

Harold & Judy

Day 22
Saturday, July 28, 1990
Stratford, TX to Liberal, KS
81 miles
8:00 a.m. - 4:00 p.m.

Lasting Vows

I woke up Saturday morning gripped by a steamy dream about an old college fling. The scenes were so vivid and the feelings so real I felt as though I had gone back in time; it was that emotional. Even as I went through my morning routine of splashing my face, stretching, and praying, the revived feelings of the long-forgotten relationship hung on as if I were in my dorm room.

After a good, old-fashioned breakfast of pancakes, eggs, and bacon I got my gear together, loaded up the bike and said good-bye to Harold and Judy in their driveway. They had been such gracious hosts and I hoped they knew how grateful I was for them stretching their comfort zone to take me in. Now, standing side by side in the driveway to see me off, they represented all that was lasting and longsuffering about a married couple. The picture stuck with me as I rolled past the neighborhood homes on my way to Highway 54.

Reaching the highway I discovered the conditions were not as favorable as the day before as I plugged along at about fourteen mph into a steady headwind. What a blessing to have covered the 126 miles to Stratford the day before. Traveling was a ton tougher now.

After covering the forty miles to Guymon, Oklahoma, I chugged into the quiet business district around 11:30 a.m. feeling drained and ready for a break. Dragging at the end of a week was common but add to that staying up past eleven o'clock and I really had the slows. Now I needed a break, and even though it was too early for lunch I decided to pull into the Kentucky Fried Chicken and grab some of their fine coleslaw for a snack. Walking up to the counter I almost lost my train of though as the cutest girl in Guymon asked me for my order. Trying not to stare too obviously, I ordered a pint of cold slaw and a cup of ice water and hoped she would take her time and keep talking as she took my money and worked the cash register. Picking up my food, I walked far enough into the dining room so as not to look conspicuous but seated myself where I could take a glance every now and then. Man, was she cute. I glanced up more than every now and then. I couldn't help it. Not that having girls on your mind is a bad thing; it's pretty normal for most guys, but this was torture; I couldn't turn it off. What would it be like to have a girlfriend like that? Why didn't I? Why was I out in the middle of nowhere, single and alone, without a girl anywhere that I was close to? I wanted personal interaction and some kind of bodily contact so badly—a hug, a handshake, a high five —something with love and friendship. I figured it wasn't going to happen at the KFC and I couldn't take the torture any longer so I decided to hit the road.

I wanted to save the rest of my coleslaw for my peanut butter sandwich at lunch but I knew it would get hot in my

Oklahoma

black panniers by the time I stopped again. Judy had wrapped my sandwich in clear plastic wrap so I took the sheet of plastic from the sandwich and made a lining on top of the coleslaw and filled the container with ice on top of the plastic wrap. Then I put the lid back on the Styrofoam container sealing the plastic around the edges so the melted ice would not mix with the coleslaw. I was impressed with the idea. I put my sandwich in a leftover baggie, stuffed it all in a Ziplock bag, and tucked it neatly in the top of my left pannier.

The next town was Hooker, Oklahoma. "Please," I thought, "can we change the subject?" The fifteen miles on Highway 54 helped. Straight as an arrow, wind in my face, and the most irritating, repetitive ripples in the road, like rows of hard garden hose, beating me to pieces, took my mind off the girls and onto survival. Add to that the smell of cow dung from the feed lots along the side of the road and my girl fantasies were now feelings of nausea.

Harold and Judy had taught me a little about feed lots. They were basically fat camps for cows; places where cattle ranchers brought cattle to fatten them up so they could get a higher price at the market. Thousands of four-legged manure machines stood around and ate specially prepared hay-twinkies all day, getting fat and going to the bathroom, some putting on three or four hundred extra pounds. One can only imagine the amount of cow crap piling up for miles along these feed lots. It was so nauseating I had to pull my shirt up over my nose and mouth as I passed a large lot, but the smell was still unbearable; the July sun beating down on the massive piles of poop made the stench nearly lethal. After passing a two-mile stretch and thinking it was safe to breathe, I became assaulted another way. Repeatedly, cow trucks leaving the fed lots would pass me up, emitting the same offensive odor and sometimes flinging leftovers from the tires. Occasionally I had to dodge a pile that had made it over to my side. What an appetite killer.

About a mile outside of Hooker I thought about stopping at a roadside table and eating my lunch but when I pulled off the road I was unsettled about eating alone on the side of the highway in the dry windy heat so I moved on. When I got to Hooker I noticed a number of little burger shacks but nothing felt right until I spotted Al's Super Burger. Without hesitation I pulled in like I was on automatic pilot. I went in and asked if I could buy a Coke and eat my peanut butter sandwich at the table. Another nice girl behind the counter smiled and politely granted my request.

As I sat down in one of the booths along the wall and began eating my coleslaw and sandwich, I couldn't help but overhear the conversation of the two men and the young lady in the booth right next to me. When someone mentioned something about the local government, I chimed in and asked where the highway taxes were being spent since they were obviously not being spent on the roads. I was an instant hero. Doug, the guy sitting closest to me was going to send my comment to the newspaper. I was serious; my back had taken such a pounding from the repetitive bumps across the road that I could hardly sit down.

After a while the girl and one of the guys got up to leave and Doug moved over to my booth to talk about my trip. He was a gas line worker in the area and was interested in helping me out with contacts he had with pastors up the road.

We talked about God and the involvement Doug had with the local youth camp. He told me how he had fallen into the wrong crowd after his drinking days in the Navy and started smoking dope and getting into trouble. Then, in tears, he shared how he turned his life over to Christ and shortly afterward met his wife and started seventeen years of family life for which he was so thankful. As we were leaving he offered to meet me in Liberal for dinner and pay for a hotel room if I didn't make contact with the Episcopal priest I had been trying to reach there. The Rev. Ashley Null from St. Andrew's had responded to my request for housing but so far all I had been able to do was reach his answering machine. Doug said he would be at the Pizza Hut in Liberal at 7:00 in case I didn't connect with anybody. If I did, no problem, he'd be there anyway.

When I pulled out on Highway 54 toward Tyrone and Liberal the comment Doug made about meeting his wife started me thinking. My mind left the road and drifted back to a time when I thought I loved a girl enough to get married. I replayed the good times we had and rehearsed how it came to an end. We certainly had some high emotion for a while but in the end our trajectories weren't heading in the same direction and I headed off to Ambridge and she got married. Seemed like the right decision at the time but out here halfway across the country alone, on a bicycle, getting intoxicated on cow dung had me thinking maybe I had missed the boat.

When I got to Tyrone I had traveled fifteen miles and could hardly remember any of the ride. I didn't remember looking in my mirror once to check on approaching trucks, and hardly remembered smelling cows.

When I got to Liberal I stopped at a gas station and asked the attendant

Kansas

for directions to St. Andrew's Episcopal Church. Oddly enough he knew where it was. Usually I get, "Episco-what?" I tried calling the church and the priest but when I got nothing but answering machines I decided to bike over and take a look around. My directions took me off the highway and back in a neighborhood where I found the church tucked neatly among the homes. I walked around the building but being after five o'clock in the afternoon didn't expect to find anyone around so I checked the service times and decided to find the Pizza Hut where Doug said he would meet me.

On the way my mind became flooded with negative and critical thoughts about my predicament. "Look what you've gotten yourself into now." "The day's over, you don't have a place to stay. What if Doug doesn't show?" The voices mocked yesterday's glory ride to Stratford and the hospitality of Harold and Judy and beat away at my lonely condition. I began asking God for forgiveness and asking for help.

When I found the Pizza Hut it was six o'clock in the afternoon and I was hot, dirty, and tired from ten hours on the road, and emotionally spent. Giving up on the St. Andrew's idea, I checked into the cheap motel across the street to get cleaned up and wait for Doug. While checking into the motel I noticed sharp, shooting pains in my lower back when I moved a certain way and became even more dejected. The roads had repeatedly pounded my back to where, at one point, I had to ride standing on the pedals to avoid the pounding. Now, what I needed was a swimming pool to ease the pain but all my econo-motel had was a parking lot. Maybe I could find one on Sunday, I thought.

Checking into my empty motel room I showered up, put on my shorts, and laid down on the bed, resting my back and looking forward to meeting Doug. That was the last thought I remember until something woke me out of a deep sleep and I leapt off the bed like a fireman. Gripped with fear that I had slept through the meeting I quickly grabbed my watch and saw the big digits -- 7:18. I stepped into my flip-flops and bolted out the door in a dazed stupor. With my brain in a fog I crossed the highway and busted into the Pizza Hut. Inside I looked around, and nearly wilted in relief when I spotted Doug sitting in a booth drinking iced tea. Since his wife and older son were out of town at his son's baseball playoff game he was in no hurry to leave and was going to wait until 7:30. He was glad to see me and suggested we go to "the best barbeque place in Liberal," so we hopped in his car and headed down the road.

The food was excellent and we had a great time talking about our lives and how the Lord had found us in different situations and blessed us in so many different ways. In his case, he had been lost in drugs and alcohol and after hitting bottom, called out to God and eventually was set free from his addictions. Soon after he met his wife and was further blessed with three wonderful children. During the conversation I kept thinking how incredible it was that two complete strangers could be talking like brothers and enjoying each other's company so quickly.

After dinner we drove around Liberal talking and looking at the sights, ending up at the motel where Doug dropped me off, giving me thirty dollars to pay for the room, then heading back to his home and family. I watched TV for the first time in two weeks, by myself, of course, and eventually fell asleep.

Day 23
Sunday, July 29, 1990
Liberal, KS

Chance or Providence

Motels are great for sleeping late. Especially when you're 1,300 miles from home and nobody has a clue where you are. I had checked service times at St. Andrew's when I rode by the church the day before and had planned to get there before the morning Bible study at 9:30. My thought was to get there early enough to meet some people before the class got started and hopefully find someone to put me up for the night.

I took my time getting ready, feeling stiff in my lower back. All packed up, I rolled my bike out of the ground floor room and over to the office to drop off my key. After checking out, as I was about to mount up for the ride to church, a red Honda Civic pulled into the parking lot and a priest stepped out. I looked at him and he at me and we exchanged names simultaneously, "Joseph?" said the priest. "Ashley?" I inquired. Sure enough, it was Ashley Null, the priest of St. Andrew's Episcopal Church that I had left messages for the day before. He was on his way to meet some parishioners for breakfast before the Bible study and saw me on my bike and figured it was me. We laughed and thanked God for working things out. I retrieved my key from the office and put my bike back in the room and climbed in the Honda to go to breakfast. Ashley had been on a youth retreat since Wednesday and didn't get home until late the night before and when he checked his answering machine and got my messages there wasn't anything he could do; he apologized and hoped I was taken care of. I told him about meeting Doug and how everything had worked out fine.

We pulled into the restaurant and joined six parishioners who usually met after the eight o'clock service. Ashley introduced me to the group and the conversation began, focusing mainly on the bike trip. People asked questions and I explained how God had met my needs in so many miraculous ways. When I finished telling the story about the events of the day before, meeting Doug at Al's Super Burger, not being able to reach Ashley in Liberal, having a great dinner and fellowship with Doug, and him paying for my hotel room, a lady commented, "Aren't you lucky?"

I paused for a split second, feeling surprised and somewhat offended that someone in the church would attribute what I had just described to luck. I had just finished telling, firsthand, how God had been taking care of my needs, consistently, without fail, every day, for the last three weeks, and she calls it luck?! The truth is I wanted to scream, but not wanting to ruin the nice breakfast,

I calmly replied, "Well, actually, I don't believe in luck. I think it was God watching over me every day." My tone was probably not as gentle as it should have been and I'm afraid I surprised her with such a direct reply, but it just came out. I couldn't attribute what I had been experiencing to luck. I didn't pray, "Dear Luck, I need help today." I had come to know a personal God who was ready to handle even the slightest detail of my life, not when the coin landed on heads, not when the stars line up right, every day. That's who I wanted to get the credit.

Another lady continued the conversation by asking how Ashley and I got connected. Ashley explained how he had checked his messages the night before and when he was passing the motel on his way to breakfast he saw a biker leaving the motel and figured it was me so he pulled over to check it out. "You mean you two had not arranged to meet this morning?" The other lady spoke up, "I would say that's pretty lucky, but you don't believe in luck."

Another lady spoke up who had a son that had just qualified for the world cycling championships in Japan. We acknowledged the simple miracle of how I would show up at the breakfast table at a time when she was thinking about her son over in Japan. He was also a Christian and hoped to use his cycling ability to reach people with the good news about Jesus. She was comforted by our "providential" conversation and hoped I could meet her son someday.

After enjoying the He-man breakfast special, Ashley and I took off so he could get to the church in time for the Bible study. He dropped me off at the motel to get my bike and check out while he bolted to the church. I grabbed my bike, already packed up for the road, checked out for the second time, and pedaled the short distance to the church, tender back and all.

When I got to the church, dressed up in my Sunday all-purpose shorts and formal T-shirt, I found Ashley in his office and asked if I could put my bike somewhere inside the building just for peace of mind. He suggested his office would be the best place and told me to wheel it in as he went to get the Bible group started. The small group was getting their last cup of coffee and finding their seats when I walked into the parish hall and took a seat. Ashley introduced me and let me explain what I was doing before he got started, saying they could visit and hear more afterwards. Of course, in the back of my mind I looked forward to talking to more people in hopes of lining up my housing for the evening but I wasn't all that concerned; the church had a good feel to it and I knew something would work out.

After the Bible study I talked with Jo Maxwell, a friendly lady whose husband was a reader for the service. I followed her into church and we sat together during the service. Afterward I met her husband Paul and after talking for a while he invited me to spend the night at their house. Then, an elderly lady, Clara, offered to take me to lunch at the hospital cafeteria where some friends sometimes met after the service. For the afternoon, another couple invited me to their house for swimming and the Jacuzzi. What a line up. And my back could

Clara, Jo & Paul in Liberal

not wait to feel the jets in the Jacuzzi.

Clara and I were joined by another elderly friend and we had a nice relaxing lunch at the hospital cafeteria. Afterwards she drove me to her house to look at the trees in her yard. That may have sounded like a boring offer some other time but after three weeks of busting it on my bike, talking with a nice lady and walking around her yard on a sunny Sunday afternoon was just right.

Clara drove me by Paul and Jo's house and stayed around to visit until Ashley dropped by to give me a ride to the pool and Jacuzzi. We arrived at a beautiful house with nice shade trees covering the yard and a separate pool area complete with exercise equipment and changing rooms. I could hardly believe it. After a quick visit I changed into my suit and hit the pool, floating weightlessly, stretching my back, and swimming around like a seal just released into his new aquarium tank. After a soothing swim and stretch I moved into the Jacuzzi and relaxed as the warm jets massaged my knotted back muscles and relieved the stiffness brought on by the rippling roads; then back to the pool for a few more laps, more stretching, and topped off with a little nap in the sun on the patio. I could not have ordered a more perfect day and literally could not absorb it all. God was too good.

The day ended with a friendly cookout at Paul and Jo's with some of their friends. Bedtime came with hardly the words to describe how blessed I felt.

Suck it up and Ride

After such a great weekend, Monday morning came with the usual thud. Sunrise was not until 6:43, making waking up early even more of a drag. I slept until 6:15 and spent more time than usual praying and reading the Bible; that is, if kneeling by the bed with my forehead resting on the open book can be considered praying and reading. More like spiritual napping. Normally I pray for the Lord to heal my body and fill me with his Holy Spirit and empower me for the day, but this Monday morning I prayed specifically for strength and healing for my aching back.

During a leisurely breakfast conversation with Paul and Jo, we discussed the scripture verse, "We have not been given a Spirit of fear but of power and love and a sound mind." We agreed that fear is not from God but we all experience it to some degree or another and need the Holy Spirit to remind us of God's love in the midst of our fear and empower us to press on. I needed a little extra love and power for some reason. We finished breakfast and I returned to my room in slow motion to complete the packing process and get ready to head out.

As we stood in the driveway saying our final good-byes, Paul surprised me by giving me fifty dollars for traveling expenses. I thanked him and tucked it in my hip pouch and rolled down the driveway, waving one last time to my new friends as I began another unpredictable day on the open road.

I had a slight delay trying to find Highway 54 but with the help of the Mac Tool Truck guy I circled around the foul-smelling meat packing plant, crossed "the two sets of railroad tracks," and headed due east. Immediately I was confronted with a strong headwind that, along with my already sluggish attitude, made me feel like pulling into the nearby motel and calling it quits. Pedaling felt more resistive than ever, as if I was pedaling through mud. At one point I actually gave up pedaling and nearly rolled to a stop, suddenly snapping to and resuming the pumping.

I thought about the three college guys Paul had told me about who stayed at his house during their cross-country bike trip. They got as far as St. Louis and the heat was so punishing they quit and flew home. "No way!" I thought.

Then I remembered the card I received in Liberal from Helen back in

Ambridge. She had mailed it there because it was a church on my list of stops and as it worked out, I got it. The card read, "The whole church is praying for you." Then, in large handwriting at the bottom, "Keep riding!" I cried out in exhaustion, "Oh God, I don't feel like riding, please help me keep going."

For some reason, thoughts about my childhood began to flood my mind. The theme this time was about all the opportunity and material advantage I had growing up. "We had it all," I recalled to myself. "Cars, boats, skis, scuba gear, surfboards, tennis rackets, baseball gloves; and you were so good at so many things; why didn't you stick with one and get good? You had the skill, you could have made it." The thoughts continued as I recounted the many different directions and side roads I had taken that kept me from focusing on a goal. Except for one major exception. I recalled that strange and wonderful season when things were different. After a major religious experience in college I had re-dedicated myself to my first love – tennis – and after graduation stayed focused for three years traveling and improving but quit at age twenty-five when I was offered a real job. "Oh God," I cried, "you gave me a second chance and I blew it. Please don't let me quit now."

My focus shifted to my childhood religious experience. Where was the dedication when I was young? Where was my devotion to God? I thought of my childhood Episcopal church. Where was the excitement about God back then, the Christian friends, the support and encouragement? Was it there and I missed it? What about the college days? Was God there on those Sunday mornings when I walked by myself across the quiet campus of Georgia Tech to All Saints Episcopal Church on North Avenue, struggling with the tension between my belief in God and my behavior at the fraternity party the night before? Why didn't I follow his ways? Why did I get swept away so easily? Why didn't the church speak to me? "What a waste!" I yelled, as I angrily belted out my frustrations over a silent church that had failed to meet my needs as a young person and was continuing to do the same to millions of kids today. The emotional steam pumped through my body and kept my mind off of the rigorous pedaling that I barely had energy for.

Earlier I had turned off Highway 54 to change the scenery and check out a no-name, two-lane back road that cut through Meade State Park. The peaceful prairie along with the absence of traffic calmed my mind and allowed me to relax. The only excitement was passing by a young calf that had slipped through the wire fence and was standing in the middle of the road. As I passed by he almost mangled himself on the barbed-wire fence trying to run away. I felt so bad I pulled into the driveway of the next farm house to tell someone about the escapee. As I rang the doorbell and stood on the porch waiting for someone to answer, wild thoughts about farmers' daughters flooded my mind. When the door opened, much to my amazement, there stood an absolutely beautiful young woman, casually dressed and standing behind the screen door. What began as a good deed suddenly turned into a torturous fantasy. As I told her about the calf I could hear my words but my mind ran wild in the background. What if she asks me to come in for something to drink? I thought. In a delightfully sweet tone she explained who she thought owned the calf. "Well, I just wanted to tell someone," I said as I backed away from the door and walked my bike back to the road and pedaled off. "What was that?" I thought. "A trap? What if she had asked you in? Dear God, lead me not into temptation," I called out.

Passing through Meade State Park and reconnecting with Highway 54, I rolled into Meade and pulled into a hometown burger joint for lunch. Actually I just wanted a place where I could sit down and eat my peanut butter sandwich and be around people. Jack's Burgers looked like the perfect local hangout. Inside, a mix of people, young and old, workers and loafers, played pool and talked while the juke box played in the background. What a happy spot. I stood in line watching the busy food preparation going on behind the counter, waiting for my turn to order. Naturally, a cute young girl took my Coke order and said it would be fine for me to eat my sandwich at a table. Was it just me or were there cute girls everywhere I went?

I took my food to a booth by the window where I could see my bike and even though I felt like an obvious outsider I relaxed and enjoyed my lunch, watching the people in the friendly atmosphere.

Finishing up and saying good-bye to my friendly waitress, I went outside to discover a huge black thunderstorm right in the direction I was heading. The wind whipped around in the parking lot and sprinkles of rain dampened the air. "I can't ride into that mess," I thought, and went back inside to wait it out. Ashland was only thirty-seven miles so I wasn't all that pressed for time but since I didn't have a place lined up to stay I wanted to get there early enough to work something out. I ordered some fries and sat back in my same seat. Lunch time was about over and the place was cleared out except for the group of teenagers hanging around the pool table and the elderly lady sitting at the next table.

I struck up a conversation with the lady, using the always exciting topic of the weather. She seemed happy to talk. I began thinking that if the weather doesn't clear up I might need a place to stay right here. She seemed like the type that wouldn't mind taking in a nice, stranded biker but when I discovered she lived about fifty miles north I scrapped that idea.

With that option closed, I decided to go outside and check out the storm. It still looked pretty nasty but there wasn't any serious lightning and the rain had stopped. Once again I knew I would look stupid riding in the direction of a storm but I didn't feel good hanging around Meade and figured a little rain couldn't hurt, so I took off.

Highway 160 out of Meade was only a two-laner but carried traffic from Highway 54 heavy with eighteen wheelers. Two-lane highways and eighteen wheelers always make for a nerve-racking experience but add wet roads to the mix and you're talking white knuckles. Trucks whipping by at sixty miles per hour threw off a sheet of wind and water that hit me like a sandblaster, causing me to hold onto my lower handlebar grips and tense every muscle in my body every time they came by. Some would come closer than others depending on the oncoming traffic and some seemed to come close just for the sport of it. What came out of my mouth for those drivers began to shock me. Eventually the traffic lightened up and the sun came out, making for a more relaxing ride and allowing my adrenaline to subside.

For the next ten miles I cruised along, keeping one eye on the road and the other on a thick black thunderstorm approaching steadily from the north. When I came to the intersection of Highway 283 south out of Dodge City I could tell the storm was gaining and I got a wild urge to outrun it to Ashland. The road was slightly downhill and with a surprising burst of energy I felt like I was flying.

The terrain reminded me of an old cowboy movie and soon I found myself in a thrilling fantasy about me as a Pony Express rider being chased by Indians as I pedaled flat out over the barren land. That lasted until the storm caught up and drenched me with sheets of heavy rain, soaking me to the bone and causing me to laugh hysterically and shout Indian noises as I continued to pedal in the downpour. Maybe too much endorphins, but I was having a blast being out in the middle of nowhere in the pouring rain playing cowboys and Indians. The rain passed and the sun came out, drying me off by the time I got to Ashland.

Ashley Null, the Episcopal priest back in Liberal, had given me the name and phone number of a Catholic priest friend whose mom lived in Ashland. He lived in Kansas City and Ashley had talked to him back in May and told him I might be going through Ashland. Ashley was going to call him that morning and let him know I was heading to Ashland and see if I could stay at his mom's house. Pretty open-ended situation but it was all I had.

I pulled into the first little mini-mart in Ashland and went inside to use the phone. There were booths along one wall next to the phone with a couple of ladies chatting and drinking coffee. When I called the Kansas City number Ashley had given me, I got some person who didn't know any Catholic priests or anyone who lived in Ashland. As I tried to explain my situation I kept my voice low so everyone in the store wouldn't hear my conversation and think I was some kind of goofball. "Do you know a Father Callahan? How about Ashley Null in Liberal? ....What do I want him for? It's a long story but I'm trying to reach his mom in Ashland. Never heard of either one? Well, thanks a lot." It was a little embarrassing hanging up the phone knowing the ladies probably heard every word I said. I smiled kindly and started walking out of the store when one of the ladies asked, "Are you looking for Mary Callahan?" Shocked and surprised, I replied, "Does she have a son who's a Catholic priest?" "Yes, that's her," she said with a smile. "She was just in here. She owns this store. Ask the girl at the counter for her number."

Dumbfounded, I walked over to the counter and the girl was glad to give me

Mary's number. I dialed the number and Mary answered. She had heard I was passing through but didn't know when. She gave me directions to her house and said she had dinner ready. She seemed used to these kind of surprises. I guess I was beginning to get used to them too.

I found the house and felt welcome before I even went in the yard. I went around the back and Mary met me and showed me the garage where I could park my bike. Andrew, the young boy she was taking care of, took to me right away and I felt like big brother coming home from college. After a shower I joined Mary and Andrew for dinner, consuming enough tacos for a small boarding house. Afterwards, Andrew wanted to go down the street to the local playground so I asked Mary if I could take him. She was happy to get a break so off we went, like father and son. I watched him swing and climb with the other kids as the sun went down on another miraculous day. My soul soared with praises to God as I stood there in the peaceful sunset with a place to stay and a family to be a part of.

I carried little Andrew home on my shoulders and after talking with Mary and having one last piece of pie, I retired to my room for a sound night's sleep.

Day 25

Tuesday, July 31, 1990

Ashland, KS to Medicine Lodge, KS

71 miles

7:30 a.m. - 3:30 p.m.

Something about the Name

Leaving Ashland, I had no idea how much of a toll Monday had taken on my body, but as the terrain developed into repetitive hills and relentless headwinds and pedaling became a torturous cycle of climbing hills and fighting wind, I realized I was in a deeper state of exhaustion than I was used to. On top of all that, for some reason I didn't pack any lunch when I left Ashland, causing my body at one point in the afternoon to just stop functioning. As if someone pulled the plug on my energy I wilted in the seat with my head hanging down and arms resting on top of the handle bars as if I was ready to take a nap. I just couldn't go any further. Slowing to almost a stop before regaining consciousness, I forced myself to press on. The problem was, when I finally limped into Medicine Lodge not only was I totally drained and exhausted but my right knee was in so much pain I could hardly rotate it through the pedal motion. For the last twenty miles I had used low gears and coasted whenever possible relying on my left leg for power and pushing down on my right knee with my right hand. The last two miles flattened out and I rolled painfully and deliriously into town.

The only contact I had was the name of a Catholic priest Mary had given me and the number for St. Mark's Episcopal Church. I pulled into the first convenience store on the edge of town to use the pay phone and get some nourishment into my system. The pay phone didn't return quarters and after trying unsuccessfully to reach the Catholic priest and then the Episcopal Church and losing my money on both I decided to bag the idea.

The afternoon sun pounded the side of the building where I used the phone and the heat was punishing. I had to find rest somewhere. A man came out of the store and was getting into his pickup and I asked him about the motel situation in town. I had Paul's fifty dollars so I had no problem considering his gift as God's way of taking care of me. The el cheapo was a couple of miles down the road in the wrong direction so I eliminated that idea, the thought of expending energy in any direction except the way home made me nauseous. The Best Western was closer to town on the highway I was traveling, which sounded good. I asked the man if there was a bike shop in town and he told me about Mr. Kutz who had a shop at his house just a few blocks down the road. I had been feeling something strange in my rear wheel and I wanted to have it checked out.

I went inside the store to get something to eat and look for a phone book. The store was set up like the one in Ashland with a section of booths along the side wall where the locals hung out and drank coffee and talked. Two older couples sat across from one another chatting and passing the time so I sat down nearby with my orange juice and corn dog and said hello. I asked if they knew Mr. Kutz the bike man. "Everyone knows Mr. Kutz. He's been fixing bikes around here for thirty years." One of the men even knew his phone number. "Tell Janie behind the counter to ring 6-3042." It was the wrong number. Janie checked the phone book; he was off by one number. The next time she tried the line was busy so I decided to just ride over. "By the way," I asked, "you folks don't happen to know any Episcopalians in town do you?" "Episco-what?" "Uh, St. Mark's Episcopal Church?" "Oh yeah," one lady said, "I think Mr. Rickert at the pharmacy goes to that church. If not, he knows everybody in town and will know someone who does." They gave me directions to Mr. Kutz's house and I decided to call Mr. Rickert from there.

Pedaling tenderly down the back road, crossing the railroad tracks and turning left at the second road, I made my way slowly toward Orval Kutz's house. The hard dirt-and-gravel driveway allowed me to keep riding down the narrow stretch leading to the full gravel section in front of the two-car garage connected to the small, one-story house. One of the garage doors appeared permanently closed for storage purposes while the other was wide open where an elderly man, who I assumed was Orval, stood inside talking with a lady and a young boy as he worked on a bike. Walking on the gravel toward the door I got the feeling Orval was the granddad of bicycles in the area and well liked by everyone. Inside the garage you could tell Orval had been fixing bikes for a long time by the bike parts, frames, and old wheels that lined the floor and walls.

Stepping inside I introduced myself and what I was doing and told him about the locals at the mini-mart that led me his way. We talked while he put the finishing touches on the old three-speed he was working on, testing the gear changing then lifting the bike off the stand and rolling it over to the lady waiting at the garage door. After a friendly good-bye he calmly turned his attention my way and asked in an unhurried voice, "Now what can we do to keep you on the road?" I told him about the strange feeling in my rear wheel and after clamping the frame in the stand and rotating the pedals he couldn't find anything wrong except a dragging rear brake, which he adjusted while talking as if it were second nature, but nothing with the rear bearings.

Orval knew Mr Rickert, the Episcopalian, and let me call him from the shop phone. I reached Mr. Richert at the pharmacy and told him about my ride and my Episcopal ties and asked if he knew someone who might put me up for the night. He said he would check around and call me back. He called back and said I was welcome to use the fellowship room at the church. He gave me directions and said he would meet me there and take me to his house to use the shower and then go to dinner.

I said good-bye to Orval and rode over to the church to check out the room at the church. The door around back was open as he said but the room he was talking about was not at all what I needed. It didn't have a couch or anything to sleep on, only thin carpet on the concrete basement floor, and on top of that the dark paneling made the place feel so gloomy I got depressed just standing there. I called Mr. Rickert and explained what I had found and suggested that I needed a bed and would probably be better off at the motel. I was hoping he would offer an alternative, like his house, but he just agreed to pick me up at the motel at 6:30 for dinner. Feeling exasperated by the whole deal, I got on my bike and limped down the road to the Best Western.

Pulling into the parking lot and casting my eyes on the swimming pool water glistening in the sun I thought I might be seeing a mirage. Suddenly I had a one-track mind. I checked in, rolled my bike into the room, grabbed my bathing suit and made my way to the man-made heaven. Walking tenderly and favoring my right knee I felt like an old man as I made my way across the parking lot. When I finally made it to the pool steps and eased my way into the refreshingly lukewarm water my whole body went limp and I sank to the bottom like a dead man. How I wanted to just lie there motionless forever but eventually I had to exert myself and come up for air, spending the next half hour floating and drifting weightlessly through the therapeutic medium.

After my motel room shower and my nice, clean, white towel I sat on the comfy bed and flopped backwards like a rag doll thinking how easily I could just lie there for the night. But not wanting to pull another Liberal, I dug deep and forced myself to flex a few muscles to sit up and finish getting dressed before the Rickerts showed up.

"Dub," as he liked to be called, and his wife Jean arrived on time and after climbing in the back seat of their large, leather-seated, four-door Buick, I immediately relaxed, feeling secure in their company. Dub reached over the seat and handed me a long, thin box containing a tube of anti-inflammatory cream that he had brought from his store and told me to go ahead and rub it on my knee right away, which I did as we drove and talked on our way to the local steak house. After a wonderful dinner where I consumed every atom on my plate plus half the salad bar, we headed back to the motel for my much-needed crash time. Dub stopped the car in front of my room and I pulled myself out of the back seat like a hospital patient returning home after hernia surgery and said goodnight. "Call me in the morning if you have any problems," Dub said before I shut the back door. "Thanks," I said, leaning my head below the roof. "I'll see how it feels." I had a feeling I would be calling. I could hardly move.

Day 26
Wednesday, August 1, 1990
Medicine Lodge, KS

Driven to Ride

I woke up after a much-needed good night's sleep feeling much better but not at all confident in my knee. My watch displayed 6:24, which meant I would have to hurry to get my stuff together, pray, warm up, eat, and get on the road by 7:30. I didn't have any food for the road, I hadn't made any contact in Wichita, and I felt tender and weak. Even still, something was driving me to push on to Wichita.

It didn't make sense; according to my itinerary I was right on schedule and today could be a rest day. Why couldn't I just chill out, take it easy, and let my body heal up? A battle raged inside of me. "Hurry up, get on the road, press on!" "It's too late to get going, your knee hurts, relax, take a break!"

I got on my knees and prayed. I read some scripture about Jesus healing many people of their diseases. Maybe that was for me. Maybe I should just believe I'm healed and take off in faith. "But I don't feel good about taking off," the mental reasoning pleaded. Then the drive to get moving would kick in and sway me in that direction. Then the rational voice, "No way, it doesn't feel right." Eventually reason prevailed and the decision was made: "We're not going. We'll have a peaceful breakfast at the Indian Grill next door, come back and relax, call Jean and tell her we can't ride and see what kind of accommodations come up. That's the decision. We're sticking with it. Amen."

After a leisurely breakfast of eggs, sausage, and pancakes at the Indian Grill, followed by a complimentary cinnamon roll in the motel lobby on my way back to the room, I laid back down in my bed and rested for an hour or so. I hardly had a choice. I just didn't have the energy to move.

Finally I rallied enough energy and courage to call Jean and tell her I had decided not to ride. Without any persuasion on my part, she invited me to stay at their house and told me Dub would be home for lunch around 12:30 if I wanted to join them. As she spoke, an immediate weight was lifted, as if someone had lifted an x-ray blanket off my shoulders.

I gathered my gear together, checked out, and gingerly walked my bike to the top of the hill leaving the motel. Carefully swinging my leg over the bar I fit my left foot in the pedal and pushed off, coasting slowly down the hill and tenderly placing my right foot in the pedal, afraid to push down at all. When the road leveled off and pedaling became necessary, I rotated my legs slowly and pushed as softly as I could in the lowest gear to see what I could do. No way. My knee was too tender. At least I knew my decision not to ride was the right one. The big question was what about tomorrow, or the next day. In my athletic career I had experienced tendonitis in knees and elbows before and generally responded well to ice and rest, but I could only hope. I had also hurt my knee and had to stay off for days. "Oh God," I whispered, "please help me. Determination and positive thinking won't get me out of this jam. I need you."

Favoring my knee and slowly pedaling through the neighborhood streets I soon came to the house. Jean greeted me at the door and welcomed me inside making me feel right at home. I needed that. Physical injuries had always been a major discouragement to me and this one was severe. Just having someone to share the situation with was comforting but to be accepted into a home and looked after by a mom figure answered my deeper need for love and care. Dub came home and we all sat at the kitchen table and had a nice lunch together talking freely about the church, Ambridge, families, and varying degrees of personal life. In less than twenty-four hours Dub and Jean had changed their relationship with me from skeptical outreach to genuine care and I couldn't have been more grateful.

During lunch I asked Dub and Jean if St. Mark's had a Wednesday night prayer service. My need for some type of spiritual interaction bordered on desperate and just about anything legitimately Christian would do. St. Mark's didn't have anything but Dub thought I might enjoy meeting another pastor in town who seemed to have similar interests. His name was Stan Tedro and he ran the Open Door Fellowship, a nondenominational church that operated out of an old motel facility and had a well-known ministry, especially to youth.

Dub located the number and Stan answered the phone when I called. As soon as we started talking something in me brightened up and I knew this connection was right on. He didn't interrogate or scrutinize my situation, but took an immediate interest in me and even offered to come pick me up for their Wednesday night prayer service. Holding the phone I relayed the news to Dub but he gladly volunteered to take me over so I thanked Stan and told him I would be there that evening.

After the call Dub went back to work and I spent the afternoon writing postcards to friends back in Ambridge and to people I had stayed with the last couple of nights. I made a point to thank the people who had sustained me on this journey since each one had played a critical role in getting me where I was. Without one of those kind people contributing in their specific way, the trip could have ended. I wanted them to know how grateful I was for their help and friendship, and also that I had made it a little further down the road.

When I had finished the cards and hung around the house long enough I decided to do something with my tires, which I knew needed attention. They were the original tires and I had put about 1,500 miles on them before I started the trip. The rear tire had become noticeably worn from carrying the weight of the panniers and more of the body weight, leaving the front tire with hardly any wear at all. Dub suggested I get some new ones but being the miser that I was I decided to just rotate them instead. I made the switch in the garage pulling off both wheels and putting the worn tire on the front rim and the good tire in the back. When it was all back together and the tires pumped tight I spun each wheel and let it rotate just to get that good feeling of everything being ready. I leaned my beauty against the concrete wall, ready for tomorrow's ride.

After dinner Dub drove me over to the Open Door Fellowship and dropped me near what used to be the motel office. I walked in with a young family who arrived at the same time and we talked as we made our way to the worship space. Everyone I met greeted me in a friendly manner and made me feel as though I was back in my home church in Ambridge; their pleasant demeanor and warm reception seemed to radiate from their genuine faith and openness to the Holy Spirit.

When the singing started I joined right in. I felt like a dry sponge softening up and absorbing the living water. As I stood there soaking in the peaceful experience I realized what I was feeling and the sponge analogy I was imagining didn't exactly fit the typical Episcopal model but the satisfying experience was undeniable and at the time nothing could have been more real, or desired. After the worship time Stan invited people to come up front and lie face down as a sign of being humble and repentant before the Lord. I went right up. Again, a little out of the ordinary, but the desire to go and my desperate need for God's help propelled me past any whisper of self-consciousness that might hold me back. Afterward Stan gave a teaching on being prepared to share Jesus with others followed by specific prayer for people's needs. I went forward for prayer for my knee and for God's favor in letting me finish the trip.

After the service, Stan asked if I wanted to go see a special project that he and a couple other churches had been working on. We drove over to an old diner they had turned into a teen hang-out where kids were talking, listening to music, and having a good time. That night they were having a birthday party for one of the kids and the love and acceptance was palpable. The ministry this little church was doing with such limited resources both astounded and inspired me. While talking with Stan I told him that I had thought of a similar place for teenagers back in Ambridge but was having trouble putting things together. He told me what they had been through and left me with the phrase, "Fail to plan, plan to fail." The statement convicted me somewhat and caused me to renew my efforts to plan better. I also felt a tinge of guilt for not having accomplished more up to this point, but that was certainly not Stan's intention. The statement was true, after all, and in the end, Stan's love and commitment for Christ and teenagers, and the work his church was doing in Medicine Lodge made a major impression on my mind. Stan dropped me off at the Rickerts' and after sharing as much as I could about my visit, I went to bed with visions of teen hangouts in my mind and how I could duplicate in Ambridge what Stan was doing in Medicine Lodge.

Day 27
Thursday, August 2, 1990
Medicine Lodge, KS to Wichita, KS
97 miles
7:00 a.m. - 5:00 p.m.

Good with Bad

I woke up completely determined to ride. I felt rested, the knee seemed relatively painless, and it was time to move on. Dub offered to take me to breakfast and then to his pharmacy in town to get something for a private itch problem I was having. We loaded up my bike and gear and headed for downtown Medicine Lodge, the Mayberry of Kansas. Dub opened the glass doors and we walked down the isles of the empty store until we located the special cream I needed. We went outside and unloaded my stuff and prepared for my departure. After a picture we shook hands, said good-bye, and I put my feet to the pedals, pushing very gently and rolling slowly down the quiet main street. The knee was a little

Leaving Dub, Medicine Lodge

stiff but surprisingly painless. As I rolled down the street marveling over the way Dub and Jean had nursed me back to health in so many ways, the name Medicine Lodge suddenly took on a new meaning and I could hardly contain my emotions. The goodness and grace from God and the people of that little town brought me to tears.

The tears subsided and the riding continued in an almost effortless manner. The beautifully overcast morning kept me comfortable, the wind blew in my favor, the road stayed nearly empty of trucks, and the greatest miracle of all -- no trouble with my knee. Granted, I was being extra careful and had put into practice a riding plan that I had devised before the trip but never used. The plan was to keep my revolutions fairly high without laboring on the pedals unnecessarily, and to get off the bike every hour for even a short time. I hadn't come even close to that plan, usually riding nonstop until my hands and toes went numb, then starting to look for a place to pull over. Now I was super conscious about riding smarter.

That included taking care of a new problem, the personal itch problem, otherwise known as jock itch. All of a sudden my case seemed terminal. The night before I had tiptoed to the bathroom in the middle of the night looking for

New resting policy

anything that might give me relief but could not find any of the usual creams. I tried Listerine, Preparation H, and finally, good, old-fashioned washing with antibacterial soap. The latter at least got me through the night, but now I needed the real stuff that Dub had given me that morning. Why I didn't put it on in the pharmacy when he gave it to me I'll never know but now I had no choice, the itch and irritation were unbearable and I had to stop. Just when desperation was setting in I noticed a small, roadside park up ahead and anxiously made my way. Pulling in and leaning my bike outside the men's room I two-stepped inside the stall and quickly applied the magical cream. Whether it was psychological or not I felt instantly relieved and happily returned to my bike, refocused on the ride to Wichita.

Having a place to stay any night was a plus but something about my accommodations in Wichita instilled a hopeful anticipation that both inspired and calmed me on my ride. Two days before I had no idea where I would stay next but while in Medicine Lodge I had given a spontaneous call to my good friend Langley, back in Ambridge, and asked if he knew anyone in the area. Not surprisingly, because Langley knew more people around the country than anyone I knew, he suggested a family in Wichita who had been supporters of the seminary and whose son was an Episcopal priest. He gave me the father's business number and left me with a reasonable hope that they would be able to help.

That day I called Mr. Wilson at his paint company and was told he was out of town through the weekend. Thinking that was a nice long-shot that missed, I was about to hang up when the receptionist asked if I would like to speak to Mr. Wilson's son or daughter. "Sure, that would be great," I said, thinking I didn't want to let go of the only thread of hope I had in my fingers. The son got on the phone as I drew a deep breath and began explaining who I was and what I was doing on my bike ride, making sure to include the important part about my friend Langley who knew his brother, Brad, the priest. Being a bicycler and Christian himself, the pleasant speaking man on the other end of the phone was happy to help and gladly gave me directions to the family ranch where he said I was welcome to stay in the guest apartment on the property. "Have a nice ride," he said. "See you soon." So it went in Medicine Lodge, another miracle associated with the town's name that I had not remotely comprehended at the time.

Approaching Wichita made me appreciate how laid back my ride in the open country had been. The once-peaceful open road abruptly turned into a four-lane business race track with uneven concrete slabs, close curbs, and all of the hot, dusty fumes I cared to inhale. Subconsciously, my once-relaxed body tensed up and my hands squeezed my handlebars in a death grip as I bounced alongside the commuters maintaining my narrow position in the intense rush hour traffic. At the traffic light at one of the mega intersections, I decided to put on my helmet that normally hung from my handlebars while riding on the open road.

When I finally got through town and past the Cessna plant on the outskirts, my body relaxed somewhat but we were still clearly not out in the country. It might have been at one time but now the area had the look of a rapidly growing suburb with new roads, new cars, new shopping centers, and, as a plus, a little more room for bikers.

When I turned into the long, tree-lined driveway leading into the ranch I felt as though I was entering a well-kept vestige of what used to be. White fences, open fields, and horses, leading into a large, tree-covered barn and stable area complete with horse trailers, a modest but stately ranch house, and a friendly dog completed my ride. I leaned my bike against the lamp post in front of the house, walked up the short steps, and knocked on the door. The dog just laid there unbothered as I waited but no one answered. The door was cracked open so I stuck my head inside and called out, "Anybody home?" No sign of life, even in the dog, so I closed the door and walked back over to the large horse barn to look around. I had always loved horses but never had I seen a barn like this one. You could tell it had been around for generations. It was big and sturdy with a long corridor lined with horse stalls on both sides. The stall doors were made of heavy wooden planks with one-inch, round steel bars chest high to look through. On many of the doors was a gold name plate identifying the enormous and beautiful creature inside. Halfway down the "T"- shaped building was the main entrance with the office on one side and the tack room on the other. The sight and the smell brought back memories of childhood excitement over riding and hanging around horses and the special thrill of checking out the different saddles and bridles in tack rooms; it was still a thrill.

Scraping up some change in my hip pouch for the drink machine by the entrance, I retrieved an ice-cold 7-Up and went outside and sat down in a folding chair under a shade tree. "What a day, what a place, what a life!" I thought as I relaxed and absorbed all the goodness surrounding me. Pretty soon a young lady in jeans and boots came around and offered to show me the guest apartment. Her name was Susan and she helped with the horses and seemed to be a good friend of the family. She gave me the number for Barbara, the daughter who lived nearby, and informed me Barbara was expecting me if I wanted to give her a call. After saying good-bye and bringing my saddlebags inside, I called Barbara, who generously offered to come by and take me to dinner whenever I was ready. Not wanting to postpone dinner any longer than necessary, I told her to give me an hour to settle in and get cleaned up. She picked me up in her large Suburban and suggested that rather than go out to eat she would make dinner at her place, which suited me fine since I wasn't exactly dressed for dinner and actually had become so sleepy I could hardly keep my eyes open. Once inside Barbara offered a huge, cushy recliner for me to sit in while she prepared spaghetti. I plopped down in the comfy chair, dropping my head backwards into the pillow-like upholstery and tried to carry on a conversation as Barb spoke from the adjoining kitchen. After a while I found myself drifting in and out of consciousness, trying not to be rude but physically unable to hold my eyes open, sometimes finding myself coming to and not knowing who spoke last. At some point Barb got through that dinner was ready and after a huge plate or two of spaghetti and some slightly more coherent conversation, we drove back to the ranch. After a tour of the main house, I slept-walked over to the apartment.

The homey little place (two bedrooms, living room, kitchen, and bath) filled with books, pictures, and other family memorabilia, together with the knowledge that the Episcopal priest son, Brad, had spent time in the little hideaway, made me feel right at home. How I wanted to meet him and hear his story about going from this magnificent life to the ministry. Maybe some day. Now it was lights out.

Day 28

Friday, August 3, 1990

Wichita, KS

About Time

I "woke up to the sound of thunder," (I think that's a song lyric by Bob Seger) and it was music to my ears. Getting to bed after 11:00 p.m. always made rallying at 5:30 a pain, so staying in bed until 8:00, dozing, thinking, stretching, and listening to the rain provided a welcome relief. My next stop was Chanute and the Episcopal priest there was not expecting me until 7:00 p.m. so I didn't feel pressed for time. Depending on the road conditions I felt I could crank out the 100 miles in eight or nine hours.

Peering out of the door I noticed Barbara's Suburban parked in front of the main house next door. Apparently she had spent the night there since her parents were out of town. I didn't blame her; the place was beautiful with a huge, open kitchen and a walk-in pantry that looked like a country store, large rooms with beautiful heirloom furniture, wood floors, high ceilings, and loads of family memories. Who wouldn't want to stay there for a night, or a lifetime?

Feeling rested but not real confident about the weather, I decided to walk outside in the puddled driveway and check out the overcast skies. Barbara stepped out of the main house and asked if I wanted to go to breakfast. My first reaction was hesitation, thinking I didn't have time if I still wanted to make the ride to Chanute, but not wanting to say no and justifying in my mind that "I needed to eat anyway," I found myself agreeing. "Sure, that sounds good, if we can make it kind of quick." So, reluctantly I climbed in the Suburban and off we went.

Instead of going out, once again Barbara decided that we go to her house instead. There she prepared a hefty pile of bacon and eggs that hit the spot just right. After one last drool over the 1967 red Jaguar in the garage, I climbed in the Suburban and Barb drove me back to the ranch on her way to work. It was now 10:30 a.m. and the rain had stopped but the clouds hung heavy and gray. Along with the clouds and bad weather another storm had begun to brew inside of me, driving me anxiously to pack up and make the ride to Chanute. Even though the decision felt uncomfortable, something kept pushing me as I packed, as if I was being propelled again by some internal force. Against all rationale, I finished packing, hooked the panniers on the sides of the rear wheels, clipped the handlebar pack in its place, and headed out despite the late time, clouds, and slight sprinkle.

A voice whispered in my mind as I left the long driveway and pulled onto the main road, "Why are you leaving a perfect set up on a ranch with your

Apartment on the farm

own apartment in order to attempt a 100-mile ride on wet roads with cloudy skies and frantic Friday traffic?" It was after 11 a.m. and I was just getting to the Highway 54 intersection after five miles of busy suburban traffic when the voice spoke louder, "This is nuts! You're tense and anxious and totally unsettled with this decision. What are you doing? What is one day? Why do you have to make Chanute today? Why can't you enjoy yourself around the ranch and get an early start in the morning?"

I couldn't go on. I pulled off the busy road into the parking lot of a large shopping center to try to make some sense out of the situation. Standing over my bike I wrestled with the monster again. One side of me wanted to do the logical and peaceful thing and go back to the farm. The other side wanted to push on as if I was running away from something. What was it? I could feel the pressure, and in some glimpse of sanity, knew what I wanted to do, but couldn't make myself do it. Frustrated to literal tears, I folded my arms across my handlebars and dropped my head on my forearms in a desperate sign of surrender, and quietly begged God for some kind of wisdom over the situation. Without an audible voice or writing in the sky, I somehow rose up with a decision that gave me peace. I would stop running, turn around, and spend the rest of the day at the ranch. If I erred, it would be on the side of rest and mental peace instead of anxiety and frantic pushing.

I pushed off for the ten-mile loop back to the farm feeling exceptionally relieved while contemplating the experience. I figured the conflict had something to do with the issue of control. I knew enough about myself to know that I was hypersensitive about being controlled by anyone, especially women. Barbara, in her sincere attempt to take care of me, had, in effect, made every decision about where we went and what we ate, to the extent that I felt like a little kid with mommy all over again. Not that being a kid with mom was a bad experience, but as an adult it brought up all kinds of powerful emotions.

All good moms want the best for their kids and mine was no different. The hard part, as with any mother and child, was finding the right balance between guidance and control that worked best with the various personalities of each child. Some kids respond well to advice and guidance and find their way somewhat painlessly; others acquiesce to parental expectations (spoken or assumed) and end up doing something they hate, with resentment; while others, like me, flee any aspect of control and end up doing their own thing, often times running away from the good part in reaction to the bad part. My mom and I had gone back and forth about my future vocation, especially as an engineer, and I bucked being saddled with such domestication like a

Allyson & Susan with Freebee

wild stallion trying to be broken for a show horse. I had marched to the beat of a different drummer from early on and resisted any and all attempts to make me do otherwise. And sometimes that came with a price. In the end, though, it was mom who gave me the book, *A Man Called Peter*, the story about the great Scottish-American preacher, that set my heart on becoming a minister, for which I was truly grateful. What a mixed bag parenting is, I thought. "Dear God," I prayed, "get me back to the farm."

I circled around in front of the main house and pulled up next to my apartment. After unpacking I wandered over to the first house near the barn to meet Allyson, the wife of the son I had talked to on the phone to arrange the stay. Barb had told me she thought they would be home today. Allyson wasn't home but a maintenance guy directed me to the stable where Allyson and the vet were checking out a sick horse. Walking up and introducing myself, I expressed how grateful I was for the apartment and how I had decided to wait out the rain and get an early start in the morning. Allyson's family were big bikers themselves and when I mentioned the strange feeling I had in my rear wheel, she offered me her car and told me where the bike shop was where their family did all their biking business. I took her up on the offer and loaded up my bike in her blue Honda Civic and took off. Judging by the number of bikes in the garage, I had a feeling the bike shop would treat me well when they learned of my Wilson connection.

Rolling slowly along the dirt road "back way" out of the property with the local Christian radio station playing and a lightness in my heart that I hadn't felt for days, I could hardly contain my happiness. Here I was, staying on this nice family's horse farm, in my own little apartment, driving a nice Honda, and listening to my favorite Christian music with peace instead of pressure, all because somehow I heard the right voices and turned back from the craziness. The scary thought of being somewhere out on the highway cranking my way to Chanute briefly flashed through my mind. What a nightmare to think I almost missed this moment. How many other blessings had I missed because of my clouded thinking?

The bike shop was located in a new shopping center and was top-notch. Allyson had given me the name of a guy at the shop, and after explaining my situation to him he told me they'd get right on it and I could pick the bike up that afternoon. Leaving my two-wheeled friend with the mechanic, I headed over to Taco Tico for a relaxing lunch. The sky had begun to clear and the day was shaping up nicely. Since I had some time to kill, I decided to head back to the farm and check out the swimming pool I had noticed off the side of the main house. Parking the Civic in front of the apartment, I changed into my suit, grabbed a towel, and headed for the pool. The water was clear, the sun warm, and I swam around without a worry in the world.

After some lounging in the sun I strolled over to the apartment, showered up, and went to pick up my bike. Sure enough, the noise I'd been hearing was a broken rear axle only held together by the quick release levers on either side.

Why leave this?

The shop returned the broken pieces and worn bearings in a baggie. No telling how long I had been riding with it that way or at what point it would have stranded me on the highway. All I knew was it was another small confirmation for my decision to stay…as if I needed one. I left the bike shop and treated myself to a strawberry-and-vanilla frozen yogurt cone in the air-conditioned sweet shop next door.

Back at the farm I relaxed and read the Bible, walked around the stable, and petted a few horses. As dinner time approached, Allyson and Susan, the nice girl I met in the barn the day before, drove up and invited me to join them at Pizza Hut. I piled into her Suburban and off we went to enjoy a great dinner and friendly conversation. Afterwards, they dropped me off at the apartment, and said farewell. A good end to a good day, I thought.

After Allyson and Susan dropped me off the sun had barely set and the sky glowed beautiful orange over the peaceful property. All alone, and not quite ready for bed, I decided to walk around the expansive property and bask in the peaceful surroundings.

Looking out across a large open field and spotting the white posts of a jump course laid out in their various heights and x-shaped patterns, I decided to head in that direction. In grade school I had taken English riding lessons after school and also rode western on my Uncle Fred's horses on his farm. I thought of those fond memories as I walked among the jumps and stood in the quiet field absorbing the silence and scanning the property for another place to visit. In the distance, among clusters of sprawling oak trees and thick, overgrown hedges I noticed a building tucked away beneath the branches. Walking closer I noticed a smaller structure hidden in another clump of trees nearby. It looked like the smaller structure was some kind of changing room or cottage that went along with the larger, screened-in recreation room and outdoor picnic tables, none of which looked like they had been used in twenty years. I could almost hear the sounds of weekend picnics and family gatherings of years gone by.

Not too far away I noticed the rectangular shape of a tall clump of bushes with a rusted fence woven among the branches. Walking closer and estimating the size of the enclosure, I thought, "Could it be?" I followed the path closer and nearly cheered with disbelief as I recognized the facility. It was a tennis court. "Unbelievable," I thought, as I walked through the overgrown gate entrance, my heart pounding with a lifetime of emotion wrapped up in that familiar scene. This one had seen better days with the perimeter closed in by thick weeds growing under the fence and even protruding through cracks in the weathered asphalt, and broken twigs and leaves covering the rest of the faded green surface. The tattered net drooped low between the rusty net poles, emphasizing the length of time since its last use. I stepped through the open gate as if I was walking back in time. As I stood on the faded baseline looking across the net at my invisible opponent, my mind rewound twenty-five years of memories: nights with dad under the lights at Grady courts, countless hours on the practice courts shuffling back and forth hitting forehands and backhands, thousands of practice serves hit from standing ball hoppers, running the lines, playing tournaments, and dreaming about getting a computer ranking. The thought of quitting during college for the fraternity life, then making a push after college only to quit again in order to get a "real job" still haunted me like a demon. My abandoned dream was as overgrown and decrepit as the court I was standing on and the regret tortured me. "Why did we quit?" I cried, as I stood alone in tears among the weed-eaten green asphalt thinking about those tennis days gone by. "What a waste! You could have made it!" I sobbed in gut- wrenching sadness, dropping to my knees with my face in my hands. "Dear God, please forgive me for quitting. Please help me make something out of my life."

Rising to my feet and wiping the tears off of my face with the back of my hands, I took one last look at the past and turned and walked through the rusty gate feeling emotionally wrung out but just a little lighter inside, as though something had been left behind. The sky had grown darker as I followed the overgrown path back to the guest house, thinking tomorrow was a new day.

Day 29

Saturday, August 4, 1990

Wichita, KS to Chanute, KS

107 miles

7:45 a.m. - 5:30 p.m.

Still There

Even after a great day off and a good night's sleep I still didn't get started as early as I wanted. Time really wasn't an issue but for some reason I was being extremely hard on myself about my late start. My plan was to leave at 7:00 a.m. but I didn't get away until 7:45 and was bashing myself like I was some kind of slug. "Damn!" I whispered. "You plan on leaving at seven. Why can't you make it happen? It's not that tough." The criticism continued as I pedaled down the road huffing and puffing about my slack nature and my inability to set a goal and carry it out. "How much more opportunity could a person have? Good parents, nice house, good neighborhood, friends, private high school, paid-for college, but look at us, thirty-three years old, single, basically unemployed, alone, and riding a bicycle in Wichita, Kansas!" I was fuming, "If only you had been able to make good decisions maybe life would be different right now. Maybe you wouldn't have given up on tennis. Maybe you would have a life. Maybe you could get your butt out of bed on time!"

Eventually the venom emptied out and I experienced some sense of release and satisfaction that it was over. Concluding the session and flowing almost naturally from my lips were the words of various scripture verses: "Who will save me from this body of death? Jesus Christ my Lord." "I no longer call you slaves but friends." "God sent his Son not to condemn the world but to save it." "I will never leave you or forsake you." As the miles rolled by the negative emotions gradually gave way to thoughts such as, "Cast your cares on him because he cares for you." And, "A broken heart, O God, you do not despise." The condemning thoughts diminished and I thanked God for Jesus my friend and the Holy Spirit my comforter.

The rest of the morning was spent enjoying the ride and thinking about the red Canondale touring bike I saw in the bike shop when I got my bike fixed. It was almost identical to one I had wanted to ride on the trip but couldn't because it was too expensive. The owner of the shop in Wichita offered to give me the one in his showroom to finish my trip but I gratefully turned him down. I guess it would have made for a good story but I had become attached to my bike and didn't want to let her go now. I thought about writing the owner of the shop when I got home and see what kind of deal he would make with me on it.

About 10:30 as I cruised along enjoying the beautiful blue sky and nice wide shoulder of Highway 96 towards Chanute, suddenly a large camper rattled by with a flat rear tire flapping, smoking, and flinging loose rubber to my side of the road. A large hunk flew off just missing my face. "What the hell!" I shouted. Do these people even know what's going on? All I need is a hunk of hot rubber smacking me on the side of my face.

Up the road a ways I came upon the group pulled over in the emergency lane with a few other cars lined up behind and people huddled around while someone worked on the tire. I pulled alongside to say hello and they quickly apologized for the flinging rubber. The whole family—grandparents, mom, dad, teenagers, and friends—were off for a week of camping and this was not part of their plan. After talking for a while about my trip they offered to meet me up the road a few miles for lunch. They knew of a good place about six miles up the road in Beaumont and would meet me there when they finished changing the tire. Sounded like a plan to me, so off I went.

About five miles up the road I saw signs for Beaumont but didn't see anything that resembled a town except for a small gas station near the highway. As I passed by I noticed one of the cars from the camping caravan parked in the gravel by the front door so I pulled in. They had had a problem with their spare and were getting it fixed. They decided it would be a while before they would be back on the road so we agreed to meet in Severy about seventeen miles further up. The station guy suggested a great diner right off the highway. The question was could I cover the seventeen miles before they could fix the tire, put it back on the trailer, and drive to Severy? Removing my shirt to keep it from getting wet from the workout, I took off, feeling ready for a good challenge. Right out of Beaumont the road began to dip slightly and I was flying. I thought if I could make it in less than an hour I would beat them. The plan seemed to be on track until the terrain changed to hills and the sprint turned into real work, their caravan passing me about three miles outside of Severy, everyone waving cheerfully out of the window. My two favorite mottos, "Winning isn't everything, it's the only thing," and, "Second place is the first loser," shot through my mind but this time I found a way to laugh it off.

Jones family & friends

My new friends were waiting for me in the parking lot of the country restaurant when I rolled in. Granddad was checking the oil in his pickup truck so I hung outside with him trying to cool down a little before going inside in the AC with the rest of the bunch. The last thing I wanted was to sit in a cold restaurant with a sweaty, wet T-shirt. After a few minutes lightly flapping my shirt across my body in a semi air-dry attempt, we went inside and joined the group.

Two tables had been pulled together to accommodate the group and I sat at the end with the teenagers feeling like part of the family and talking openly about our mutually shared Christian faith. They were from Wichita and loved the Christian radio station I had listened to while cruising around in my Honda getting my bike fixed. We talked about high school, graduation, jobs, and living the Christian life in a teen culture of parties and having the nicest car. After a huge country meal and a great time laughing together we all went outside for a picture by the family boat and our final good-byes. Not used to such a huge lunch, I felt like hopping in the camper and napping the rest of the way to Chanute, but that not being an option we said our good-byes and headed on down the road at different speeds.

Somewhere along the way the road had narrowed considerably and the once-wide shoulder had been reduced to about eighteen inches of safe space on the right side of the white stripe with the edge of the asphalt sloping off at a forty-five-degree angle a foot higher than the dry, sandy, ground below. There literally was no way to pull off the road without stepping off of the asphalt slope into the sand and weeds. So with the afternoon sun beating down on my post-lunch, groggy body I felt confined to my thin roadway and sentenced to continue riding until a suitable pull-off showed up. As I methodically trudged along a car approached from the opposite direction and a lady waved out of her window at me. Caught by surprise at her friendly gesture I quickly lifted my right hand from the handlebar to wave back and lost my balance, steering the bike toward the edge of the road and teetering on the slope and trying not to go over the drop off. Flexing my muscles and trying to lean away from the slope I thought I had regained control when my back tire slid off the edge and down the slope, fishtailing the back end around and pointing the bike out into the highway. I thought for sure I was going down but by some miracle I kept my balance, steering the bike across my lane and over the center stripe into the opposite lane before gaining control and steering back to my side of the road. With my heart beating audibly in my chest and adrenaline racing through my entire body, I tried to continue pedaling normally and regain my composure as sweat dripped from my face and my right leg shook uncontrollably. To make matters worse, glancing down at the road I noticed my rear wheel wobbling from the hit.

Still confined to my narrow riding space, there wasn't anything to do but keep riding and pray for a place to pull off and rest. Stopping in the sand and weeds in the heat with no shade and no place to sit was not even a consideration; at least while I was moving I had a breeze. Even in the trauma I rolled along thanking God for sparing me the wipeout and from being mangled by traffic. What grace. What divine intervention. Maybe even an angel or two. Oh, God, did I feel thankful.

Just ahead on the left I noticed some big shade trees with a small picnic table underneath. As I pulled off the highway into the paved drive I noticed a small church set back among the trees along a river bank. I felt as if I had found the Garden of Eden. I went straight to the table, took off my shoes and socks, and flopped down on one of the side benches like a rag doll, exhausted.

After some unknown amount of time I was startled out of a deep sleep by the buzzing sound of a weed whacker but remaining somewhat comatose and unable to move, I continued napping. At some point the engine stopped and I awakened to the presence of the operator who had walked up to say hello. "Sorry to disturb you," he said, in a genuine and friendly tone. "My name is John." At first I figured he was a member of the church just taking care of the grounds but after we talked a while, I learned he was the pastor, trimming the grounds and cleaning up around the building he and some of the members had built. He also was a biker and knew there wasn't a bike shop anywhere nearby that could fix my wheel. The shop he used was totally in the wrong direction. After a pleasant visit, I decided to hit the road, asking him to pray that I might find someone in Chanute to help me fix my bike.

The rest of the ride was spent in quiet thought and prayer, giving my situation to the Lord and asking that his will be done. I felt totally at his mercy and pretty much at peace. Entering Chanute I pulled alongside a pay phone outside a mini-mart gas station and called Fr. Harold Payne, the Episcopal priest who had agreed to put me up. Next to the phone was a man cleaning the interior of his car who stood up and began asking questions about my trip. His name was Reverend Brown, the Methodist minister in town, who had always wanted to take an adventurous bike trip but wasn't sure about going solo. Without going into detail about my day, I encouraged him to seek the Lord and maybe try a group if that's what he wanted to do. No way was I going to gloss over what I was doing and recommend it to anyone.

Reaching Fr. Payne I scribbled down directions to his house and strolled on over. He welcomed me like an old friend and after accompanying me in unloading my gear and putting away my bike, showed me to my little guest room where I showered off 100 miles of sweat and road dirt, emerging refreshed and very thankful to be safe in the comforts of a home. Inquiring about my appetite, Harold suggested we go to his favorite Chinese restaurant where the portions "are always more than one person can eat." I proved him wrong as we sat and talked while he marveled at how much sweet and sour pork one person could consume. After a quick tour of the town we drove back to the house and talked until my eyes started drooping. Unable to fight it, I excused myself and staggered to my room and poured myself into bed, instantly passing out for the night, so thankful that tomorrow was Sunday, a much-needed day of rest.

Day 30
Sunday, August 6, 1990
Chanute, KS

Sabbath Rest

It's amazing what a little bike ride can do to help one understand the word "Sabbath." I woke up Sunday morning from such a deep sleep I literally could not remember where I was. As I looked around my little room and the fog began to clear, the pieces came together – Harold's house, Chanute, Kansas. Next, my senses woke up and I began to feel how tight every muscle in my body was as I stretched, twisted, and yawned, trying to loosen the lactic acid and get some blood flowing through my exhausted cells. The emotional and physical relief from not having to get back on the road could not have been more comforting. Other than going to church, the only thing on my mind was getting my bike fixed.

Placing my feet on the floor and slowly pushing myself upright, I stretched to the ceiling before moving slowly to the bathroom to wash up. Harold had been up and was waiting in the kitchen, ready to begin preparing his special French toast. After a friendly breakfast together in the sunny kitchen nook by the window we put the dishes in the sink and headed for church.

Arriving early, as pastors normally have to do, Harold went about his pre-service duties as I hung around by the front door talking to a few early birds. One of them was a young man who looked to be in his twenties but intellectually acted much younger. At first I thought he was mentally retarded but as we talked he shared the tragic story behind his mental handicap.

One night, as a normal, vibrant teenager he was riding around on his motorcycle with his girlfriend. They were flying down some dark back road when he lost control and wiped out in a ditch. They were both hurled through the air, crashing through a fence and landing in the woods unconscious. A passing motorist found them and called the ambulance. The boy lay in the hospital in a coma for a year before coming to. Through the incident he had lost most of his memory and basically had to start life over. He seemed to be making reasonable progress given the circumstances and was grateful to God for being alive and able to go to church. I felt grateful just listening to the story as this young man struggled to construct thoughts and sentences that otherwise would have been easy for a person half his age.

During the church service my mind wandered from the day before when I could have been a bug on someone's windshield, to the night in junior high when I went racing around the neighborhood on a girlfriend's brother's dirt bike when her parents were out for the night. Once again I recalled the famous line, "There, but for the grace of God, go I." The other thought floating around was what to do about my bike; I couldn't ride the next day with my wheel wobbling from my near wipeout.

After church a man approached me and started asking about my trip. In the course of the conversation I

Fr. Harold Payne

made sure to tell him about my near wipeout and need for repair work. "Do you know about Mr. Elder?" he asked, with an excitement in his voice. "He used to have the bike shop in town where everybody got their bikes before the store closed down. I think he still lives in town, does repairs at his house. If he's home," the messenger from God concluded, "he just might be able to help you out."

As soon as Harold and I got home from church I looked up Arnold Elder in the phone book and gave him a call. I held on to the receiver, praying that he would answer. "Hello," a male voice answered. "Hello," I replied, in nail-biting anticipation, "is this Arnold Elder's home?" "Yes," the soft-spoken voice replied, "this is Mr. Elder." My insides felt like busting into back flips as I tried to restrain myself and explain my story in a way that he might consider worthy of his immediate attention. "Hi Mr. Elder, my name is Joseph Martin and I'm a youth minister from Pennsylvania riding my bike across the country and a man at church this morning said you might be able to help me out." So went my introduction followed by an explanation of my rear wheel problem. "Is there any way you could take a look at my bike today?"

"Well," he said with hesitation, as I held my breath, "I'm going out for the afternoon but if you want to drop it by now I'll look at it when I get back. Will that work?" "Yes sir," I said, "whatever works for you." What I was really thinking was more like, "Yahoo! You're the best, I love you! I'm leaving right this second!" After a few quick directions since he was only a few blocks away, I hung up, told the good news to Harold, raised my hands in victory, and headed over to Mr. Elder's house.

He was a delightful man and seemed confident that he could fix my wheel as long as the rim didn't need to be replaced. He told me how another cross-country biker had come through needing a wheel and the only one available was a near fit off one of Mr. Elder's old bikes hanging in the garage. He fixed the biker up good enough to get him down the road to a bike shop that had what he needed. The biker carried his old wheel with him to the next town, got it fixed and left Mr. Elder's wheel in the shop for them to mail back. The biker was amazed that Mr. Elder would trust him enough to send him off with a nice wheel but that was the kind of man Mr. Elder was, and the wheel got mailed back. He told me to call him later that afternoon. Walking home through the quiet neighborhood I thanked God for his absolute goodness.

Arriving back at Harold's house, I grabbed my Bible and spent the afternoon on the front porch reading and thinking about life. Harold joined me at some point and we talked about the Episcopal Church, religious ceremony, and lukewarm faith. He wasn't as critical or alarmed about the situation as I was, but I had become used to that. My spiritual fervor was on hyper drive and I couldn't expect everyone to rev up to my 24/7 monastic life. Most people would be waking up tomorrow for another typical Monday morning thinking about the normal concerns and demands of the day, not riding a bike meditating on God all day. "Even still," I said to Harold, "a Sunday church experience focused on the God of the Bible doesn't seem to be asking too much."

I called Mr. Elder around four o'clock and he said my bike was ready. Walking down the quaint neighborhood sidewalk under a beautiful sunny sky I felt like skipping and singing like a school kid as my gratitude and total wonder over God's involvement in this situation overtook my emotions. As I approached

The great Arnold Elder

Mr. Elder's one-story house with a well-kept lawn, shade trees, and walkway to the front door I wanted to pinch myself. It seemed too good to be true. But it was true. I knocked on the door and Mr. Elder came out and led us across the lawn to the garage where he fixed bikes and also did wood-working. Along with tools and bike parts, hanging by thin black strings on the pegboard above his work bench were a variety of Christian symbols he had cut out of wood and made into necklaces. They were hints of a Christian faith that became more evident as we talked about his life and some of the struggles he had been through lately. I could have talked with him all day. When the time came for me to leave I asked him if I could have the fish necklace with the cross cut out of the middle. I offered to pay him for it but I knew he wouldn't accept my money. He handed me the wooden fish with the thin black rope and I slipped it over my neck right there and dropped it inside my shirt. He also didn't charge me for the repair. We went out in his front yard and I took a picture of him next to my bike under a large shade tree. After another sincere thank you, I pedaled off slowly, turning back to wave as he stood in the yard. I think we both knew there was something providential about our encounter.

Harold had invited a young couple from the church over for dinner and after a wonderful home-cooked meal made with vegetables out of Harold's garden and some more friendly conversation I hit the sack, floating on a cloud of God's goodness.

Day 31

Monday, August 7, 1990

Chanute, KS to El Dorado Springs, MO

90 miles

7:20 a.m. - 5:30 p.m.

From Harold to Hades

The morning was surprisingly cool as I pulled out of Harold's driveway and made my way toward Route 39 out of Chanute, my bike rolling perfectly and my brain surprisingly clear for a Monday morning. Inside my shirt hung the wooden fish reminding me of Mr. Elder and my astounding stay in Chanute.

Crossing a bridge over the Neosho River I came upon some road construction where the two-lane road had been reduced to one with the traffic alternately passing through at the instruction of the sign holders. As I approached the checkpoint traveling along with the other cars in my lane, the female sign holder turned the sign around and gave me the "STOP" side. Normally the right front fender of a car would be stopped where I was, making a comfortable distance between the driver and the sign holder, but there we were, standing right next to each other, hardly able to ignore our awkward closeness as we waited for the other cars to come through. "Good morning," I said, trying to start a simple conversation. The kind of conversation all female construction workers have with bikers at 7:30 in the morning. "Good morning," she replied back, in a surprisingly sweet and friendly tone, her brown eyes and pleasant smile displaying a cuteness not at all deterred by the hard hat and orange vest. Her day was just getting started and she wasn't too excited about standing eight more hours in the hot sun turning a sign back and forth and I couldn't blame her. Standing up all day, breathing construction dirt, and getting eyed up by every guy that passed by wouldn't seem like a female dream job, but it was all she could find at the time. We talked a little about my ride until the oncoming traffic passed by and it was time to turn the sign around to "SLOW" and let me pass. I asked her name and said I would pray she finds a job that fits her style a little better.

When I got to the other end of the construction I passed another cute girl holding a sign and my mind started churning. What were two cute girls doing holding traffic signs at a construction site? "Was that a sexist question?" I thought. Would I date a female construction worker even if I found her attractive, or would a nicely dressed corporate woman be a better candidate? Of course I leaned toward the nicely dressed corporate girl, at least that's what I always thought, but why? Who set the categories? As I left the construction site and rolled through the peaceful back roads I prayed that God would someday bring me the woman of his choosing.

The morning passed by peacefully as I traveled under green, shady trees on a peaceful, two-lane back road. Along the way I approached a simple, black-and-white "Train Crossing" sign with a lonely track cutting across the road and disappearing into the woods in both directions. The scene was so Disney-like I had to stop on the tracks and stare down the rails as they disappeared into the woods just to try and capture the moment in my mind. Pushing off and pedaling a few strokes I turned around to get one last look; it was just too perfect to leave behind.

Around noon the fantasy ride ended as my two-lane back road reconnected with Highway 54 entering Fort Scott and my tour through Wonderland abruptly turned into a stint in the Demolition Derby. The sudden change in intensity caused such a shock to my nervous system that I decided to pull into a Wendy's for some peace. Stepping inside the quiet refuge I ordered a single with everything and a large iced tea and sat down at a little table by the window where I could watch my bike. Just as I settled in an elderly lady walked by my right elbow carrying her yellow tray, immediately followed by undoubtedly the most beautiful girl in Kansas. Trying not to gawk as she walked by, I turned my gaze to the window and stared at the traffic to refocus my mind. "Thank goodness they're sitting behind me," I thought. I didn't want them to see my jaw hanging open. But just knowing she was back there made it hard to concentrate on my food. Pretty soon they left and I stayed another hour watching traffic and trying to get motivated to tackle Highway 54 to El Dorado Springs.

"At least my housing is covered," I thought, as I forced my exhausted body back on the bike, recalling how miraculously my contact had worked out. Back in San Diego before the trip began I had been at a Fourth of July party where some people were asking me about my route and out of the hundreds of towns I would be passing through I for some reason mentioned El Dorado Springs. One of the guys in the conversation spoke up, "El Dorado Springs? I know everybody in El Dorado Springs! I worked in a body shop there for years and my mom and dad still live there." We all laughed and had a good time with the coincidence and then the guy gave me his dad's name and phone number and said he would let him know I would be calling when I came through.

While in Chanute I had called Mr. Mitchell in El Dorado Springs and told him I would be coming through on Monday and asked if he could put me up for the night. He hesitated for a while saying that he lived twelve miles off the highway but then agreed for me to call him when I got to town and he would meet me at the highway.

That was the only spark of hope I had as I approached the town. Other than that, the closer I got to the city limits the more and more uncomfortable I felt.

The heat was suffocating, the drivers violent and rude, and even the scenery was offensive. An eighteen wheeler thundered by so close I could touch its wheels, blasting his horn and about blowing me off the road. Next, a rusted-out, blue pickup truck roared by with the passenger hanging his head out the window shouting four-letter instructions about getting off the road, and one driver went so far as to turn around after one pass from behind and swerve right at me head on from the opposite direction, giving me the finger and shouting some form of inbred, incomprehensible dialect as he drove by.

Still a ways to go

By the time I reached a traffic light at the edge of town I was convinced the place was literally a stronghold of the devil. I pulled into a Quickie Mart gas station and sighed in relief to be off the road. Practically wobbling inside, I called Mr. Mitchell in hopes of getting out to his place as soon as possible and being treated like a human being.

Using the phone inside the store I knew the girl behind the counter was listening as I talked to Mr. Mitchell who, much to my utter astonishment, weakly explained that his wife was working late that night and he was scheduled to work as a volunteer at some club he belonged to and it just wasn't possible for me to stay at their house tonight. "Maybe next time," he said, sounding as if he wanted to end the conversation before he had to make up any more excuses. Dumbfounded and too shell-shocked to make a response, I slumped against the phone in silence, searching for words. I didn't know what to say. Thoughts raced through my mind, "Maybe next time?! There may not be a next time! I might not get out of this stinking town alive." Frustrated and deflated I squeezed out the words, "Thank you very much," and politely hung up.

The girl behind the counter tried to act like she wasn't paying attention but as I got up and went over to ask for a phone book she gave me a deer in the headlights look that said, "I've never heard anything like this before." I took the phone book and looked in the yellow pages under "Churches" and decided to look for an Assembly of God Church. I had never been a member of an Assembly church but my experience at their services told me I could at least find committed Christians there. I found a listing but at six o'clock on a Monday evening thought it would be a miracle to find anybody there to answer the phone. Before I dialed I asked the girl if she knew where this particular church was and she said it was just a few blocks off the highway not far from the store. I dialed the number and waited. One ring, two rings, then, much to my surprise a man answered. Surprised by his voice I tried to introduce myself and explain my situation without sounding like a vagrant.

He was the pastor and just happened to be working late but was on his way out the door. I could tell he was skeptical as any pastor who gets calls regularly from transients looking for free food and money would be, but after a few questions and some conversation he said he would wait for me to ride over and would pray about what he could do. Hanging up the phone I smiled and said good-bye to the girl who, by now, was at a total loss.

I followed the directions easily enough and pulled around to the church office. The pastor greeted me at the door and immediately I knew he would help. It wasn't the first time that I had met people with genuine faith in Jesus and our spirits connected. Pastor Dana and I were about the same age and from the start we just clicked.

The church had recently bought an old house nearby that they planned to use for emergency housing for displaced or needy families after they fixed it up but it wasn't ready for use. Even still, Dana seemed convinced that my situation was just what they had in mind and I could be the first occupant. So, digging through a supply closet, he gathered up some sheets and a blanket and off we went, he driving slowly and me following the short distance close behind. Pulling into the gravel-and-grass driveway alongside the heavily shaded little farmhouse and walking around to the overgrown backyard, it appeared the place had been vacant for a while. Unlocking and pushing on the sticky back door confirmed the look. The inside was a cluttered mess; but the cleanup had begun and at least one bedroom was cleared out enough to see the floor, and the water and electricity were both in service, a lot more than I had an hour before.

Dana had to get home to his family and offered to bring me back dinner if I wanted, but I had seen a Pizza Hut near the mini-mart where I used the phone so I told him I would just go there and save him the trouble. He agreed and said he would drop by later to see how I was doing.

After a nice shower in the musty, rust-stained bathroom I put on my civilian shorts and my next day's riding shirt and walked toward the big red roof. It was kind of a long walk but I was so happy to have my housing taken care of and a sense of belonging affirmed by Dana's kindness, I enjoyed the stroll. At seven thirty in the evening the temperature was pleasant and I didn't have a worry in the world. At seven thirty it also had been a long time since that Wendy's single back in Fort Scott and I was ready to chow down. For some reason I had a craving for anything with red sauce and when I walked in the door my mouth actually began to water. After a couple of large plates of the All You Can Eat Spaghetti deal along with garlic bread and multiple trips to the salad bar, the craving was satisfied and I strolled back to the farmhouse completely content.

Probably not much profit for Pizza Hut on their $4.99 special that night.

The sun had set and the sky was turning dark by the time I completed the slow walk back to Green Acres, ready to hit the sack. Dana came by on his motorcycle and we talked and prayed together like longtime buddies. I told him about my demonic experiences coming into town and he was not surprised at all. He had experienced the strong spiritual warfare going on in El Dorado Springs and was burning out in his ministry trying to fight it. None of the mainline churches in town seemed to have a clue what he was talking about and he felt alone in his struggle. After we prayed together, he took off and I got ready for bed.

My room had a 1970s vintage, brown-vinyl waterbed with a wood stained frame made of 2 x 12-inch boards that took up half the floor and at first glance looked promising -- until I climbed in. With low water and no heater my butt hit the floor and the icy cold vinyl enveloped my body and sloshed around in a way that redefined the word misery. I decided to spread the sheets on the same vintage carpeted floor and try to get comfortable but just couldn't fall asleep, dozing off into some semi-conscious state at some unknown hour of the night. This uncomfortable state lasted until I was awakened by a noise somewhere in the house that perked me up and caused me to lie there motionless in my now moonlit room, listening intently for another sound. When the tiny noise squeaked again my heart started pounding and I quietly reached for the tire pump from my bike which I had rolled into my room for security. Then, armed with pump in hand, I quietly sneaked through the hallway toward the back door where I thought the noise was coming from.

The drab, unfurnished rooms gave me the creeps as I crept along the walls and made my way through the kitchen to the back door. Of course, lurking in my mind were visions of some Freddie character busting out of the pantry with a long kitchen knife to slice me up but, rebuking such thoughts and praying under my breath, I made my way to the back door. Reaching for the old, round doorknob, I confirmed that the door was locked just as I had left it. Feeling relieved, I peered through the back door glass at the gently blowing trees and my shower-washed clothes waving eerily on the clothes line. This night could not end soon enough.

Back in my room I became so sick of the situation I wanted to pack up and leave right away but decided riding at night was not a good idea. With no other option, I laid down and dozed off on the hard floor waiting for the sun to come up. At the first hint of sunlight, I got up and wasted no time packing and getting on the road. Rolling my bike out the back door and into the overgrown backyard, I prayed for Dana Taylor as I made my escape from El Dorado Springs as quickly as possible.

The Longest Day

Not surprisingly, the road heading out of El Dorado Springs was as big a pain as the town itself. In my anxious fury to flee for my life, I left without eating or filling up my water bottles and soon found myself on a narrow, truck-infested, two-lane highway with about twelve inches of paved shoulder barely wide enough to keep me off the road. The heavy truck traffic rumbling past my left elbow became so intense I had to pull over after a few miles and reconsider my route. Actually, I wasn't supposed to be on this road in the first place. In my original route submitted to the California AAA, Highway 54 through El Dorado Springs had not been recommended. The prescribed route had me exiting Highway 54 after Fort Scott, bypassing El Dorado Springs on a small, winding, back road away from the main highway. At the outset of the ride I had decided to stay on 54 after Fort Scott because it was a straight shot and would save some time. Now, after a night from hell and an early morning barrage of nerve-twisting trucks, I was rethinking that decision.

Actually, there was not much to think about. Highway 54 had not been recommended for obvious reasons and what I needed to do was get off as soon as possible and connect up with the prescribed route. Shortcuts usually look better on paper than in real life and in this case my shortcut was about to kill me. I slowed to a stop and walked my bike off of the pavement into the sandy shoulder far enough away from the traffic to look at my map.

Road K toward Roscoe looked like my best shot. A short distance ahead I reached the sleepy side road, waited for an opening in the traffic, and bolted across, feeling as though I had busted through the wardrobe in Narnia to another world. In an instant, the trucks, noise, and stress ceased, and in its place, trees, peace, and contentment, as my anxiety level dropped and my whole body relaxed in the new scenery. Up the road a little way a herd of wild turkeys scampered across the road right in front of me and disappeared into the woods. Now we were back on track.

The only problem with the peaceful back road was the fact that I hadn't eaten, filled my water bottles, or gone to the bathroom. After covering fifteen miles the little farmhouses scattered along the woods started to look inviting as I imagined nice elderly couples sitting around round, wooden, kitchen tables enjoying crisp bacon and steamy pancakes, sipping coffee and reading the newspaper. Surely they wouldn't mind a visitor. Passing by a particularly cozy-looking farmhouse I pictured a little old lady stepping out of the side door in her apron, waving me in for breakfast. Other than that, my hope rested on Roscoe, a little dot of a town five miles ahead, that I pictured would have one of those hometown diners with a parking lot full of pickup trucks and plenty of local folks inside packing in lumberjack specials.

So much for my hope in Roscoe; the place didn't exist. I'd have to keep riding another ten miles to Osceola, and hope it had something. Which it did— a mini-mart gas station—and that was it. But I didn't want packaged factory food with a one-year shelf life. I wanted cooked food. Something that was alive sometime within the last year. I asked the woman at the counter if she knew of a diner near by. "There might be one up the road," she said, pointing out the plate glass window, "but I'm not sure he's still open." With dehydration setting in and low blood sugar, my first thought was, "How could you not know? There's nothing else in this town but a mini-mart and maybe a diner. It's not like one of the five diners across town might have closed." Thankfully I kept my thoughts to myself. As a consolation, I grabbed a bottle of OJ and a bag of peanuts and sat outside on a wooden bench to ponder my situation.

Okay, I had strayed off course, and yes, I had left El Dorado Springs in haste without thinking about food for the day. I messed up. Now I was trying to get back on track. "Please Lord," I confessed, "I've strayed again. Please get me out of this jam." A verse came to mind reminding me that there is "no condemnation for those who are in Christ Jesus." A comforting thought settled in and I decided to fill my water bottles and hit the road.

After ten more miles of back road, I came to a fork in the road. The map said I was in Harper just as it said I'd been in Roscoe but the town didn't exist. The only sign of life was a small, white, one-room schoolhouse, sitting in the grass in the middle of the fork with a few ladies standing by a car in front. We looked at each other curiously as I approached and since they seemed like a nice bunch I decided to pull into the grass and say hello. Actually, I wanted more than to say hello. It was almost noon and I hadn't really eaten since the Pizza Hut the night before and I was famished.

"Hello there," I said, rolling into the grass and trying to appear as harmless as possible. "Do you ladies know of a restaurant anywhere nearby?" As they discussed the issue among themselves, my options sounded pretty dismal. As kind of a last option, one lady said they could fix me a tomato sandwich inside if I wanted.

My first thought was to politely decline, thinking, "That's nice of these friendly folks to offer me a tomato sandwich but I've got some serious food needs here," but hearing a sensible voice I accepted the offer for a tomato sandwich. They invited me inside the little schoolhouse and explained that it was Election Day and they were monitoring the voting booths all day and since there weren't any stores close by they had plenty of food. To my mouth-watering amazement, the menu of tomato sandwich turned into homemade wheat bread, cheese, cold cuts, Fritos, fruit, breakfast sweet rolls, lemonade, homemade cookies, and watermelon. They shared it all with me and seemed to get a thrill out of my appetite as we talked and greeted the few locals who dropped by to vote. The atmosphere was so friendly and relaxing I thought about staying the rest of the day, or the week if someone had asked me, but it was time to move on. Stepping outside we took a picture on the front porch of the schoolhouse and I pedaled off on road U, stuffed to the gills and in total awe of God's mercy and provision. Another five miles and I'd be back on my prescribed route.

Without a place to stay for the night and no contacts anywhere nearby I decided to keep on Road U until I reached Route 66 and stay on my prescribed route until something showed up. After my feast in Harper my faith level was high and the housing issue didn't worry me at all. I would enjoy the ride and trust God that things would work out.

The first test of that confident attitude came about two miles down the road when I came upon a road construction crew laying tar and gravel over both lanes of the road. With fresh gravel covering the road I thought about turning back and finding another route toward Highway 66 but was so determined to get back to the prescribed route and stay on it, I decided to push on. Just to

Voting is good

make sure I asked a guy on the road crew if the tar was dry enough for me to ride over and he shrugged with a "shouldn't be a problem" reply. With only about a half mile of new road to cover I considered walking in the high grass by the ditch but didn't want to waste the time so I made the plunge. And what a plunge it was. The heat had kept the tar wet and as I rolled over the sticky surface little globby rocks stuck to my tires and flung all over my bike, my socks, my chain, and the back of my shirt. My anger boiled with each pedal rotation and every pinging sound of rocks hitting my bike frame until I was steaming. When I couldn't take it any longer I dismounted and walked in the high grass, carrying my bike on my right shoulder.

By the time I reached a dry section of road and a place to sit in the grass to pick the rocks out of my sprockets, my lunchtime high had evaporated into thin air. As I wove around lakes and multiple campgrounds seemingly going in circles without making any easterly headway, the faith high had turned to dust and I was ready to call it a day. The late afternoon sun still gave me plenty of daylight to push on but when I came upon a campground with lots of kids and camp counselors swimming and having a good time, I pulled in, thinking they might welcome a fellow youth worker and put me up for the night. It was only three o'clock in the afternoon but after the night I had had I figured a little swim and recreation might be fun and maybe I could meet some friendly people. Boy was I wrong. The camp director was away for a couple of hours and the counselors were as cold as the popsicles they were sucking on; not even a friendly conversation; we're talking a complete stiff arm. Having been a camp counselor myself I felt totally frustrated that they wouldn't receive me but there was nothing I could do. Shaking the dust off my feet, I hit the road in search of hospitality.

A few miles ahead I came to a fork in the road and in my frustration over the windy back roads and personal rejection I decided to head toward the main highway instead of continuing through the boon docks. I reached Highway 65 in a town called Warsaw and headed north. Even though I had broken my pledge and left my route I was determined to keep riding until God provided the right place to stay.

Immediately the tension of highway riding was back. Highway 65 had practically no shoulder and tons of speeding trucks making for the most intense riding so far. In some places the pavement crumbled off into rocks and weeds right on the edge of the white stripe. Every time a car or truck blew by I squeezed the handle grips and flexed every muscle in my body. On one occasion I looked in my handlebar rearview mirror and took note of an eighteen wheeler barreling down on me from behind. Looking ahead I noticed cars approaching in the oncoming lane ahead. Doing some instant calculations, for the first time during the trip I felt an extreme urge to get off the bike and get out of the way. Quickly braking and swinging my leg over the seat, I grabbed the bike and hopped off the road into the gravel. The car approached in the other lane and the truck roared by with his wheels covering the stripe where I had been riding. My knees went weak; I was stunned. I cried out, "Lord I've done it again! Please spare my life and find me a place to stay."

Further down 65 I pulled into a truck stop, which basically made up the town of Lincoln. It was five o'clock so I decided to try the church idea for a place to stay. On a billboard advertisement for a church I made note of the pastor's name and called him at home. He said he was supposed to be on vacation and would like to help but didn't want his congregation to know he was home. Huh? I didn't know what to say.

Five miles later I exited 65 and headed east on a small gray road toward Cole Camp. I pulled into a little neighborhood gas station and hung out, talking to the manager and hoping something would come up. After about an hour of talking and eating free tortilla chips from the Nacho oven, I was still without a place to stay.

By now it was seven o'clock and I had been on the road almost twelve hours. The next big town was Versailles, twenty miles away and even though the math added up to a very grueling day I had no other choice but to go for it. I said good-bye to the station guy and tortilla chips and pushed on.

By the time I hit Stover, ten miles down the road I considered checking into the sleazy motel next to the beer store but the message on the bright yellow portable sign, "Beer Sold on Sundays," and the witch-looking woman standing outside the rundown market across the street, convinced me to move on.

By this time the sun had set behind me as I headed east toward Versailles and through my mirror I noticed the glow of the orange and purple clouds reflecting the sun's colors. Turning around to look at the brilliance I was awestruck by the beautiful display and something inside me came alive and rejoiced in God's handiwork and praised him for his greatness. Turning back around and scanning the lights of the houses in the dark countryside, I felt the strangeness of riding a bicycle down a strange, two-lane highway in the dark without a clue where I was staying for the night hit me head on. Approaching Versailles I passed some nice houses with lights in the windows looking very cozy inside. If only someone would wave me in. It didn't happen.

By the time I pulled into the Conoco station in Versailles it was 9:00 and completely dark. A group of teenagers was hanging around the little store talking with their friend working behind the counter. I asked for a phone book and sat down at a table across from two boys. They asked about my ride as I located an Assembly of God church in the Yellow Pages. The guy behind the counter commented that his girlfriend knew the pastor and volunteered to give her a call. After talking to her on the phone he dialed another number on his store phone and handed me the receiver. A man answered and once again I found myself explaining my situation in the company of strangers who couldn't help but listen. He seemed like a nice guy but given the late-night circumstances and his kids already in bed, he just didn't have a solution. Just as he was ending his apology and about to hang up, he paused for an instant, then perked up with an idea. "You know, there's a place not too far from you called something like 'The Sound of Calvary' or something like that; it's

Sunset leaving Cole Camp

an old school building they've turned into a teen center. I think they even house some boys there. They might be able to help you out." He gave me directions to the school and we said good-bye.

I confirmed the directions with the kids who knew of the place and meandered off into the pitch-black neighborhood. After a little hit-and-miss and some help from an older guy out for a walk, I came upon a huge, dimly lit school building. The front was totally dark so I went around back where a lonely street light lit up the back parking lot. Dim lights shone through the back door window but it was locked.

Sounds of Calvary: Jim, James, & Rick

Looking around I noticed a mobile home in the side yard with some lights on inside. Leaning my bike against the handrail by the short steps, I knocked softly on the door. A lady came to the door and I introduced myself and briefly explained my situation. "Well, you've come to right place," she said without hesitation, explaining their ministry of housing and guidance to young people who needed help getting their lives on track. "Let me get you some sheets and things and we'll get you fixed up." Disappearing for a short time and returning with sheets and a towel under her arm and keys in her hand, she cheerfully introduced herself as Linda as we walked over to the school door I had checked earlier and went inside.

While I was filling out a registration paper, her husband Jim came in with two teenage boys, Mike and Tim, who had been helping him in his auto body shop. A third boy, James, passed through on his way out to work. After a good time of chatting and getting to know one another they showed me the showers and invited me to join them in the kitchen after I got cleaned up. I felt like I had come home. After showering off twelve hours of Missouri, I emerged clean and ready to hang out with the guys. In the makeshift kitchen area with a couple of teenagers, a pastor, and a box of microwave burritos, we made a night of fellowship out of the strange meeting and put a happy ending to a long, mixed-up day.

The friendship was so refreshing I could have talked all night but by midnight my eyelids felt like fishing weights and I told them it was time to call it a night. They congratulated me on setting the record for the most microwave burritos ever eaten in one sitting and showed me to my private room—an entire classroom—sparsely equipped with one bed and a night table placed against the blackboard-covered wall. The opposite side was the typical window-covered wall with all the panels wide open and a cool breeze blowing gently through. As I settled into my cozy single bed staring at the moonlit sky through the wall of windows I realized there might be some significance in my sleeping in a classroom. "Oh God," I prayed. "This is too much. Teach me what I need to know."

Day 33

Wednesday, August 8, 1990

Versailles, MO to Hermann, MO

73 miles

8:00 a.m. - 5:00 p.m.

It Just Never Ends

Going to bed after midnight, after the fourteen-hour marathon, after the El Dorado Springs nightmare made for one tired morning. I just didn't have any get up. After a short prayer time and some stretching I went to the kitchen to see what I might rustle up for breakfast and, not having the energy to make anything, settled for a prepackaged turkey and cheese sandwich from the fridge. James, the guy who passed through on his way to work the night before, had just come home from his graveyard shift and joined me. I'm not sure which one of us was more out of it.

After packing up my bike and rolling it outside into the cool morning air I knocked on Jim and Linda's trailer to say good-bye. They came out and we took a picture and said our farewells. As I got ready to leave I realized my gloves were missing. Jim opened the office where I had registered the night before but no gloves. After searching everywhere with no success we stopped shortly and Jim offered a simple prayer asking God to help us out. During the prayer I got the idea that the gloves were at the Conoco station where I made the phone calls the night before. I wasn't positive but having exhausted all the other possibilities I decided to say my final farewells and head back to Conoco.

Riding without gloves would not be possible. Not only did they pad my hands and keep my fingers from going numb, they also protected the tops of my hands from frying in the sun. I had sunburned them one summer working as a water ski instructor and the gloves were essential, along with my white baseball hat, handkerchief covering my neck, long-sleeve T-shirt, and daily doses of sunscreen and lip gloss to keep me from sizzling.

At the table where I sat the night before and talked with the teenagers were two elderly men drinking coffee and talking about farm prices. I didn't even have the energy to say hello much less engage in any kind of polite conversation so I just smiled and scoped the scene for gloves as I walked by. Nothing.

I walked up to the counter and before I could even ask I saw my faithful companions lying in a box below the register. A sense of relief rushed through my body that perked me up and gave me a boost for starting the day's ride. The nice lady handed me the gloves and off I went.

Feeling relaxed and peaceful I mounted up and headed out in the cool morning air on road C toward High Point. There I would hook up with my prescribed route — and follow it till the end. "So help me God. Amen."

At High Point I pulled off the quiet road and strolled inside a small, rustic country store to get some OJ and celebrate being back on track. The spacious old place with well-worn wooden floors, high ceilings, and large mirror behind the counter was right out of the Old West, except for the Frosted Flakes and Twinkies on the shelves. As I drank my OJ and talked with the lady at the counter she excused herself and returned with a scrapbook of newspaper articles of bikers who had passed through town. A nice article with a happy group shot of the "Wondering Wheels," a well-known biking tour group who had passed through town, caught my attention. What a different scene to be riding with a group of bikers, chatting on the road, and hanging out in the evenings with relaxed meal times and preplanned accommodations. Different from my trip but still encouraging to know I was traveling where other bikers had been before. I paid for the OJ with my next-to-last $20 traveler's check and said good-bye to Jean.

Money had not been an issue so far but now it was. The Matthew 10 scripture where Jesus sent out the disciples and told them not to take gold, silver, or copper in their belts, no bag for the journey, and no extra tunic had inspired my strategy, but now, with $36 left I was thinking more seriously about it.

Around noon, peaceful Road C connected with four-lane Highway 54 into Jefferson City. At a major intersection of 54 and 50 on the outskirts of the city, a huge Assembly of God church with a humongous, black parking lot caught my attention. A church van and two cars were parked along the curb near the big, glass entrance with a few kids and adults milling around so I pulled in. My ongoing need for companionship and conversation had become chronic.

Leaning my bike against the wall next to the glass doors I walked inside and was kindly greeted by two nicely dressed men I assumed were pastors standing in the carpeted lobby. Introducing myself as a youth minister and explaining my trip turned into an easy conversation as they took interest in the trip and shared their own stories of ministry and mission trips. Since lunch time was approaching I thought it would be nice if we could all go to lunch together so I asked if they knew of a good place nearby, thinking they might take me up on the idea. A nice girl walked up and joined the conversation, making the idea even more inviting but no one took the hint, instead giving me directions to "one of the best lunch buffets around." Before heading out I asked if either one had a business card so I could write them when I got home. The younger pastor went to his office and came back and handed me a business card with a folded-up bill underneath that he placed discretely into my hand. "Have a good lunch," Pastor Blondo said, saying the rest with his eyes. Catching a glimpse of the number 20 on one corner, I was speechless. There was no way I could explain to him what that money meant in light of my situation and my stretched faith. I pulled out of the parking lot rejoicing over the faithfulness of God working through his people.

The directions to the Golden Corral led me down a steep hill and into the frantic lunch hour traffic. The only problem was the restaurant was located on "fast food alley," which was a left turn at the bottom of the hill, but the way out of town was to the right. There was no way I was going to take a left turn and fight the hectic traffic in the opposite direction I needed to go and then cross back over the road and come back in the right direction. I turned right and headed toward Highway 94, which took me on a bridge over the Missouri River and away from the food district. Major road construction

Along the Missouri River

had closed one span of the bridge causing me to merge in with the single line of traffic and cross the dusty span pumping like mad and gripping my handlebars with white knuckles six inches from passing cars on my left side and barely missing construction barrels on my right. One clip of a handle bar and I'd either be under a wheel or train wrecked in the construction equipment. When the rush was over the traffic subsided and soon I found myself out of town on peaceful 94 along the banks of the great Missouri River.

The road was wide and flat with trees on the left and soybean fields along the river on the right. The air was even refreshing — what a relief. My nerves were wearing thin from life-threatening city traffic. I grabbed a quiet lunch near Wainwright and relaxed in the little ghost town along the river before pressing on toward Herman. In some of the curves in the river the water cut so close to the high rock mountains there was no room for the road so it had to be routed up and around the hills and back to the other side. Nothing caps off a long day of riding like a few steep mountain climbs. I approached Herman physically exhausted.

Before taking the bridge over to Hermann I decided to pull into a grocery store to get something to drink, relax, and decide my next move. The fact that I didn't have a place to stay for the night somehow hadn't bothered me much during the day but at 5:00 in the afternoon with the sun still beating down on the black asphalt parking lot and heat radiating to about 100 degrees, I was starting to think about calling it a day. Parking my bike right outside the main entrance to the grocery store and quickly grabbing a quart of Gatorade and a nectarine I returned and situated myself right inside the door on a stack of fifty-pound bags of dog food, making myself strategically visible. After a while a lady walked by and, in a kind, comfortable tone struck up a conversation about my ride as if she had some experience with bikers. Then, as if she knew what I was thinking, asked, "So what are your plans for the rest of the day?" Somehow knowing this was my Godsend, I simply told her the truth. "I was just trying to figure that out," I said, giving her the option. Without hesitation she suggested that since she had raised a family of twelve, and only a few still lived at home, there was plenty of room if I wanted to stay for the night. "Uh," I thought, "let me think about that for about one millisecond." She said she needed to grab something in the store and then I could follow her Jeep to their farmhouse just a couple of miles down the road. Waiting for her by the door I was so overwhelmed with joy I was almost laughing out loud.

When she came out she said, "I'm Maxine, by the way." I followed her to her Jeep and then the couple miles to her driveway and up to the rustic-looking, large, farmhouse. What a great old place. She showed me one of the older kid's room who no longer lived there and told me dinner would be ready in about a half an hour. "Towels and soap are in the bathroom." The door shut and I just stood still, gazing at my wood-paneled bedroom with private bath as if it were my own room. How much more could I take? I dropped to my knees and buried my head on the bed.

After a nice long shower I put on my trusty shorts and next day's T-shirt and walked to the kitchen. A couple of young boys showed up and we all sat down to a great feast of grilled hamburgers and all the extras — just like one big happy family. We sat around the table talking about the trip as I politely consumed three hamburgers, baked beans, and everything else the kids didn't eat until the kids got antsy and wanted to go outside. Mr. Witte came home from work and he and I took a walk around the property as I digested the dinner he wouldn't be getting tonight. As soon as the sky grew dark I opted for an early bedtime and we said goodnight. My eyes shut before my grateful and exhausted head hit the pillow.

Day 34

Thursday, August 9, 1990

Hermann, MO to Alton, IL

95 miles

9:30 a.m. - 6:30 p.m.

What Color Do You Want?

Even after a good night's sleep, I woke up in Hermann with glassy eyes and swollen glands, usually my body's way of telling me it was run down and needed more rest. On top of that, when I went to get dressed for the day's ride I couldn't find my second pair of biking shorts.

Looking over my little pile of belongings I realized I hadn't seen them all day during yesterday's ride. Normally, after a day's ride I take my padded shorts into the shower with me and wash them thoroughly and let them hang overnight. The next morning I put on the second pair and strap the wet pair on top of the rear panniers and let them air dry during the morning ride. After they're completely dry I put them inside the panniers ready for the next day. As I pondered the situation I concluded that I had left them hanging in the shower back in Versailles.

Trying to stay calm and trust God in this discouraging situation, I went into the kitchen where Maxine was fixing breakfast. Being as tired as I was and thinking that the ride to Alton would be somewhat easy, I was in no hurry to get on the road. With wet shorts I wasn't sure I wanted to ride at all.

During breakfast Maxine showed me an article in the morning paper about a church group that was bicycling through the area and had stayed overnight at a church in Hermann. She knew where the church was and offered to take me and my bike over there so I could meet the group and maybe ride with them a while if they were going my way. Sounded like a good idea so we loaded up the car and drove over the bridge to Hermann.

A thick fog hovered over the town as we crossed over to the southern side of the Missouri. Maxine knew the town well and explained its history as we took the scenic route to the church. Apparently, during the rise of the great river cities like St. Louis, Cincinnati, and Pittsburgh, the founders of Hermann envisioned their city also growing into a commercial giant. The boom didn't happen and Hermann remained a successful but small German settlement now preserved as a historic tourist community. As we drove up the hill toward the church a part of me regretted not having ridden over the bridge the day before like I had planned. When we pulled up to the church and I saw the kids and leaders milling around the property and loading up their gear in the supply trailer my regret deepened. How cool it would have been to have hooked up with the group the day before. If only I had followed through with my plan and crossed the bridge. Then again, my accommodations had been absolutely perfect and I was thankful for all Maxine had done for me. But the regret persisted. Did God have a better plan and I missed it?

Pulling alongside the church and unloading my bike among the buzz of biking activity, we both knew this meeting was something of a divine intersection. Me, riding across the country from San Diego, a youth group on a week-long trip, crossing paths in Hermann, Missouri. It was so right. Saying our final farewells, Maxine and I hugged and parted company. Once again I felt as if I was saying good-bye to a longtime friend. She drove off and I walked over to meet the group.

In the back of the trailer was a young guy loading the gear who I assumed was the youth minister. He's usually the one rushing around like a maniac while the rest of the crowd mingles about talking and enjoying themselves. I introduced myself and we connected immediately as youth ministers and fellow bikers. As we talked at the back of the trailer surrounded by duffle bags and food supplies a light came on in my head regarding my bike pants dilemma. I explained my situation of leaving my pants back in Versailles and asked if he thought anyone in the group might have an extra pair. He and a few kids standing nearby laughed and said in unison, "He needs to talk to Tom." One of the kids led me over to Tom and I introduced myself and explained my situation. He was one of the pastors of the church and was well known among the kids as "Mr. Biking Gear." By the big smile on his face I could tell he was amused by the problem and offered to help if he could locate his duffle bag. Digging through the pile by the trailer we uncovered the bright blue, mammoth-sized bag and, unzipping the five-foot-long clothes locker, Tom chuckled and asked, "What color do you like?" We all had a good laugh as I chose the blue Canondale pair right near the top. They were his favorite but he was happy to let me use them. He gave me his card and told me to mail them back when I finished my trip. I was ecstatic and immediately excused myself to the bathroom and changed out of my wet pants.

It was about time to ride and the pastors invited me to join them inside the church for their morning devotional and final briefing. Glen, the youth pastor, welcomed me and presented me with one of the group's official T-shirts, "Riding for the deaf and hearing impaired." I told the group about my trip and how God had used them to solve my pants problem and encouraged them to keep the faith. As part of their morning ritual we all put our helmets in a pile and gathered around to ask God for protection during our ride. Since we were traveling in different directions we gathered outside for a picture, said our farewells, and rode off in separate directions, the group with their multiple riders, friendships, conversations, and support vans and me… well, just me.

I headed back over the bridge and caught Highway 94 alongside the Missouri River, cutting peacefully through thick, green soybean and corn fields growing along the river on the right and steep, rocky cliffs with hawks soaring high above the pine trees on the left. Much of the ride was flat and easy, making the travel just right for my groggy physical condition, while the picturesque natural setting provided the perfect backdrop for my

Youth group in Hermann

melancholy emotional state that had drifted into a meditation on the fantasy I was living.

The party ended when the road ran out of riverbank and had to turn up from the flat valley into what had been the scenic mountains on the side. The grade was so steep and long I barely had the strength to climb up. Using the lowest of my eighteen speeds and creeping along slower than a walk, I felt I was on the verge of stopping. Having never in my biking memory given up on a hill, I grabbed hold of my pride, panted prayers through my breath, and labored on each pedal as it came around. Approaching exhaustion but refusing to quit, an idea crossed my mind to begin steering back and forth from one side of the road to the other to give me a break from the constant uphill grind. Every pass across the lanes was as flat as I wanted to make it providing regular intervals of rest until I got to the edge of the road and had to U-turn up and back across. The only drawback was crossing both lanes of the road and having to keep an ear out for approaching traffic. The switchback method continued for each new climb as I made my way to the top of one hill then coasting to the bottom of a new one, only to start the process all over again. The dread of reaching the bottom after a nice coast and having to pedal up another hill felt like a form of torture as I was forced to exert myself and press on when my body absolutely wanted to quit.

When I finally came out of the last set of mountains and the road leveled off I had only covered fifty miles for the day. Thinking I might get a chance to cruise for a while, my bubble quickly burst as my peaceful, two-lane mountain road turned into a congested, four-lane industrial highway connecting Highway 61 with Interstate 70 near St. Charles. The fast-paced traffic and tight curbs required emotional and physical energy I just didn't have and when the tension became unbearable I exited into a mini-mart gas station to get something to drink and let my nerves settle.

Alongside the concrete block building near the metal men's room door a young black boy sat on the curb with a dejected look on his face with his bike lying on the ground in front of his well-worn tennis shoes. "What's going on, big guy?" I asked, feeling sorry for the young guy. "My bike got a flat and it's too far to walk it home."

Identifying with my fellow biker, I chirped out, "Well, what do you say we just fix that flat and get you back on the road?" His eyes lit up as he said with a glimmer of hope, "Can you fix it?" "I think so," I said, "but first let's get something to drink, what do you say?" We went inside and picked out what we wanted, my Gatorade and his Pepsi, then returned to the heat, fixing the flat under the shade of the roof extending from the store over the gas pumps. The job provided a well-needed distraction from the road stress and a long-lost feeling of helping someone and being appreciated. We finished the job and after thanking me and happily vowing "to go to church on Sunday," Deandrea pedaled off on the worn walking path along the side of the highway.

Job over, it was time for me to face the inevitable -- five o'clock, four-lane commuter traffic outside St. Louis – and it was a nightmare, especially the stretch of Highway 94 intersecting Interstate 70. The congested and hectic traffic stampeded by as pushy drivers fought for position on the cracked up, four-lane concrete slab with a twelve-inch asphalt shoulder scattered with rocks, glass, and flattened pop cans. Sucking down exhaust fumes and pumped full of adrenalin I squeezed the handlebars and pedaled machine-like, fixing my eyes intently on the pavement ahead, looking for gaping cracks in the concrete and dodging debris, feeling every car that whipped past. I was beyond my limit. I felt as if my body had kicked into emergency auto pilot with me just along for the ride. It was a zone like I had never experienced in any athletic endeavor and as close to an out-of-body experience I had ever come.

After an immeasurable segment of time I passed through St. Charles and gradually the frenzy subsided. Turning onto road H, a small, two-lane asphalt path cutting through residential homes and farms, I found myself singing, laughing out loud, and talking to animals along the road. It was kind of fun but I felt borderline delirious. After a few miles the high settled down and I pushed along quietly.

My contact for the night was in Alton, Illinois on the east side of the Mississippi River. A few miles before the bridge, in West Alton, I pulled into a gas station to call the Episcopal Church that had agreed to put me up. Coasting into the parking lot, I leaned my bike against the large, glass front of the station and walked inside. A young attendant sat at the desk while a few of his buddies hung out near the door to the garage, shooting the breeze and waiting for quitting time. They were interested in my ride and after talking for a while one of the guys commented that no bikes or pedestrians were allowed on the bridge over to Alton. "That thing is so old and beat up," he said, "some people drive twenty miles down river just so they don't have to drive over it." "Twenty miles," I thought. "There is no way I'm adding forty miles to this day just to get across the river."

I called the church but no one answered. I tried the priest's house and left a message on his answering machine that I was heading to Alton and would try to call again. I didn't see any other option than to go over the bridge. One guy had a pickup truck but backed out of his buddy's suggestion that he drive me over the bridge, so off I went.

As I approached the bridge, sure enough, a sign read, "No Bicycles Allowed on Bridge." Feeling a little guilty about breaking the law but feeling even more desperate about getting across the bridge, I decided to go for it. It was 6:15 and the traffic was moderately low but taking one look at that bridge sent a rush of fear over my entire body. I could not believe my eyes. For a major highway this bridge could not be real. It looked like something from the History Channel before the industrial revolution. I was looking for hoof prints. The two lanes were undivided and narrow, there was no emergency lane, and the guard rail was made out of one row of 2 x 12-inch boards supported by rusty steel poles that wouldn't stop a wagon from going over. The lane was barely wide enough for traffic to get around so I hugged the waist-high rail and pumped as hard as I could. Adrenalin flowed again as I chanted, "Lord help me, Lord help me," in repetitive sequence, one after another. Looking down out of the corner of my eye I could see under the rail to the river below, which looked to be about thirty feet down. One good bump and I literally could tumble under the guard rail to the water below.

A few cars made it around me when the on-coming lane was clear but by the end of the sprint they had decided to follow on my tail until I reached the other side. Crossing the finish line on the other side the road widened and I had room to get out of the way and slow down to catch my breath. My heart pounded and sweat drenched my body as my hands and arms shivered on the handle bars and both legs shook uncontrollably. Pulling over to the side the road and coasting to a stop I tried to gather my senses, standing over my bike and leaning forward on the handlebars, still quivering and dripping with sweat. After ten minutes or so the shaking subsided and I pushed off to find my destination.

I found the Episcopal Church downtown but nobody was there so I pedaled down the street to the police station and sat outside. Across the street I noticed a church with a steady flow of people going inside carrying what looked like Bibles in their arms. Young and old, black and white, they looked like a happy group and I was drawn to them except that they were going inside a Unitarian Universalist Church. Knowing that Unitarians generally don't believe the Bible as Christians do, I wasn't all that eager to go over, but the urge was irresistible so I crossed the street and introduced myself to a young guy walking down the sidewalk. "Excuse me," I asked, "can you tell me what's going on inside?" "Oh, it's just a Bible study for our church," he said in a welcoming tone. Still perplexed I asked, "What kind of church is it?" Realizing my confusion he smiled and happily explained, "Oh, we're a Christian church just using this building." Ta da. Thank you very much. I'm not crazy after all, I thought. He invited to come inside if I wanted so I followed him in.

Inside the lobby area people welcomed me right away and let me use the phone. I left another message on the priest's machine with the phone number of the church. After explaining my situation to some guys who seemed to be about my age, they offered to put me up at their house if nothing came through. We went into the service and sang worship songs and enjoyed a solid teaching on the parable of the Prodigal Son. I was so hungry for lively Christian faith and fellowship I soaked it up like a sponge.

During refreshments after the service someone yelled above the crowd, "There's a phone call for Joseph Martin." It was the priest from the church who told me he had made arrangements for me to stay with a family from the church and they would be right over to pick me up.

I hung out with my new friends until the son of the family showed up and offered to load my bike into his pickup truck. After saying good-bye to the friendly crowd and thanking the guys who offered to put me up we took off and headed out of town for the family home.

Man, did it feel good to sit down and let someone else do the driving. Gus and I talked the whole way home as I watched the scenery go by on our way to their new house, knowing once again I had been placed in good hands. At the house, the family welcomed me like one of their three boys and after showering up in my own room I joined them for a fantastic spaghetti dinner, talking freely and enjoying the divine arrangement. At some point every cell in my body began shutting down and I excused myself for bed.

Day 35

Friday, August 10, 1990

Alton, IL

Family

Not surprisingly, I had decided the night before I would not be riding on Friday. John and Jane Kudros had taken me into their brand-new home and treated me like a family member, giving me free run of their gorgeous house for as long as I needed to recuperate. I thought a year might do it.

View from the Arch

The newly finished house out in the country had all the new smells of carpet and paint along with new appliances, intercoms, and bathroom fixtures. Waking up in my new room, with my new family, and with no pressure to ride felt like a vacation. After a splash on my face in the new sink and a little stretching, I headed down stairs for a typical breakfast of everything I could find in the kitchen followed by a little lounging on the couch in the large family room. Gus and a friend showed up and we spent some time outside talking and throwing the Frisbee barefoot in the green grass next to the pond on the spacious side property.

That evening John and Jane invited me to join them for dinner in downtown St. Louis along the newly renovated river walk area. Sitting in a nice restaurant and being served by polite and professional waiters never felt so good, or so strange. The feeling of being out of step with normal life hovered over the whole experience, making me super-conscious about my surroundings. I noticed everything. After dinner, as we walked along the riverfront in the fresh night air toward the Arch I felt like Tarzan among the city people. Did any of the other people walking by feel like an alien or a misfit? How many felt lonely or outcast? I wondered. Could this be how it feels to be a minority? Walking around looking normal

John & Jane

and doing things everyone else is doing but inside feeling like you don't fit? Being a white, middle class American all my life and never having to think about such things, I was struck by the strangeness.

Aside from my alien feelings, the evening out with friendly people doing normal things was a total delight and a great reprieve from the lonely biker routine. I had been on the road for over four weeks now and I think the Kudros realized I needed a pick-me-up.

Arriving home we sat in the living room for a while before I retired to my new room, in the new house, thinking of my new family and wondering if I would ever live like this.

Day 36

Saturday, August 11, 1990

Alton, IL to Olney, IL

120 miles

7:30 a.m. - 7:30 p.m.

More Short Cuts

T he morning air had a taste of coolness in it as I loaded my bike in the pickup and said my final farewells to Jane and my latest adopted home. John drove me back to town and dropped me off at the 76 station on the now-quiet main street where I had come in on Thursday. We passed the intersection where I had pulled over trembling and sweating after pedaling for my life across the worst bridge in Mississippi River history. Now, early on a Saturday morning, the scene was quiet and peaceful.

John stood next to the car as I went through my routine of attaching panniers, pumping tires, and loading water bottles for the day's journey. We didn't talk much about the ride but kept things light, maybe subconsciously avoiding the concern most people have about the ride I was taking. Soon everything was set to go and John said good-bye and headed home, as once again I found myself standing alone with my bike at a strange gas station in a strange town getting ready to take on another day of unknown adventure.

I pushed off under a hazy sky and enjoyed a nice flat ride over the forty miles to Mulberry Grove, a classic Mayberry RFD town. By that time the sun was straight up, signaling lunch time, so I pulled into the little grocery store for some orange juice and raisins to go with my PBJ sandwiches. Checking out at the register, I commented to the lady what a nice town Mulberry Grove was. She accepted my compliment enthusiastically and asked me if I knew about the annual festival happening today. "The stores in town close at noon and everyone goes to the park where we have food booths, music, and even a parade in the afternoon," she stumped, "and you have to try one of the festival's famous pork burgers grilled by the fire department." Let me think, PBJ or grilled pork burgers? "So where's the park, again?" I asked. After all, I wasn't pressed for time and was always open for a little hometown culture, so I followed the lady's directions and pulled into the park. As I walked my bike through the entrance toward the food booths I was quickly accompanied by four young bikeriding boys excitedly asking questions about where was I from, why did I have so many water bottles, all the obvious questions. When I answered that I had biked from San Diego, California, one boy responded in amazement, "You mean you rode your bike all the way from California to come to the festival?!" Obviously the

The good people of Mulberry Grove

festival was a major event and it seemed appropriate that anyone who showed up for the festival did so on purpose, so I cheerfully told him, "Of course, let's go check it out."

As we talked, a jolly man walked by, catching wind of our conversation and finding the idea of someone riding from California to the festival a real knee-slapper. I played along with the spoof, adding that I really rode all that way for the famous pork burgers, which he loved. So much so that he escorted me over to the ice cream booth to get his friend to go find their local newspaper photographer, then led me over to the fire department tent where the pork burgers were grilling and introduced me to the men there, who happily offered me a complimentary pork burger and drink as we shot the breeze. They had a good time with the "riding cross country for a pork burger" story and when the photographer showed up we all gathered around the grill for a picture. They invited me to ride my bike in the parade later on but I felt I needed to get on the road to Olney where the Episcopal church there was expecting me.

Before I left I stopped by the ice cream booth and talked with the friendly ladies and some fine young folks from the Methodist church. The entire experience was uplifting and a large part of me wanted to hang around for the parade but I decided to take off, pulling back onto the main street and pedaling on to Olney.

After another forty hot, flat miles I pulled into a little wooden grocery store tucked neatly under some large shade trees on the side of the lonely highway to get something to drink. Inside, a few local old timers sat around a small table passing time. When I told them where I was heading and the route I was taking they commenced telling me of a shorter route that would save me "a hell of a lot of time." Being hot and exhausted in the middle of the afternoon I was open to anything that would make the day easier so I thanked them for the tip and took off.

Backtracking about a quarter of a mile, I found the "first hard road past the big white house" like they said and turned left. The road was nice and quiet and the riding peaceful. Five miles from that intersection I took another left and found the riding equally pleasant for the next ten miles until the nice hard surface turned into fresh tar covered with loose gravel. The tar had pretty much dried and where car tires had passed over were two paths of more compacted gravel but the little rock edges were still sharp, causing my tires to ping with every inch and making me feel like the rubber was being shredded right off as I grinded over the prickly surface. I began to fume.

If that wasn't bad enough, after a few miles the loose gravel turned to loose, golf ball-size rocks, which were impossible to

Peaceful 185

ride on. By then I was out in the middle of nowhere with no other roads in sight and too far in to turn back. I started walking my bike over the big rocks, praying for God's guidance and wondering how I might send hate mail to the little grocery store. A mile or so up the road I passed by a farmhouse where a man was helping his wife unload groceries from her car. A hard road was in sight and I asked them where I was and how I could get to Road 3 to Olney. They assured me Road 3 was just up the road and was paved all the way. At five o'clock in the afternoon with twenty more miles to cover I was in no mood for another good ole' screw up. Thinking I actually considered waiting around Mulberry Grove for the parade at four o'clock gave me the creeps; my day would have been shot. How could I have even considered such a stupid idea? What's worse, how could I have made the stupid decision to get off the route again?

Finally getting back on a decent road, I began thinking about my inability to stay on track. Even though I determined in my mind to stay on track, I got off anyway. It reminded me of the apostle Paul when he said, "For what I want to do I do not do, but what I hate I do." Was that me or what?

Passing through another small town I encountered another festival with the local park packed with people. Bands were playing, grills were smoking, and kids mingled everywhere. At a stop light on the edge of town a group of teenagers hung out on the corner and we talked as I waited through a couple of lights. A couple miles down the road a car whizzed by and the same kids waved playfully out the window. "God watch over them," I whispered. At the next light a pickup pulled along side of me blasting some dark heavy metal music right in my ear. Maybe I was at the end of my rope but it just felt evil and I was in no mood to be harassed, especially by the devil. Looking down at the ground I whispered, "Satan, I rebuke you in the name of Jesus. He is Lord and has risen from the dead and you have no power over me." Eventually the light turned green and the misery stopped.

All day I had been looking forward to a weekend in Olney in the vicarage by myself. The pastor had resigned and I was told the house was empty and I could relax, write, kick back in comfort, and rest up for the last leg of the trip. When I reached Olney I called Deacon Armstrong from the mini-mart on the edge of town. He gave me directions to the church and agreed to meet me there. It had been twelve hours since I left Alton and I was a zombie. I didn't hurt anywhere and wasn't dragging but I felt lightheaded and wanted some comfort, peace, friendship, and relaxation really bad.

Deacon Armstrong met me at the church and informed me that the new pastor was in the process of moving in and I couldn't stay there. Instead they had fixed me a cot in the basement of the church. While we were talking on the sidewalk, a sister from the Catholic Church walked by and after hearing about the trip offered me a place to stay. Thinking everything was covered I declined and went into the church with Army. When we walked down the basement steps my heart sank as I surveyed the small canvas cot set up in the corner near the children's Sunday school table in the wood paneled and otherwise stark, depressing bunker. As I stood there dumbfounded over the drab accommodations, Army informed me that there was a committee meeting in the basement at 7:00 a.m. and he would come get me for breakfast at 6:00. There was a bathroom with a sink but no shower.

I could not describe my feelings as I stood there like a statue analyzing my situation. Was I angry, disappointed, disgusted, betrayed, or all of the above? I wasn't sure, but I was fuming. Trying to stay calm, I told Army I really needed a shower and after some thought he agreed to let me in the vicarage across the street. When we walked inside my first thought was, "So tell me again why I can't stay here?" But I kept silent and just grumbled inside about their lack of faith and hospitality. During my shower I decided to look for the sister and take her up on her offer so I could rest comfortably and not have to get up at 6:00 a.m. after a nice night on a canvas cot. By the time I finished up and walked outside, the dusk was turning to dark and a lady from the church was waiting to take me to dinner. Trying not to sound rude or ungrateful, even though I was feeling both, I explained my decision and asked if she knew where the sister lived that had walked by earlier. We walked down to the convent house, then over to the parsonage, carrying my stuff around like a vagrant but with no success. Completely convinced I was not sleeping on the cot in the basement, I asked Ruth if there was a motel nearby that might work. She agreed with the idea, like I knew she would. God forbid letting an Episcopal youth leader stay in an Episcopal parishioner's house or anything.

After dinner, Ruth dropped me off at the motel and said she would be back around 9 a.m. to take me to church. I poured myself into bed trying to make sense out of the craziness and soon was fast asleep.

Day 37

Sunday, August 12, 1990

Olney, IL

Encountering Evil

Ruth came by at nine o'clock and after a pleasant breakfast, drove me to church. Walking into the small, old church building I got the feeling that nothing had changed inside the place in thirty years. It looked like a museum and felt about as spiritual. The service verified the feelings as I painfully endured the dreadful message and lifeless ritual. During the prayer time as I buried my head in my hands and wrestled with the discouraging thoughts flooding my soul, a mental picture developed of a large fist gripped tightly around the church. During announcements I raised my hand and shared the picture with the congregation and asked them to pray about what it meant. To me, there was no doubt what it meant – as if I were interpreting a dream, I felt the picture represented an oppressive hand of control over the congregation by a small number of people and possibly Satan himself, but I kept that to myself.

During the coffee hour following the service I was confronted by a handful of elderly members puffing their cigarettes and explaining their interpretation of the picture. "We believe," the half-smiling, half-smirking matriarch explained, "that the picture represents the hand of God holding our church in his care." The others chimed in and the interaction became so unsettling and spiritually disturbing I chose to peacefully agree and move on to another section of the room.

Shortly after, a young couple approached me and with welcoming expressions and gentle spirits explained that they were fairly new at the church and had found the atmosphere to be terribly rigid and resistant to change. "The church seems to be controlled by a few older people who have been here all their lives and won't let go," they said with desperation. My heart sank and I assured them I would pray for them. It was time for me to leave.

I mean, really leave. The experience had felt so disturbing and controlling, an urge came over me to do something I had never even considered during the trip, to ride on Sunday. I just had to escape. Ruth was ready to leave and without going into any detail I told her of my plans to ride and asked her to drop me off at the motel.

My mind was spinning with the decision. Something was wrong with the idea but I pushed forward anyway. With each clothes item folded and each riding piece put on, I grew increasingly uneasy with the plan. After everything was ready and the time had come to roll out of the motel room, the bubble burst. I couldn't go through with it. Wilting on the bed and begging God to please help me, a peaceful clarity settled over my mind and I began to think rationally. It was too late to get started, I had no arrangements for the night, and I was in no mood to endure a hard day of riding. In a glimpse of sanity I decided to scrap the idea, change into my street shorts, and look for a quiet place to have lunch and figure out my next move. Unhooking the panniers and leaving everything in the room, I climbed aboard my mechanical friend and slowly meandered toward town in search of a friendly meal.

Passing a few fast food joints and opting out of the empty home-style diner, I noticed a hospital sign and remembered Clara in Liberal, Kansas, who took me to the hospital cafeteria for lunch after church. The atmosphere then was bright, the food cheap, and we had a great time. Why not, I thought, and followed the signs to the main entrance. While contemplating the best way in and where to leave my bike, a minister and his wife walked up on their way inside. "Excuse me," I asked, "do you know if the hospital has a cafeteria?" "That's just where we were heading," they replied cheerfully. "Would you like to join us?" "Sure, if you don't mind," I said, but really my thoughts were more like, "Thank you, yes, please, I beg you. I'll do anything for some friends!"

They showed me a little patio around the side of the building that could be seen through the cafeteria windows – a perfect place to keep an eye on my bike. Inside, Reverend Ray insisted I go first through the line and get whatever I wanted. He and his wife followed and shortly another couple from church showed up and the five of us enjoyed a great lunch together sharing stories, laughing, and filling up on way too much pie. My heart soared. They would never know what a joyful rescue operation they had just performed and how grateful I was for their company.

After lunch we talked with some kids hanging out on the patio looking at my bike and reminded them of God's love for them personally and his great gift of love – Jesus. One never knows the effect of such sharing but our motivation as older people wanting kids to find meaning and direction in life early instead of squandering so many good years like some of us did was at least genuine. Finally, the time came for us to depart, so we said our good-byes and off we went in our separate directions.

Faced with a new plan and not knowing where else to turn I called Deacon Army and told him I had decided it was too late to ride and asked if I could sleep in the basement of the church. Paying for another night in the motel was out of the question. He gladly agreed to meet me at the church and let me in. The nagging question in my mind was why he and the others were so resistant to putting me up in someone's house. We got along fine and seemed to enjoy talking with one another but I still ended up in the basement. After rolling my bike down the short steps and "settling in" to my empty room, we talked for a while and he offered to come back later and take me out to dinner.

Thinking that a nap might be a good idea I stretched out on the cot and rested – sort of. Feeling restless and depressed in the dungeon, I decided to walk around the quiet neighborhood and process my swirling thoughts. What had happened today? How could I be treated so kindly by some people and feel run out of town by others? What made me so uncomfortable that I nearly left town? I didn't have any answers. All I knew was I wanted friendship and love so desperately I could taste it; someone to sit down with and exchange common thoughts, someone to share my emotions with, to be close to, to touch, to hug. But where? Who? How? My situation had become desperate and I was powerless.

Army came back along with his wife and Ruth and we shared a pleasant dinner together. They dropped me off at the church and gave me directions to a breakfast place near the highway where I could meet them in the morning on my way out. We agreed on 6:00 a.m. and said goodnight.

If loneliness had skin on I would have bumped into him when I stepped inside the basement door. Walking down the steps to the empty room with painted gray floors and my little cot in the corner felt as if I were entering a jail cell. I did have refrigerator and phone privileges though, so before going to bed I tried to call a friend who had graduated from the seminary in Ambridge and who was now pastoring a church in Bedford. We had a tentative arrangement due to my unpredictable schedule and I looked forward to firming it up. The opportunity to talk with someone I knew also motivated the call.

Nobody answered at his house or the church so I left a message on the home answering machine. Then it was back to the silence again -- me and my friend Lonely. Man, did I want to talk to somebody who could understand my feelings. Who could I call? My friend Langley was out of town and it was too late to call my pastor friend Joe. I finally laid down on the cot and stared at the dated ceiling tiles with the small round holes in them, the sound of the dehumidifier humming softly in the corner now more evident. I guess at some point I fell asleep.

Day 38

Monday, August 13, 1990

Olney, IL to Brownstown, IN

120 miles

7:00 a.m. - 7:30 p.m.

Still a Man of Unclean Lips

Waking up and sitting on the edge of my cot I noticed my bike had a flat tire. I called Army and told him I might be late for breakfast. A part of me wanted to tell him I wouldn't make it at all and just get on the road but I resisted. I needed to eat anyway and I didn't want to hurt anybody's feelings.

Thanks to Larry at the Ambridge Bike Shop, fixing the flat was quick with my plastic tire tools and foolproof peel-and-stick patches. Finding the hole and removing whatever caused it was the critical part. Running my thumb along the inside of the tire, I located the pesky metal sliver and pushed it out from the inside with my trusty mini-pliers and then pulled it out from the outside. The hole was easy to find with a little air in the tube and before long we were climbing out of the basement into the fresh morning air. I felt like a hostage being released from solitary confinement as my eyes adjusted to the daylight.

The restaurant was located in a hotel on the edge of town right off Highway 50 and after a pleasant breakfast with Army and his wife and another nice couple, we took pictures outside in the parking lot, said our farewells, and off I pedaled toward the 50 overpass. Overcast skies loomed in every direction and the pavement glistened with moisture as I cut along the freshly paved, four-lane highway and wondered if more rain waited ahead. Just happy to be motoring along swiftly east, I resolved to give thanks to God and not worry about it.

After all, with the traffic light and a smooth, four-lane highway with a two-foot shoulder all to myself, what more could I ask for? Everyone had plenty of room and there was no need for anyone to cause me any stress, especially since the inside lane was usually empty and reasonable drivers could move slightly left to provide even more cushion.

That seemed to work just fine until about 10:00 a.m. when the truck traffic showed up. I don't know what caused it but all of a sudden those thundering beasts dominated the highway, and often with little or no notice that I even existed. On one occasion, with all lanes open and no oncoming traffic, a monstrous rig whizzed by in the right lane with his wheels covering the white stripe right next to my shoulder, nearly blowing me off the road with a misty blast. I raised my open palm in a questioning gesture and shouted, "What are you doing a_ _ hole?! What a piece of s_ _ _." I caught myself, repented of my language, and tried to settle down. All I needed was some psycho in a ten-ton truck chasing me across the country.

On top of the truck invasion the road situation changed dramatically. The smooth, four-lane highway with nice wide shoulders reduced to two lanes with a puny, one-foot shoulder. Keeping my eyes alert I noticed two, huge, eighteen-wheel rock haulers approaching in the on-coming lane. These were the biggest trucks I'd ever seen. As they thundered by at no less than sixty miles per hour one lane over, I was met by a wall of wind and sand that knocked my hat off and caused me to pull off the road and stop. What came out of my mouth was worse than before. I began to wonder how I might deal with my language problem but, more importantly, how to survive my truck problem.

In all my life of driving I had never seen so many huge trucks. Eighteen-wheel gravel haulers, fourteen-wheel dump trucks, cement mixers, flat beds, loggers, and house-size freight movers, all making time on two-lane Highway 50 two feet from my left ear.

Every now and then a sand hauler would fly by, blasting a fine spray of dry sand across my body that felt like needles. I shouted at them too. "What the hell do you think you're hauling jerk? Why don't you cover your bleep-ing truck?!"

Other times I could see the monsters converging on me through my mirror

A good sign and a bad sign

while also being aware of oncoming traffic. Knowing it would be a tight squeeze for all three of us, I would hug the edge as far right as I could, flex every muscle in my body, and brace myself for the blast. Instinctively I would duck my head as if curling into a ball as the shock wave of wind and dirt blasted by. In a twenty-mile stretch I lost count how many times I repeated the curling drill.

Around noon I crossed the Indiana line into Vincennes and quivered into a Kentucky Fried Chicken, nerves raw with abuse. The sky threatened rain when I walked inside but after a drumstick and some coleslaw I moseyed back out to blue skies and puffy white clouds, a fully loaded gravel truck thundering by as I stepped out of the door, reminding me of the nightmare. My hope was to get to Bedford and make contact with a seminary friend, Ron.

By early evening the truck traffic subsided, I suspect, due to dinner time and quitting time, and I cruised along methodically, hanging closer to the lane stripe where the road was usually cleaner. My general late-in-the-day cruising posture was to droop my head low staring at the road stripe and the pavement right behind my front tire for direction while keeping my ears open and taking an occasional glance at my handlebar mirror for rear approaching traffic.

Sometime after five as I cruised along methodically near the right lane stripe, hanging my head down and keeping an eye on my mirror, I looked up suddenly to discover an oncoming car side by side with the car it was passing, heading straight for me. As I whipped to the edge of the one-foot shoulder I caught a glance at the face of the young girl driver as she blew by twelve inches from my handlebar, never honking or slowing down. With immeasurable fear and frustration I belted out the big "G_ _ D _ _ _ it! You *#@&*&^%$!" Shaking uncontrollably I pulled off the road to gather myself. Dropping to one knee while holding onto my bike, I tried to stop shaking while crying out, "Oh God, please forgive me of my pride and stupidity. Please get me home safely, please." After some amount of time I gingerly mounted the bike and pushed on.

Getting closer

Finally in Bedford, I stopped at a tiny, roadside ice cream drive-in to use the phone and get something to drink with ice in it. Once again nobody answered at Ron's house so I ordered a large lemonade and sat down on the picnic table in the shade of the patio awning and pondered my next move. A young, college-age guy buzzed in on his crotch rocket and ordered a milkshake and sat down at the other end of my table. Looking like one of those buff guys on a Gillette commercial, he asked where I was heading and we talked for a while. He was on his way to visit his girlfriend and was just grabbing a snack since he had some time to kill. He also enjoyed bicycling and was fascinated by my trip. I was fascinated with the thought of visiting a girlfriend.

Not that I had a particular girlfriend I was missing at the moment, but the thought of this young guy meeting up with his girlfriend and spending time together touched the same raw nerve that had been flaring up for weeks. I wished him well before he sped off, then turned back to my more immediate thoughts of where I'd be spending the night.

With options seemingly exhausted in Bedford I decided to call my contact in Cincinnati to at least confirm my stay for the following night. Surprisingly, the friendly male voice on the other end was actually a person and after a brief introduction our souls seemed to connect and the conversation flowed as if we were lifelong buddies. Explaining my inability to make contact with my friend in Bedford and my urge to make a run for Brownstown, Stan suggested that we pray. We asked the Lord to give me safe travel and a place to stay in Brownstown along with a safe trip to Cincinnati. "Amen," we concluded, hanging up our respective phones under totally dissimilar circumstances: Stan, preparing for dinner with his wife in the comfort of their home and me, mounting up for a twenty-five mile jaunt to Brownstown without a clue what awaited.

By now the twelve-inch round clock hanging above the ice cream pick-up window showed 5:15. Rolling out of the crumbling parking lot and shifting gears to pick up speed on Highway 50, I actually felt invigorated for the ride, and with the truck traffic diminished and car traffic thinning with every mile, the twenty-five mile trek clipped by completely uneventfully.

On the outskirts of Brownstown I pulled into a supermarket and put the "Hermann strategy" into effect. Hanging out near the front door drinking my Gatorade and snacking on peanuts, I had a strong sense that my decision to ride to Brownstown was the right one and that God would provide. After sitting on a bench outside the store for nearly an hour my confidence began to wane. "Should I just pick someone walking by and tell them my situation?" I thought. "Could you give me just a little sign, God?" Another half hour passed. Darkness settled in and I needed to make a move.

Maybe it was a sign or just coming to my senses but realizing the grocery store plan was not working, I got the idea to leave the outskirts of town and find the actual heart of the community, a town square or something.

Following the urge and pedaling down Main Street in complete darkness, I noticed a tall, white steeple reaching through the trees a few blocks over on my right. Turning right on the next street and left two blocks later, I located the steeple and pulled up to a large, but dark, Methodist church. Walking my bike along the sidewalk around the side, I noticed a light on above the side door. The door was unlocked and inside, coming from the stairwell to the second floor, I could barely hear voices muffled in the distance so I decided to investigate. Climbing the stairs to the second floor, I followed the soft chatter to a doorway to what seemed to be a meeting room with a group of people gathered around a large table.

Noticing me through the doorway, one of the men excused himself and came to the door. "Sorry for interrupting your meeting," I whispered. "I'm a youth minister biking across the country and my contact in Bedford fell through so I came to Brownstown hoping to find a place to stay." With sincere eye contact and a gentle and welcoming voice, Pastor Don explained that the meeting was about over and he would be glad to help if I would hang around for a minute.

The words flowed into my parched soul like water from heaven, soothing my vibrating nerves and uplifting my drooping spirit. I hung out with my bike on the sidewalk as the people filed out of the side door on their way home, to a normal life. Don came out last and walked me next door to his house and introduced me to his wife and two sons. He showed me the bathroom with the shower and clean towels and invited me to take my time. When I emerged clean, dressed, and in my right mind he gave some money to his teenage son, Daryl, and sent the two of us down the sidewalk for dinner. We walked a couple blocks to Shoneys and had a great time talking and eating together, just like I had done hundreds of times with kids back in Ambridge; this time the context was slightly different.

When we returned, Don and the boys walked me over to the church with sheets and a pillow to a comfortable, well-decorated den with a large couch where I could sleep and get an early start for Cincinnati. They didn't plan on waking up as early as I planned to the next morning, so we said a short prayer together and exchanged our goodnights. Sleep came gradually as I stretched out in the peace and quiet of the cozy church den, basking in the love of God and barely able to absorb what had just happened. Coupled with the nerve-racking and near-death incidents on the road, and my mind could hardly compute what I was doing.

Day 39

Tuesday, August 14, 1990

Brownstown, IN to Cincinnati, OH

100 miles

7:45 a.m. to 6:00 p.m.

Not Now, I'm Working Too Hard

Beautiful, blue skies greeted me as I emerged from the church not as early as I had planned but rested and eager to get to Cincinnati. The crisp morning air was almost cool enough for my light gortex jacket but I opted out of that idea, knowing that shortly the body heat would more than compensate for the mild chill. Pedaling peacefully through the neighborhood and slowly out of Brownstown, the mood was ripe for a satisfying ride.

Even Highway 50 was peaceful for a mile or two until an eighteen wheeler thundered by, rumbling and hissing like a locomotive. "Oh, God, I'm just not ready for this yet," I moaned, like most people who get to work early in the morning. They show up, get some coffee, maybe chat a little with co-workers, and then settle into work. Nobody appreciates walking in the office door to be met by a loud boss waving file folders and shouting about the day's work before they've had time to warm up a bit. That's what I thought anyway, but nobody else cared, especially the trucks.

By 9:30 my bottomless pit of a stomach screamed for breakfast and Seymour, Indiana, located at the intersection of 50 and Interstate 65, got the nod. Rolling down Main Street I noticed a nicer looking restaurant obviously open for breakfast but when two business-dressed ladies walked out, I lost interest, feeling self-conscious about walking into a fancy place, full of well-dressed working people with real jobs, in my biker shorts.

That was my option in Seymour and before I knew it I had passed through town and was back on the open road. Ten miles later without an option for breakfast, a sign read, "Versailles 20 miles." Kicking myself for passing through Seymour and too hungry to wait twenty more miles I vowed to stop at the next place that had food -- no matter what I felt like. The next place, just a couple of miles up the road, was called the Midway and looked like an abandoned mobile home in the middle of a gravel parking lot. Even though I lost my appetite just looking at the depressing place I pulled in, determined to keep my vow.

Walking slowly across the potholes and uneven gravel and feeling a bit reserved about the Midway I looked down the road and spotted a yellow portable sign in front of another place that looked much more inviting. The inner voice perked up and the decision to head over was unanimous. Drawing closer I read the sign, "The Swing Inn," and the closer I got the better I felt. This was the place.

I took a booth by the window and was greeted by a very cute, dark-haired waitress with a pretty smile whose friendly, talkative nature made me feel right at home. She asked about my trip and we continued talking across the small dining room as she went about her business refilling shakers and wiping tables. The breakfast rush was over and the one customer sitting on the other side of the room also joined in the conversation. After delivering my sweet-smelling order, Tanya walked back to the kitchen and returned with her brother Tim, the cook, both pulling up a chair from the next table over and joining me in friendly, uplifting conversation that nourished my needy emotions.

They suggested I might enjoy visiting the old post office down the road that still processed mail with a hand stamp, and even though it sounded interesting, there was no way they could understand the tunnel vision I had for getting to Cincinnati and the unlikelihood that I would stop. My goodness, I couldn't stop for food and rest, much less a novelty stop.

When it came time to leave, they gladly offered my breakfast on the house and wished me well. We all went outside and I asked John, the one customer, to take a picture of Tim, Tanya, and myself before taking off. Reaching the highway I turned back and waved to my Swing Inn friends, thanking God for steering me in the right direction.

The riding became hot and tiring as the miles clipped by and the cool, crisp morning turned into a typical, muggy, August afternoon. What's more, the smooth, "city" highways turned into desolate, crumpled construction zones, so bad during one stretch I had to walk my bike over the chewed-up asphalt to keep from beating my bike to pieces.

Around midday, with the sun beating down from straight overhead, breakfast long gone, and the eating machine growling for lunch in the middle of nowhere between Elrod and Dillsboro, a roadside fruit stand appeared. Unwilling to pass up this lonely sign of civilization, I pulled over and talked with the friendly farmer lady in the shade of the makeshift wooden awning as I consumed enough bananas, plums, nectarines, and dried apple chips for a small family. I expressed my thankfulness for the fruit stand and in the course of an otherwise dry conversation, asked the lady if she and her husband were

My breakfast friends Tim & Tanya

involved in a local church. "My sister is into church and all that," she replied, "and takes my little girl to Sunday school, but we work too hard to have time for church."

My attempt to communicate even the tip of the iceberg of my belief in God and His involvement in our daily lives, I'm sure, came across preachy and discomforting as I started to feel the "I'm not interested" vibes, and my nice farm lady began fidgeting with the fruit. "Well, thank you for such a great stop, you really helped me out," I said, trying to ease her uneasiness. "I enjoyed talking with you." "Yes, you too," she said, politely and insincerely. It was time for me to leave.

With an improved road surface and a belly full of fruit, the legs pumped strong and the miles ticked by stress free just like I hoped every ride would be, that is, until this pee wee pickup truck screamed by, hugging the right stripe and nearly taking my leg off. I was totally shocked. There was no traffic in the oncoming lane; the highway was wide enough for both of us and there was no excuse for such an asinine move, and I immediately said so, shouting as quickly as I could get the words out, "What are you doing a_ _ h _ _ _? What a bleeping jerk!" This time the thought of him turning around didn't even register; I didn't care. But I did feel something was wrong with my attitude and felt I needed to address it, but not now; I was just too drained.

Actually, I didn't have time to deal with it. As I was leaving the boondocks and approaching Cincinnati, Highway 50 turned into a divided, four-lane, concrete slab with uneven joints and cracks that repeatedly beat my tires like a sledge hammer. Bang-bang, bang-bang, bang-bang came the jolt on each rock-hard tire as it passed over every joint between every slab, every twelve feet. The repetition was punishing and exhausting as I had to flex my whole body to support my back over every bump. It also started to become painful on my spine. Add to the physical pain the aesthetic downer of the dirty and dilapidated industrial zones along the Ohio River and my taste for Cincinnati soured like rotten fruit.

Picture on the bridge

Following my map closely through the industrial outskirts, I finally made my way into downtown and on a bridge overlooking the city I stopped and asked a homeless-looking black man walking across the bridge to take my picture with the city in the background. Startled by my request at first, he gladly accepted and lined me up with the city and pressed the button. I thanked him and we departed to our separate lives.

Weaving through the public housing area I waved at some little black kids fixing their bikes on the sidewalk. I wanted to stop and help but was too tired and wanted so badly to get to Stan's house. Pulling over to a phone booth in the middle of a scary ghetto district, I got directions from Stan's wife and pressed on through town and followed my scribbled notes into a modest neighborhood with large trees, quiet streets, and, finally, to Stan's house.

Stan's wife Carol stood in the driveway and welcomed me with the kind of warmth that I could usually associate with true Christian believers. My spirit relaxed and I somehow knew I was in for a positive stay.

Carol showed me to my room with the nicely made bed, towels, and private bathroom. She went downstairs as I made my way to the shower to wash off the day's ride and soothe my body under the refreshing water. Returning to the living room feeling clean and peaceful, I relaxed and talked with Carol as we waited for Stan to come home. We also took a look in the garage where Stan maintained an old Porsche for sport racing. When Stan got home we had a good dinner and talked like family about racing, biking, and our shared Christian faith until bedtime. I went to bed feeling as though I was sleeping in my own bed while the peaceful presence of the Lord settled upon me like a dream.

Day 40
Wednesday, August 15, 1990
Cincinnati, OH to Circleville, OH
93 miles
8:45 a.m. - 6:00 p.m.

Friends Forever

E ven though I needed the sleep I woke up early and went with Stan to a Bible study that met at a local breakfast place. Stan and I had so much in common and talked the whole way, like longtime friends. Not only did we both enjoy auto racing, biking, and tennis, we both loved the Lord and talked openly about our faith and the work of the Holy Spirit in our lives. To me, Stan was the kind of role model any young man would want as a friend and mentor.

After the Bible study we drove home and got ready for the day's ride. So much of me wanted to stay but I could smell the finish line and wanted to get one day closer. Besides, Stan was looking forward to us riding together as he escorted me out of town on one of his favorite routes.

What an absolutely beautiful morning as we rode and talked together like biking buddies who had been sharing the road for years, building each other up in faith and friendship with every mile. Surely an experience I needed to boost me into another day's ride.

Instead of riding on major roads the whole way, Stan took us on a "Rails to Trails" route that cut through woods and backyards of neighborhoods on a smooth, level, asphalt surface completely free of distracting motorized traffic. We cruised along side by side, talking and enjoying the ride like any two good friends would do on a nice morning bike ride.

After about fifteen perfect miles Stan had to turn back and get to work so we rolled to a stop, dismounted, and hugged on the side of the trail, saying good-bye like brothers and expressing the hope that our paths would cross again. The emotions of the departure caught me by surprise as that familiar, choked-up feeling came to my throat and additional moisture filled my eyes during the final handshake before pedaling off in opposite directions. Once apart, tears actually began rolling down my cheeks as a deep sense of God's love and goodness enveloped my emotions and the confirmation of all that I believed was once again reestablished through the experience of an authentic Christian friendship. Soon spontaneous songs and prayers flowed joyfully from my mouth as my soul seemed to bubble over with peace and gratitude.

Settling into the ride I couldn't help but contemplate on how some relationships along the way had been so uplifting and positive while others were just the opposite. In the case of Stan, surely our similar personalities, closeness in age, and mutual interest for bicycling and auto racing fueled our friendship, but there was more, definitely something deeper. I had known a number of people who loved bikes and cars, and even called them friends, but the bond that Stan and I shared touched the spirit and the soul and connected us at a level indescribable in human terms, a level that found its expression mainly in conversation about Jesus and the Scriptures, and our

Stan my friend

heartfelt knowledge and love for both. For me, nothing was sweeter, nothing more comforting and uplifting.

After lunch, the sweet contemplation of Christian friendship gave way to hot, demanding highway biking and I began to feel the weight of fatigue settling in. The newly paved road with wide shoulders and a slight downgrade had helped for a couple of hours but by 3:30 in the muggy afternoon I trudged along like a zombie, my mind in a fog without feeling or emotion and my pedaling motion lifeless and burdensome. My knees ached with each downward rotation to the point where I lowered my gear and pedaled as if I were on a stationary bike with zero resistance. The ride into Cincinnati had apparently beat me up more than I realized and in my relief and excitement of staying with Stan and Carol I failed to notice how physically drained I had become.

As I plodded along in my late afternoon, depleted posture, head down, staring at the painted road stripe, and watching my mirror occasionally for back traffic, I looked up instinctively just in time to notice an oncoming pickup truck passing another car and hugging the white stripe in my lane. I jerked to the right just as he whizzed by at probably seventy miles per hour, two feet from my left shoulder, sending a powerful burst of wind and fear over my body that felt like death. In a tingling state of shock I turned around and with an explosion of anger and exhaustion screamed out, "What the *#%* are you doing?!! What an a- -!!" Turning back around and hitting my fist on the handlebar I shouted to the world, "Damn it! God help me!" The trauma of being surprised by a two-ton mass of metal approaching at high speed and passing by two feet away was beyond description. And even though I felt most of it was the driver's fault, the problem of my attitude and language troubled me.

As the afternoon wore on, I felt for the first time that I could actually fall asleep while riding. At times I would close my eyes and rest for about three seconds at a time, opening one eye just long enough to look for traffic. In New Holland, a quiet Mayberry-type town seventeen miles from Circleville, I stopped at a little drive-in burger stand for a Coke. Stretching out on the wooden bench under a tree alongside the white-block building, I wilted like a wet noodle and soon slipped into a day-dream about spaghetti, Christian friends, and worship music. Never before had I needed physical and spiritual nourishment like I needed it under that tree. After a half hour or so I flopped my feet to the ground and stood my groggy body up to make one last push.

The ride turned out to be easy and uneventful and as I approached Circleville, the road even tilting slightly downward and I cruised at eighteen to twenty mph with hardly any effort at all, rolling into town with a noticeably peaceful feeling in my spirit -- the complete opposite feeling I had when riding into El Dorado Springs where the oppression clung to me like a plague.

So close

But not in Circleville. The Episcopal priest there, Father Jim Slack, had responded to my postcard before the trip and when I called him the day before to let him know I'd be coming, he had given me directions to his house, which was right next to the church, and was there to meet me when I pulled into his driveway. Leading me through his garage full of bikes and showing me where to park mine, he asked about my day and waited for me to unhook my panniers before escorting me inside. Following the scrumptious, mouth-watering, spaghetti-sauce aroma we made our way to the colonial-style kitchen where Mrs. Slack and their teenage daughter stopped what they were doing to greet me and give me my dinner options. The family had just finished but if I wanted to get settled into my room and cleaned up, they'd have it ready when I came down. My entire being -- body, soul, and spirit -- relaxed and rejoiced as if I had come home.

Heading up the stairs and into my well-furnished bedroom with queen-size bed and family memorabilia, I could tell I was walking into a haven of childhood memories, most likely that of a son, judging by the décor, and I felt loved just standing there. Stepping into the long and narrow bathroom with another door for the adjoining bedroom, I washed nine hours of weariness down the drain using every skin, hair, and body product a teenage household could offer, emerging refreshed, excited about life, and hungry. Resisting the temptation to lie down on the comfy bed for fear I would never get up, I meandered downstairs and sat at my neatly arranged table setting and talked with Jim and his daughter as Mrs. Slack served the most well-received plate of spaghetti in history.

During dinner they informed me of the Wednesday night prayer and praise service that started at 7:30. I was shocked and elated. Rarely do Episcopal churches have Wednesday night services, let alone prayer and praise with a live music team. We walked over to the church together and split up as Jim got ready and we sat in the front pew. Not long after, the music team opened up with the first worship song. After the music and a brief message the intimate congregation of about twenty was invited to come up for prayer. I went forward for strength and healing in my knees and for a new attitude toward offensive drivers. After a tender prayer by a gracious lay person, I rested right on the floor in the peace of the music for a good ten minutes while they prayed for others and arose feeling perfectly refreshed.

During the prayer time a thought ran through my mind that I was to speak words of blessing to the irritating drivers rather than curse them. I held on to that thought and considered giving it a try if the opportunity arose.

The entire service was a total blessing. Nobody trying to control me or question my faith, nobody doubting my character or worried about their safety; just relaxed and genuine worship with people enjoying the presence of the Lord and one another's company. Jim's message about the Holy Spirit present and available for young and old alike invited everyone into ministry and encouraged everyone in their current vocation.

After the service a few friends came over to the house and we talked and snacked until my bedtime, when I excused myself and marched slowly up the stairs to my room, crawling into my big bed full of "the peace that passes all understanding," just as the service had said. It didn't get any more peaceful than this.

Day 41

Thursday, August 16, 1990

Circleville, OH to Zanesville, OH

60 miles

9:45 a.m. - 4:30 p.m.

Love Your Neighbor as Yourself

Knowing I had only sixty miles to get to Zanesville I didn't even set my alarm and slept in without a hint of concern for time. When I finally woke up at 7:30 a.m. the feeling of peace was so comforting I just laid there basking in the comfort, while beams of sunlight shined through the window shades, lighting up my room. It was a beautiful new day without a trace of anxiety and I relished in the unpressured schedule of having breakfast with Jim and getting on the road when the time came.

The night before, Jim had offered to take me to breakfast and was waiting for me in the kitchen when I came downstairs. The fact that he had suggested I sleep in and get all the rest I needed made me feel good about not rushing. Now that I was rested and ready to go and Jim was content with waiting in the kitchen, we headed out on foot toward the main street and his regular breakfast place. Arriving at the home-style diner we seated ourselves at an open table as a friendly waitress walked by, obviously respectful of Jim and looking forward to serving us.

As we talked I could see why people would want to be around Jim. He was pleasant, honest, straightforward, and full of wisdom. Not only did he show genuine interest in my life and the bike ride, he went a step further to ask questions about my future and what I planned on doing after the trip, the kind of questions that made me think about the facts of my situation and articulate a way forward. Whether it was Jim's strategy or God's way of speaking, the exercise of talking about my place in life and offering a plan for the future forced me to take a look at the real picture.

Just talking about my lack of income back in Ambridge, my thirty-three-year-old, single status, my shoestring ministry, and my apartment in the church office painted a portrait that begged for a plan. And the truth was I had one; it just wasn't moving along at the normal pace. I wanted to get married, I wanted to get ordained, I hoped to have a family some day and an income to take care of them, but the pieces weren't falling into place as quickly as I wanted.

Jim seemed to understand all I was saying and had the spiritual insight to know that God was working and would continue to work in my life, but somehow his questioning stirred up determination in me to take more initiative and not wait for the pieces to fall, but rather to move into action. I told him I had hoped the trip might help me hear God better and inspire me to get moving when I got home, but even that was more than I really knew, and, if the truth be known, was said more as a kind of false confession to what I knew everyone thought – that my life was abnormal and I needed to change – than a solid belief. Even still, I was thankful that someone cared enough to listen and wanted to help.

I guess we could have talked all morning but the road was calling so we headed back to get me ready to ride. We walked by the bike shop on our way home but it hadn't opened yet. Jim knew the owner and suggested I have him check out my bike before I left, but I really didn't want to take the time, plus, I knew old Bessie could make two more days and I was ready to get on with it.

Back in the kitchen, Jim and I made some peanut butter and jelly sandwiches and headed out to the garage to pack up and get me going. After attaching the panniers, pumping tires, and rolling out into the bright warm sun, I said the final farewell, hugged my new priest friend, and pedaled down the concrete driveway. Once again my stay had been more than I ever expected and gratitude overflowed from my heart.

The morning ride clipped along beautifully as I covered twenty miles of blue skies, rolling hills, and farm land all the way to Lancaster. There I planned to stop and say hello to Father Rademaker, the Episcopal priest who had offered to put me up but his location just hadn't fit the schedule. I rolled in around 11:00 a.m. and found the large, old, church and walked through the plush halls to the minister's office. He was in a meeting and asked the maintenance man, Ron, to show me around until he could get free.

As Ron and I walked around the humongous building he shared how he had hoped one day to do something like my ride but was afraid something might happen. I couldn't disagree with his logic and advised him to listen to his gut feel and ask the Lord to show him what would be best. The last thing I wanted to do was give him the impression that what I was doing was best for him.

What I did want to know was if he believed in Jesus and had trusted him for the forgiveness of his sins, and I did talk about that. After explaining the cross and Jesus paying the ransom for our sins I went ahead and asked Ron if he believed. "I guess so," he said, "but how does a person really know?" "That's a good one," I said. "I guess at some point we come to a place where we realize we have a sin problem and need a Savior, then we call out and place our trust in Christ." He said he was baptized in the Catholic Church and went through Confirmation but still didn't understand "all that." And since I didn't want to press the issue, we went back to find Fr. Bob.

After a short visit, I left Lancaster and resumed an absolutely beautiful ride with only light traffic, hardly any trucks, rolling hills, and Amish farms spread out in postcard fashion. A pleasant lunch was spent under a large shade tree near the road in the front yard of a small farmhouse.

Later in the afternoon as the heat intensified my body began to wear down. It wasn't a physical thing like muscle fatigue, it was a sleep issue. My mind and body needed more rest than I had given it over the past five weeks and all functions wanted to stop. As I plugged along on a lonely stretch of highway, a little ice cream stand appeared so I pulled in and had a large, ice-cold lemonade. What a treat. All I could think of was how perfect and free from hassle the day's ride had been. I thanked God for his goodness even in my tired condition.

Riding further down the two-lane highway I commented to myself what a totally "unmolested" day it had been. Just as the rarely used word passed through my mind I looked up ahead along the grassy edge of the highway and noticed a sheet of paper conspicuously out of place in the fresh green grass. Passing by I curiously glanced down to see what kind of litter had made its way to the roadway, and zooming in, noticed the glossy black-and-white page from a porn magazine.

A little further down the road more of the glossy pages appeared and I was ticked off; of course, a part of me wanted to look, but another part was disgusted with the pornography industry for trashing the highway and trashing lives. The memory of a porn magazine that a kid in junior high showed a group of us came vividly back to my mind. How could I remember a picture from so long ago? I thought. Now, on a beautiful day, along a perfectly scenic roadway, my mind had been assaulted by the filth in a way that could not have appeared more intentional. Clearly the work of Satan, I concluded, rebuking his evil scheme and asking the Holy Spirit to cleanse the images from my mind and restore the beautiful ride I was enjoying before the interruption. Spontaneously breaking out in song, I belted out the classic praise song, "What a Mighty God We Serve," as I approached Zanesville.

In Zanesville, Fr. Jeff Barnes, the Episcopal priest, and his family welcomed me into their home and treated me with the same warmth of hospitality I had enjoyed the previous two nights. We had a great dinner together and talked like family until I started to fade, literally unable to keep my eyes open during the conversation. Apologizing for my condition, I excused myself, and for the first time during the trip, went to bed at 8:30 in the evening.

Day 42
Friday, August 17, 1990
Zanesville, OH to Wheeling, WV
92 miles
7:45 a.m. - 5:00 p.m.

It Could Have Been Different

Going to bed at 8:30 made all the difference in the world. I could actually feel the energy. But why did I wait until the second-to-last night of the trip to figure that out? I lamented. Actually, I didn't figure it out; many nights during the trip I had felt the need to go to bed earlier than I did but stayed up talking with my hosts, and paying for it the next day, and the next. Why didn't I intentionally do what I knew was right? Even last night was involuntary – I physically couldn't hold my eyes open anymore so I went to bed. Why couldn't I just choose to go to bed early on my own? Where was my will power?

Such were my thoughts as I knelt by my bed for my standard morning prayer time, asking God to forgive my weaknesses and give me a stronger desire to do what I knew was right.

Shirley was up and waiting for me when I strolled into the humble kitchen to the smell of homemade sweet rolls and scrambled eggs. We sat around the three-foot-round, wooden kitchen table and enjoyed a delightful breakfast as we talked about light topics such as Minnesota, grits, black coffee, and sundry other topics other than Jesus and faith, giving me the impression that St. James Episcopal in Zanesville was at a different spiritual place than St. Philips in Circleville. That may or may not have been true, but it was too early to plow into anything uncomfortable, plus I was so thankful for the hospitality and pleasant conversation, and totally psyched for the day's ride.

The only detail left was locating Rt. 146 out of Zanesville, which was different from Rt. 22 on my way in. I guess I wasn't surprised when Shirley told me it was the next street over from their house. "Things are lining up for the home stretch," I thought, as I loaded up, said good-bye, and rolled down the driveway.

Everything was lining up, that is, except the two slow-moving dump trucks filled with used barn straw that pulled out in front of me on the edge of town, taking forever to build up speed while suffocating me with the most foul smelling barn waste I had ever encountered in my life, even worse than the feed lots, causing me to gag and nearly lose my breakfast. I pedaled as slow as I could until the sputtering clunkers finally pulled away.

Actually, that wasn't the only thing not lining up. Leaving town by way of steep,

Sunrise, Zanesville

tree-covered hills and gray, low-settling fog gave things an eerie London feeling as I pumped my way east. Climbing up the narrow road beneath overhanging branches, I could barely see the sun straight ahead as a dim, white ball behind the gray fog. That, together with the hay encounter, and my exuberant departure from Zanesville had been squashed.

Ten miles later, though, the fog cleared and the landscape came alive with green rolling hills, blue skies, and somewhat strange-looking farmhouses hanging onto the edge of the road supported by stilts as they suspended out over the steep drop-off. The thought of someone going to so much trouble to hang a house on the side of a hill instead of finding a flat place baffled me, but they made for entertaining scenery.

And as pretty as the rolling hills were to look at, they were murder on the knees. I began to get concerned since there seemed to be no relief from the landscape, and quitting wasn't an option. Using low gears, I rotated the pedals fluidly without much resistance, asking God what he wanted for the remainder of the trip. Would I ride into Ambridge triumphantly, signifying the magnificent way in which he had taken care of me during the entire ride? Or would I wobble across the Ambridge Bridge like a wounded soldier dragging himself back from war? I knew what I wanted, but at this stage I tried to calm myself and accept whatever he brought my way. It truly was out of my hands.

With a lot of day left to ride, I decided around 10:30 to take a break at the white, concrete-block, gas station with the mechanic stalls converted to a convenient store. As I stood by my bike alongside the building drinking my orange juice and eating peanuts, the attendant passed by and struck up a conversation, volunteering his own interest in biking, "Try to get in about fifteen miles a day during the week and more on the weekends," he said, unknowingly setting himself up for a shock. "So," he continued, "how far are you going?" "Well," I said, trying to play down the inevitable astonishment, "Ambridge, Pennsylvania. It's near Pittsburgh." "That's pretty good, where did you start?" he asked. "Uh, San Diego," I said with a smile. "San Diego! Man, I've always wanted to do something like that. How long did it take?" As the words, "six weeks" came out of my mouth it was as though a highlight tape flashed through my mind replaying every high and every hardship that I had encountered and causing me to drift from the conversation. Coming back, suddenly I had no desire to talk about the trip or parade it in any grandiose way. "Just make sure you seek the Lord before you decide," I said. "The gravel trucks alone are enough to scare you to death." There just was no way I was going to glamorize what I had been through and encourage anyone to do what I wasn't sure I would ever consider doing again myself.

He watched me pull back onto the quiet two-lane highway as I pushed on toward Wheeling, beginning to feel a completely different mind-set coming on than I had experienced the whole trip. Rather than being occupied with the thrill of the unknown and the deep thoughts of the day, I was becoming more reflective, thinking back on the events of the trip and feeling overwhelmed with having actually made it this far. No longer was I in a strange land wondering what would happen next; I was on my way to Wheeling, a place I had visited before – one day away from home – and my focus on finishing could not have been more intense.

Lunch, Seneca Lake

With my housing in Wheeling secure and only one routine ride left, I felt like a horse heading for the barn.

Winding around Senecaville Lake I looked for a peaceful, scenic place to eat the bag lunch Shirley had fixed me. Half praying and half talking out loud, I asked the Lord to lead me to a nice place, and after passing several roadside possibilities that just didn't feel right, I noticed a small path leading into the woods from the road. I quickly pulled off the road and walked my bike down a narrow path toward the lake. The path led through tall pine trees to a small clearing on the edge of a cliff overlooking the lake. The view, some thirty feet above the lake, was absolutely perfect. I sat in the shade overlooking the water, just staring at the scenery, memories of the trip flashing through my mind as I tried to absorb it all. But it was just too much. After finishing my lunch I laid back in the grass and closed my eyes and let the thoughts flow. Whatever "never-never land" feels like, I think I was there.

Back on the road approaching Wheeling in the muggy late afternoon heat and humidity, I started feeling physically weak and shaky, when a little jiffy store appeared on the outskirts of town. I pulled in for a banana, OJ, and an Almond Joy. My body had become an eating machine and it was all I could do to keep it fueled up as I fought the traffic on Highway 40 toward the Ohio River.

My revised policy of how to react to offensive drivers had been tested and seemed to be working. Whenever a car whizzed by too close or honked in my ear, instead of yelling the usual obscenity, I found myself saying the same line, "Bless him Lord, bless him Lord," repetitively until I settled down. It sounded better anyway, and even felt better. After all, Jesus did say, "Bless your enemies and pray for those who persecute you;" funny how his ways always work better. If only I could pull them off more often.

Finally I arrived at the Ohio River and walked my bike to the middle of the old Wheeling suspension bridge overlooking the historic industrial valley. Looking out over the majestic waterway, a feeling of significant accomplishment flooded my body as if I were joining the ranks of the famous pioneers. I had crossed the Rio Grande, the Mississippi, the Missouri, and now, the Ohio. "Unbelievable!" I gasped to myself. "A nobody from Tampa, Florida, standing over the Ohio River, one day away from a cross-country bike ride." Could anyone in the rush hour traffic possibly understand what I was feeling? My emotions were spilling out all over.

Crossing over the bridge into Wheeling and calling my Episcopal contact, the Cowells, from a pay phone downtown, I spoke with Eleanor, Fr. Curtis's wife, who gave me directions to their house. A couple of miles through the business district, then gradually making my way into a residential neighborhood, and finally into their quiet driveway, and I had made it to my last home on the road -- hardly a long-distance phone call away from Ambridge.

As I walked up the sidewalk toward the front door, a car pulled alongside the curb and out stepped Fr. Curtis and his teenage daughter, Marla, to welcome me. They seemed genuinely happy to see me and escorted me excitedly into the front door. After the final road shower I headed for the dining room where Eleanor served up one more of the most well-received spaghetti dinners in biking history, her fine china putting a perfect touch on the last family meal of the ride.

Talking about the day's ride I mentioned the concern I had had for my knees early in the day but how the pain disappeared in the afternoon. Eleanor said she had been moved to pray for me around 1:00 and thanked God for taking care of me. Sitting at the table like a family member with a loving group of Christian believers once again brought waves of gratitude to my soul. There was no way they or any of my hosts could know what I felt to be at their table.

After dinner we hung out on the back steps and relaxed as the sun went down. Marla's friend came by and talked for a while then off to a movie they went like typical, carefree teenagers. Typical except for the extreme advantage they had of being raised in a loving Christian family that lived out the faith they professed. What a blessing. I was happy for them – and maybe a little envious.

The rest of us made plans for breakfast and went to bed early, although I could hardly sleep thinking about tomorrow's ride. I didn't even have categories for the emotions flowing through my head. What had just happened over the past six weeks? It seemed like a dream as more flashbacks replayed in my mind: water coolers in the desert, food from stranded motorists, hospitality from complete strangers, all coming together to get me where I was -- lying in a bed in Wheeling, West Virginia, ready to ride home the next day.

The love of God flooded my thinking beyond my capacity to contain it. How could it be? A sinner like me, faltering at every turn, putting myself in danger, near death; what kind of love allows such a person to receive such favor and blessing? "Dear Jesus, thank you," I prayed as tears rolled down to my pillow.

The original plan when we all went to bed was to wake up at 6:00 a.m. for breakfast so I could be on the road by 7:00, even though Saturdays were Curtis and Eleanor's only day to sleep in. The only problem with the early plan was my inability to fall asleep.

After a few more hours of dreaming, I heard little Hannah, the five-year-old, pitter patter past my room to the bathroom. When she flushed I looked at the dim, blue lights of the clock that read 3:00 a.m. At that point I decided there was no need to be in a hurry in the morning and we would all be better off sleeping a little longer and taking our time enjoying breakfast.

I got out of bed and wrote a note to Curtis and put it under his bedroom door. "Dear Curtis, It's 3 a.m. and I haven't been able to sleep. Can we sleep in a little in the morning? Thanks, Joseph." Sometime after that I think I fell asleep.

Day 43

Saturday, August 18, 1990

Wheeling, WV to Ambridge, PA

60 miles

9:30 a.m. - 3:30 p.m.

Not Always Sunshine

Waking up and looking out of my second-story bedroom window I discovered the nightmare of nightmares: the sky was overcast and drizzling rain. My first reaction was controlled disappointment, thinking what a drag it would be to grind out the last day in the rain instead of cruising in the pleasant sunshine, but then, an even gloomier thought came over me, like an omen, that said maybe this wasn't a good day to ride. That thought was sheer horror and one that I was not even able to consider for more than a second. Regrouping my thoughts and thinking through the situation, I recalled the scripture, "The rain falls on the just and the unjust," and decided not to allow ominous thoughts to rule my day. If I thought it was unsafe to ride I wouldn't; if I wanted to face the challenge, I would. But I was not going to try to decipher the spiritual meaning behind a rainy day. Overwhelmed by the situation, I knelt down by my bed to pray and calm myself. I began writing the following thoughts in my journal:

"Lord, it's hard to express what I'm feeling right now; so many thoughts are racing through my mind. It's been an incredible trip and I thank you for teaching me so much about my weakness and your goodness. Please continue to teach me and never let me forget the lessons of this trip. Help me, Lord, to continue to walk with you and get to know you better. I want to serve you and live for you in a way that pleases you. Please be with me today. Amen."

The decision was clear: I had my Patagonia rain jacket and it was time to suck it up and press on. I was riding, rain or shine.

The smell of breakfast cooking came to me from downstairs as Curtis prepared his famous waffles, along with eggs, oatmeal, OJ, and fruit. After a pleasant time of feasting and talking that concluded around 9:00 a.m., I gathered up my gear and all of us moved the party to the sidewalk where I loaded up and prepared to pull out. The drizzle hung in the air as more of a mist, making standing outside more of a nuisance than anything. Now, all packed up and wearing my lightweight pullover rain jacket, I turned to the family for one last good-bye before heading out on the wet pavement. Once again I felt like a family member leaving home after a holiday visit; the love we shared was genuine and heartfelt. Fighting back the emotions, I swung my leg over old faithful and pushed off.

Except for the refreshing rain in the desert it was the first time I had ridden in the rain the whole trip and the first time I had had to use my jacket. Three miles down the road, though, the drizzle lightened up to barely a sprinkle and the heat was too much for the jacket so off it came. Giving thanks to God, I voiced one more prayer, "Please, dear God, let me know you are in charge of this day."

Adding to the downer of the overcast skies, the route that took me out of Wheeling was about as unsightly as any road I had ever traveled. And to make matters worse, as I passed through the ugliest industrial district in the country, I felt my back tire turn to mush and flatten down to the rim. "Rain, ugly, now a flat tire!" I moaned. "Will I ever get out of this stinking town?"

At that moment a determination rose up in me and I concluded that this was a spiritual battle that required focus, attention, and constant prayer. Nothing was going to keep me from finishing. "Jesus, you are able," I cried. "I trust in you to get me home."

Of all the businesses to have a flat in front of, I considered it a blessing that I was in front of a tire business. Rolling my bike to the glass front door, I went inside and asked the guy behind the counter if I could fix my flat in his garage. "No problem," he said, kindly. "Things are pretty slow right now, go ahead and use the first bay."

At this stage of the trip, I thought I had become pretty good at fixing flats but for some reason this one was not working out. After removing the rear wheel, slipping off the tire, pulling out the tube, applying the patch, putting everything back together, and pumping up to pressure, I tried to control my frustration as I discovered air continuing to leak. Taking a deep breath, I methodically drained out the air, dismantled the tire, and removed the tube again, quickly finding a second small hole that I had overlooked. Applying another peel-and-stick rubber

patch, and then running my thumb along the inside of the tire to check for missed prickly objects, I reassembled the whole deal, pumped up to my usual "almost-as-hard-as-I-can-pump" tire pressure, hung the panniers back on the rack, and rolled out of the garage ready to press on one more time.

Curtis & Hannah

The sky was still overcast and gray, and the road wet but as I passed through the little towns of Short Creek, Wellsburg, and Follansbee my attitude began to change. I started singing and smiling and, actually enjoying the ride. My legs felt strong and I pedaled smooth and hard along the flat asphalt. For some reason, thoughts of my family back in Tampa flooded my mind. The feelings grew stronger until I was overcome with the urge to give them a call. For the last couple of days I had not been able to reach anyone so I decided to try at the next opportunity.

Not too far ahead appeared one of those half-size, talk-from-your-car-window phone booths, so I pulled alongside and dialed the number, collect, of course, since I didn't have enough change and because Mom and Dad always expected collect calls. I couldn't wait to tell them I was almost finished. The phone rang ... and rang ... and rang. Not even an answering machine. That's odd, I thought, as I hung up, dejected, and got back on the road. Then a thought hit me. What if they had gone to Ambridge to meet me! I had read an article before the trip about a group of people who biked across the country on one of those supported tours and when they arrived at the other end they were surprised by wives, husbands, and friends waiting to congratulate them. Could it be? I pushed off and continued the push, passing under Route 22 to Pittsburgh. I was so close. Weirton was my next town. After that, it was home free.

Riding into Weirton, I couldn't believe my eyes. I thought Wheeling's industrial district was offensive but Route 2 through Weirton was downright scary. At one point I was totally engulfed overhead and on both sides by a steel mill. It was literally an industrial tunnel. For blocks, maybe miles, all I saw and heard were huge smoke stacks, clanging metal, mammoth metal beams, and rusty pipes towering overhead and spewing out smoke and gas. I didn't even want to breathe. After six weeks of open space, clean air, and blue skies, the culture shock of the steel industry jolted my senses.

When I finally emerged from the belly of the overgrown locomotive, and was able to look out toward the open road ahead, for some strange reason, I had to turn my head around and get one last look at the industrial beast. With my head turned over my shoulder, I lost my directional bearings and drifted off the edge of the concrete highway, getting both tires caught in a deep groove between the edge of the concrete road and the gravel-covered, asphalt shoulder. In a split second of deadly fear jolting through my

Weirton

body, I gripped the handlebars like a bodybuilder, somehow bouncing the front tire out of the groove, fish-tailing my back tire sideways in the loose gravel, then finding traction in the right lane of the highway and gaining control of the bike without going down.

With my heart pounding in my chest like a bass drum, I started screaming at myself in frantic anxiety and frustration. "Wake up, damn it! What are you doing? Come on, pay attention. Don't blow it now. Sh_ _!" I looked down and noticed my back tire wobbling like it did in Chanute, which made me even more furious. Quickly repenting for my foul language, I called out for Jesus to forgive my outburst and help me make it to Ambridge. I denounced Satan out loud and demanded, in the name of Jesus, that he leave me alone. My concentration increased and I determined that the power of hell itself was not going to keep me from finishing.

I approached a road sign that read, "New Cumberland 4." My excitement level soared as I recognized that sign that I had seen once before during the end of my training back in June when I rode to New Cumberland and back to Ambridge in one day. I was on familiar ground.

Pedaling strong and trying to stay focused, I rode right past a side road that I had discovered on my training ride that wasn't on the map. I turned around and took the little back road through the overhanging trees and quiet creeks that looked refreshingly familiar. I was so close I could hardly take it in.

Passing through Raccoon State Park and coasting down the steep hill to Route 18, I pulled into a little convenience store where I had eaten lunch during training. I leaned the bike against the building like I had done before and walked inside for some OJ to go with the sandwich Eleanor had made for me. I didn't mention a word to the guy behind the counter about what I was doing -- I just couldn't talk about it, my emotions were off the chart. Back outside I sat on the curb and ate my lunch in the same spot I had eaten two months before. A man pulled up and went inside. When he came back to his car I asked him to take my picture without going into any explanation. I was beside myself -- fifteen more miles to go.

I threw my trash in the metal drum by the curb and headed out. Five miles up the road, as I crested the top of a long, gradual hill, I looked ahead and noticed a motorcycle coming my way. As it got

Last lunch

closer, my mind clicked and I realized it was my friend Bob, who had dropped me off at the airport six weeks earlier. My emotions exploded and I almost jumped off my seat. He waved from a distance and I responded by straightening up in my seat and pumping my fist frantically over my head, shouting like a wild man. He rode past, then circled around and came along my left side and we slapped high fives. We shouted greetings back and forth and then he took off to tell the welcoming party I had been spotted.

Further down the road a car pulled alongside me from behind as the passenger leaned out of the window. "Are you Joe Martin?" he asked, reaching out his hand for me to slap. "You made it!" I didn't know the guy but looking through the window I could see the driver was a friend from seminary. The two of them were on their way home from Raccoon State Park and just happened by at the right time. "Can you believe it?!" I shouted. "This is unreal. See you back in Ambridge." I was in orbit.

Then it came, the home stretch. After cresting the hill at Five Points and coasting down 151, I turned left onto Highway 51 and headed toward the Ambridge Bridge. Up ahead a teenage boy sat on his bike on the side of the road waiting for me to pass by. Spotting me, he excitedly mounted his bike and pedaled alongside. "Unbelievable!" he shouted. "I can't believe you made it! There are lots of people waiting for you at the bridge." "Really?!" I could hardly contain myself.

We pulled onto the bridge and my eyes focused straight ahead. I noticed some of the young boys from the church who had run the length of the bridge to meet me. I started yelling at the top of my lungs, "Wooowhooo!" By then I was in the middle of the lane with a string of cars following behind and I didn't care one bit. I came over the slight rise in the middle of the bridge and spotted Eleanor from the church snapping away with her camera while other people from the church gathered at the end of the bridge with a "Welcome Home" banner. My mouth could not smile big enough; the fountain of joy welling up inside was just too much to express.

At the end of the bridge I coasted off the road and turned right into the tire store parking lot in the middle of the excited crowd. Expecting a barrage of hugs and happy greetings, I was caught off guard when everyone kept their distance and we all just looked at each other for an awkward moment. I guess no one knew what to say.

The homecoming: Ambridge

Party at the Vitunics

Breaking the suspense, I spoke out, "Somebody hug me." Pastor Joe's wife, Cindy, was closest and everyone else followed.

We hung around the parking lot exchanging personal greetings until Cindy invited everyone over to the Vitunics' house for a welcome home party. It felt so wonderful but so strange being back in normal life. All the familiar people were there but I felt so different and distant. We talked around the living room and I shared a few stories but my mind was in another world; all I wanted to do was thank God for all the wonderful things he had done. The gratitude kept welling up inside and I couldn't think of anything else.

The trip was over. I had actually made it. And I believed with every fiber in me that Jesus, himself, had been my companion the whole way and had provided for my needs. His presence had been as real as the shoes on my feet and I was dying to communicate that reality with everyone. I think that's what I did for the next hour or so until everyone gradually went home.

Like my second family, the Vitunics had planned on me staying the night, which I was glad to do. After showering off the last of the road dirt and packing in my final post-riding feast, I retired to one of the kids' rooms that had graciously and lovingly been prepared just for me, one last time. I'm not sure how long into the night I replayed the previous forty-three days before I fell asleep, but it really didn't matter. The ride was over and I was resting in heaven – tomorrow I would get on with the rest of my life.

My Church of the Savior family

Twenty Years Later

Dear Reader,

What I want to say in this epilogue is so personal I've decided to write it in the first person.

The truth is, reading the story of my bike ride twenty years later literally makes me want to cry. The reason is because I remember the guy twenty years ago who genuinely loved God and tried to do everything he could, even ride a bike across the country, to feel loved and approved by Him, but could never seem to do enough. And to watch him try so relentlessly and painfully is truly heartbreaking.

Having grown up with an inherent drive to seek the approval of all significant people in my life, it was only natural that when I became a Christian, I would transfer that drive toward God and seek His approval, along with the rest of the Christian community, by being the best Christian I could be. What that meant was trying to eliminate all "worldly" influences that might draw me away from God, while adding all those religious activities and practices that might make me more pleasing to Him, all the while thinking, maybe even subconsciously, that He (and they) would love me more, the "better" Christian I became. Not that trying to please God is a bad goal, but when the motivation is to earn His love and approval, the striving can be exhausting and the result devastating.

Now, clearly, that was not the only motivation for making the ride—God only knows what motivations reside in the recesses of the human heart—but suffice it to say that the guy riding his bike across the country loved God and wanted so much to feel His love in return, he would have done anything to achieve it. The heartbreaking part is watching a guy trying so hard to earn something that I have now come to understand was there the whole time, offered as a free gift from a gracious and loving God, and the trying was intensely grueling and painful.

When I returned home from the bike trip this striving for approval kicked into high gear as I sought to "put into practice" all I had learned and experienced about God, passionately trying to be the Christian I thought I needed to be and giving my all to ministry the way I thought was expected. In this twisted and taxing understanding of the Christian faith, I felt that, even as a forgiven sinner, it was now up to me, with God's help, to try to "measure up" to the extraordinary expectations of a holy and perfect God, trying harder and harder to reach the carrot at the end of the stick, but never succeeding.

The intensity of this "holy striving" reached a pinnacle five years after the bike ride as I tried to build my youth ministry and seek ordination with all of my might, at one point fulfilling the requirements for the ordination process, remodeling a large house as a youth meeting place, holding weekly youth group meetings, and taking a full load at the seminary at the same time! The exhaustion and loneliness I felt at times was crippling. But I "pressed on."

Oddly enough, six months after I had returned from the ride, I attended the ordination of a friend, and at the reception had been introduced to a cute, brown-eyed, flight attendant scheduler for USAir who attended my friend's church. We spoke for a short time (around the hors d'oeuvres, no doubt) and that was about it. For five years we saw each other at the YMCA and spoke casually but nothing more. One time I did ask her if she would like to attend a youth meeting and maybe help out but she declined, not appearing to be that interested. Imagine that, not interested in one-track striving for God's perfection through ministry and holy living! Five years later she told me all she wanted was to be asked out on a date.

That finally happened, but it didn't come easily. After five years of effort, establishing the youth ministry, completing all but two weeks of my seminary degree, and fulfilling the final requirements for ordination, I received the most crushing news of my ministry life that brought it all to a screeching halt – I was not being recommended for ordination. When the bishop spoke those words in our meeting it was as though someone landed the most penetrating sucker punch to my gut that had ever been delivered. Gasping for air and thinking that I would have to fulfill some new requirement that would postpone my life's goal for maybe another year, I asked sheepishly, "So what do I have to do now?"

If the first delivery was a sucker punch to the gut, what came next was the right hook that put me on the mat. "There is nothing you can do, Joseph. The commission has dropped you from the process, the file is closed." My body went numb. I had no words, no feelings, no thoughts. The meeting ended with no recourse and no consolation. Even though no specific reason was cited, I gathered, between the lines, that being thirty-eight years old and single had much to do with it. "For goodness sakes," I thought to myself. "I've known this for years, and prayed and begged God regularly for help; but a life-stopper?" I was totally blindsided and literally destroyed.

Actually, I had had an inkling that something was awry after my final meeting with the commission two weeks earlier. Having finished all my requirements for the process, I went into the "final passage" meeting feeling pretty good about my qualifications for ministry and my devoted service to my church and the diocese for eight years, and expected the commission to feel the same way. Not long into the meeting I detected the feelings were clearly not mutual. What I assumed would be a friendly and affirming conversation about my gifts and calling, soon became an inquisition about my singleness, my work experience, and even my workout routine at the Y. At one point I felt like a boxer covered up against the ropes just trying to fight off the punches. "Can you explain why you feel the need to go to the YMCA four or five times a week?" "Can you tell us how you plan on handling being a single priest?" And so it went for an hour and a half. On the way home, my sponsors commented that I had become defensive at times and that, over all, "the meeting did not go well." "Defensive?" I thought, I was fighting for my life!

Little did I know how heavily influenced the commission had been by two final reports that they had been waiting for before the meeting. The first, prepared by a summer hospital program supervisor, emphasized, among other things, that I was "very black and white toward my belief that Jesus Christ was Lord and Savior." Not surprising coming from an ex-Catholic nun-turned-Methodist-minister, with Unitarian theology. I couldn't tell from our meetings during the summer who she thought was Lord, if anybody. The other report, a psychological evaluation from an admitted lesbian who had left her husband and children to pursue her same sex partner, commented that I had relational issues. Not that I had any special animosity toward Unitarians or lesbians, nor were their comments completely off, but never in a million years would I have thought that their evaluation of my qualifications for ministry would influence the calling I believed God had on my life so profoundly. I was wrong. Armed with those official documents, the commission delivered the negative verdict to the bishop who, in turn, passed it on to me, somewhat like a hot potato, but having the effect more like a grenade.

Later that afternoon, as I burned off immeasurable amounts of depression and anger on the stationary bike at the Y, I found myself riding next to the brown-eyed girl on the Stairmaster. When I finished my workout I stood next to the Stairmaster pouring out my broken life to my five-year acquaintance who continued to pump the pedals as she listened politely and caringly. I left the Y that day feeling better about a lot of things.

That night, as I shared my Y experience at dinner with the Vitunics, Joe, in his infinite and practical wisdom, asked a profound question: "Why don't you ask her out?" That was a Thursday. The next day I returned to the Y at the same time and asked Heidi out for Saturday night. We were married sixteen months later.

A year after that, the new bishop of the Episcopal Diocese of Pittsburgh, the Right Reverend Robert Duncan, agreed to meet with me and Joe Vitunic to discuss my future in the Diocese of Pittsburgh. A year later I was ordained to the Episcopal priesthood, the highlight of that experience coming when the new head of the Commission on Ministry, the Reverend Geoff Chapman, offered an apology for the treatment I had received from the previous commission. When he spoke the words, practically everyone in the room—Heidi, myself, the Vitunics, and my new sponsors—broke out in tears as the love and forgiveness of God filled the room and brought healing to a deep, deep wound.

I'd like to say that after those back-to-back miracles the holy striving for God's love and approval disappeared but that wasn't the case. Sadly enough, the striving continued into my family (now with two young children) and my ministry (minister of my first parish) in such an intensity that I almost destroyed them both, reaching a place of total exhaustion, developing ulcerative colitis and other health issues, and burning out to a level that many might say verged on a nervous breakdown.

At this exhausted and stress-filled point in my life, in His love and mercy, God reached out in the form of a simple talk, delivered at a typical clergy quiet day, and literally saved my life. The message, delivered by the Rev. Dr. Paul F. M. Zahl, was what I have come to understand as, "the Gospel," the Good News that God intended all the world to hear regarding his Son Jesus Christ. Of course, I had heard most of it before, but this time it came from a man who unashamedly emphasized his own sinful human nature along with the universal brokenness of all human beings, INCLUDING CHRISTIANS, and rather than offer more exhausting ways for me to become a better Christian (for which I didn't have the energy anyway), placed all of the focus on what God had done "for me" on the cross, through the sacrifice of Himself, to not only completely and sufficiently cleanse me from my sin and declare me "not guilty" before Him, but also to deposit into my account the total sinlessness and perfection of Jesus himself, making me completely acceptable and lovable in His sight, EVEN THOUGH I CONTINUED TO STRUGGLE WITH MY SHORTCOMINGS, FAILURES, AND SINS.

What that meant for me that day was that my striving to earn God's love and approval was over; that even though I remained a sinful man, God's grace was truly sufficient for my everyday living and His love much more abundant than my ability to earn or achieve it, and I could rest. That day I experienced what the song writer must have meant when he said, "My chains fell off, and I was free."

In the years that followed I immersed myself in this "Reformation" understanding of God and the Bible, and lapped up every ounce of teaching and scholarship I could get my hands on. I soon discovered that not only had God's love and complete forgiveness been available all along but so had the biblical scholarship that articulated it so well. This vast body of knowledge, developed during the sixteenth century by the likes of Martin Luther, John Calvin, Thomas Cranmer, and others, and carried on for 500 years by subsequent generations of quality theologians, had been there all the time, explaining and confirming the original meaning of the scriptures in a way that set people free and allowed them to rest in the assurance of God's love and acceptance. For some reason I had either never heard it or perhaps never been in a position to listen to it if I had.

To help me in this crucial time of growth and study, it just so happened that a seminary student answered an ad I had placed at Trinity School for Ministry for a worship leader and began leading worship, along with his wife at my church. For the next three years Nick and Aya Lannon not only blessed our church with their music but Nick became the friend and study partner I needed to take hold of this life-giving theology. As the parish priest I was supposed to be the mentor in the relationship but as a full-time seminary student, Nick processed more theology and biblical insight in a short period of time than I could have ever comprehended, and interacted with me in a way that brought us both to a deeper understanding of the gospel—for which I will forever be grateful.

During that time we were joined at my church by other students from the seminary that had also been set free from the holy-striving treadmill and, likewise, longed to hear the freeing announcement of the Gospel. Jady and Liza Koch, Jacob and Melina Smith, David Browder, and Matt and Lisa McCormick became to me like guide wires on a newly planted tree, holding me up until my roots could grow stronger, and being the friends that Heidi and I needed during that special three-year period. It was during this time that Matt McCormick suggested we read and discuss a book titled *Thomas Cranmer's Doctrine of Repentance, Renewing the Power to Love*, by the Rev. Ashley Null. Loving the book, but having completely forgotten about the priest I met in Liberal, Kansas, twenty years earlier, I didn't make the connection until two years later when I went to hear him speak and he mentioned something about his early days in Liberal. Obviously, we have reconnected (he wrote the forward) and he has become a true friend and encourager in this wonderful grace-filled life.

Another invaluable source of teaching and support that continued after the seminarians graduated and moved on was a group of theologians with a radio show called the White Horse Inn. Driving around in my car listening to CDs of these four guys discussing Reformation theology and the all-sufficient sacrifice of Jesus Christ became like living water to me. Oftentimes I would find myself driving along with tears of joy streaming down my face just from listening to a group of intelligent Christians that could identify with my painful striving and remind me of the biblical basis of my freedom. It's hard to express the comfort and confidence that ministry has provided over the years.

Through those and countless other authors, friends, and teachers, I've learned a number of important lessons. First of all, I've come to understand how limited and frail the progress of Christian holiness is in this life, and how futile it is to try to accelerate the process through human effort. The cross of Christ allowed me to become a Christian by dying to self in the first place, and is completely sufficient in bringing about my progress, however great or small, in the same way. Secondly, being grounded in the assurance of God's love and total forgiveness, and free from the heavy burden of "doing my part" to compliment God's saving work, I find myself motivated to please God by a deep sense of gratitude for what Christ has done, instead of by the need to earn His approval. In fact, I've come to realize that true growth in Christian living is more about understanding the depth and degree of my sin and selfishness as God reveals it to me, and living in humility and repentance, than it is about overcoming, improving or eliminating the very human nature I live in.

Of course, I still struggle with my natural tendency to strive and achieve, but the words of the gospel always bring me back to a place of comfort and rest. God's sovereign control over my life and His abundant and unchanging love soothe and settle my soul on a daily basis. I just can't hear it often enough.

Thank you again for reading my story. My prayer for all of us is that we understand and believe this great work that God has done for us on the cross, and that we serve Him with all the energy we can muster, knowing that His love for us doesn't depend on our effort, but on His great mercy, and His will for our lives lies not in our great wisdom and know-how, but in His infinite love and compassion.

Blessings to you all,

Joseph

PS. At the printing of this book, as a lifelong Episcopalian, I have been removed from ministry in the Episcopal Church for my stand for the biblical gospel with my bishop, the Most Rev. Robert Duncan, now Archbishop of the Anglican Church in North America. As a result, my wife, Heidi, and our two children Wesley and Madeline risk the loss of our church and home because of a lawsuit from the Episcopal Church, and wonder what the future holds. I know many of you face the same kind of uncertainty with your jobs, homes, families, and the general state of the world. May we all learn to trust the sovereign God of the universe and find peace from the One who guides our paths and provides for our needs, even as we stumble and fail in our efforts to serve Him. To Him be all honor and glory. He will get us where He wants us to go.